Tony Vagneur is a master at crafting beautiful words into vibrant memories, emotions and scenes. The heart of a common man living an uncommon life beats within each story, taking the reader to places they never thought they'd go. With cowboy roots running deep and real, you won't want to miss this.
   – Julie Carter, author, photographer and cowgirl

Tony Vagneur tells us of cowboys, horses and dogs he has known. He tells us of his grandfather and father who taught him the ways of ranching. He tells us of his favorite ski runs on Aspen Mountain and his grandmother's little house on Bleeker Street. The stories all tell us of his deep love for the land and for Aspen.
   – Mary Eshbaugh Hayes, former editor of *The Aspen Times*, author of *Aspen Potpourri* and *The Story of Aspen*, and writer of *Around Aspen*

As an armchair westerner, reading Tony Vagneur is a transformative experience, taking me through a stand of aspens, or along a rugged but beautiful ridge. Vagneur deconstructs the cowboy life, revealing what it is to be a man hewn from the earth. Wordsmith, poet, cowboy, saddle philosopher, Aspen native and historian, Vagneur is a true voice of the American West.
   – Kanani Fong, writer and film documentary outreach specialist

Tony Vagneur is the modern-day cowboy poet, but he's no one-trick pony. For years, Tony's prose has dazzled readers of *The Aspen Times* by recalling his exploits as die-hard skier, his rabblerousing in honky-tonks, and his tomfoolery as a young boy growing up in a mountain town that changed all around him. He's not afraid to show his tender side, too. Tony's writings are a must-read for anyone who wants to relive the old days of Aspen and understand its modern age as well.
   – Rick Carroll, Editor, *The Aspen Times*

ASPEN: THEN AND NOW

Reflections of a Native Son

by

Tony Vagneur

ISBN: 978-0692339060

Library of Congress Control Number: 2014921125

Tony Vagneur
PO Box 154
Woody Creek, CO 81656
ajv@sopris.net

Available from Amazon.com and other retail outlets

Published by Woody Creek Press, Ltd.
Woody Creek, Colorado

Cover Design by eBook Cover Designs

These columns previously appeared in *The Aspen Times* over a ten-year period, 2004-2014.

Cover Photo by Margaret Wilson Reckling,
Tony, Drifter and Topper, May 1, 2013

Back Cover Photo by Greg Poschman

Dedicated to those in whose steps I follow

Acknowledgments

It would be impossible to thank everyone who had a hand in this book. Not everyone has a name in my columns, but all the people (and animals) therein have a face and distinct personality, which makes them forever unforgettable in my heart.

Many thanks to Georgia Herrick Taylor Hanson and Pat Bingham for suggesting early on that I write a column for *The Aspen Times*. And thanks to Allyn Harvey and Jenna Weathered for taking a chance on publishing my column, Saddle Sore. Additionally, thanks to the entire editorial staff of *The Aspen Times* for keeping an eye on me each week. Also, credit goes to fellow Aspen Mountain ski patrolman and writer, Tim Cooney, for coming up with the name Saddle Sore. Special thanks to David E. Stapleton and Wayne Vagneur for being reliable research sources.

Doug Franklin, professional photographer, artist and life-long friend, displayed extraordinary patience wading through hundreds of family photos and scanning the ones you see in this book. He took the photo of the 1980s skier in the Highland Bavaria photo. And thanks to Greg Poschman, photographer and film maker, who took the back cover photo, the result of many days filming and photographing this writer for the Aspen Hall of Fame. Thank you to Aspen High School friends, Terry Morse and Lawren Ethridge Bradford, long-time readers who suggested early on that I publish this book.

Special thanks to Ann Gordon, for being an understanding editor and critical eye during formation of this book for publication.

Most importantly, kudos to Margaret Wilson Reckling for being a constant sounding board for my incessant ideas about almost everything under the sun and without whose support I would have never made it this far. Thank you, Margaret!

Thank you to everyone who shares a love of Aspen and the Roaring Fork Valley and who encourage me each week to pen another column. This coming together over its special history helps keep Aspen alive in the minds and hearts of those who have traveled this road with enthusiasm and an eye toward special memories.

Preface

I was born in two worlds, it seems, the ranching life in Woody Creek, and the town life of Aspen. It might be safe to say that on some days, Woody Creek had more going on than Aspen, although Aspen has managed to create its own star in the sky of well-known places.

Some people like to think I'm part of "old" Aspen, but they really have no idea. All four sets of my great-grandparents arrived in either Aspen, Ashcroft or Woody Creek in the 1880s, and down through the generations, we've remained. Vagneur, Stapleton, Sloss, and Prindle, names you may have heard if you've been around town for long. My grandson, Cash, is the sixth generation of my family to live in Woody Creek.

On some level, I've always fancied myself a writer and had a large collection of material from high school and college, but alas, it disappeared with the help of a jealous hand and besides, I was too busy making a living and enjoying the night life to concentrate much on writing.

One fateful, beautiful spring day in Aspen, I parked in the West End, waiting for my daughter to finish a gymnastics class and, facing Aspen Mountain, a flood of memories began to overtake me and I started to make a soundless, solitary game out of how much I could remember, re-living my life from my earliest recollections, starting at about two years old.

These I began to write down in three- or four-paragraph tales, and instead of telling stories all night long in the Red Onion or the Eagles Club, and through some sort of mutual serendipity, the Aspen Times asked me if I would like to write a weekly column. A precious gift, that was.

Ten years into the column business, I can only say that my desire is to cast a different eye on the history of Aspen and the surrounding area and those people who have made it what it is today. Genuflection toward the prevailing status quo and historical interpretation turns off my creative instincts, and my most significant contribution is perhaps writing about those seldom-celebrated people who have greatly contributed to the town of Aspen, those people you may never have heard of before.

This book is a collection of some of those columns, ones I think you may like. There are a few scattered photographs for visual relief.

Anita's New Book

"I have a belly, alabaster skin and no ass," I said as I sat down to sign the model release form last Saturday. "Oh, Tony, you'll be surprised," said Anita, showing me paste-up shots of other nude models, mostly women who might make Playboy wonder how it missed such pulchritudinous heartland beauty, women who made me want to be part of the project, even if I did have to take off all my clothes to do so.

The inexperienced mind works in odd ways, and in the hours leading up to the nude photo shoot, I wondered what I should wear. It was a western theme and there were horses involved, I knew, but it never occurred to me that I might want to take along some kind of prop to cover up the essence of my maleness - forget the clean shirt and jeans.

You can't be shy about such things, and upon arrival on the set, I doffed my clothes in the grass, retaining only a clean Stetson, a pair of gloves and a bandanna. Oh, yeah, and a smile. I sauntered into the pasture to meet the horse owner, a lovely woman dressed in tight jeans, who would look good as Lady Godiva, and who held onto two handsome Friesian geldings. Waiting for the photographer to gear up, we chatted over the back of a horse, talking cattle and horse breeds as though one of us really wasn't naked. She suggested I also wear my 16" tall cowboy boots, which was a lifesaver.

There was no script, other than they wanted to get some good shots of me interacting with those two magnificent black beasts and almost immediately, the younger of the horses got stung by a bee or something, and suddenly there I was, a lead rope in each hand, trying to keep these normally gentle giants from hurriedly prancing away and the photographer softly telling me that maybe I should try to cover up, "just a little." I know what you're thinking.

Lest you think I'm the only male starring in this book, please be advised that there are other curmudgeons of the sort whose names would be immediately recognizable should I reveal them, but

I've always believed a man's business is his own and it's up to him how he wishes to expose himself to the general public.

I don't know if you've ever done an outdoor nude photo shoot, but there are some things that don't get mentioned, not even when they happen. Take a couple of horses, a naked man, a slowly dying sun, the largest population of mosquitoes we've had in years and get them all together in the same spot and it's tough on the two-legged one without a tail. It didn't bother me that the horses were getting restless and kept circling and rubbing up against me in their not-so-subtle hints that we should give it up for the day. "Just a couple more," Robert the photog kept saying with a smile (that's what they always say), and we kept up a running commentary of nonsense between us just to keep our minds off the swirling bugs.

I'd like to tell you more, but the book is still in the production stage and to say too much would be jumping the gun. However, if you've been a fan of Anita Witt's recent books about ranching, cowboying and history, you'll be sure to find this an excellent treatise in a new direction, an expanded, first-class venue. There are still some crusty old cowpokes in this one, but I think the enticing young women will upstage the men by a long shot. The horses aren't bad, either.

What can you say? Upon leaving, I told the delightful horse owner (and her good-natured husband), who made us all feel incredibly welcome and at ease that, "it was nice getting naked with you." I'll keep you posted on how this all turns out.

A Dark Shroud of Miserableness

After reading a column about the happenings at Owl Farm in Woody Creek, and in the way that weird thoughts happen, I was struck by how intrigued my deceased parents would be at seeing the name "Woody Creek" mentioned in the national media. Years ago, while living out there, my dad ran an ad in the Wall Street Journal for some forgotten reason, and the editors suggested he use the phrase "close to Denver" to describe our address because they didn't think readers would have any idea where Aspen was, let alone Woody Creek.

The hard part for me, I suppose, is seeing the conjunction of two intertwining things, an event and a location, in print almost incessantly: Suicide and Woody Creek. It brings the pain up from a place too deep to stop the flow and then the familiarity of it all rolls around and around in my psyche.

I suspect that those who had never heard of Thompson will read almost as much about his death as those who either knew or had heard of him, or maybe had read a book or two he'd penned. The draw is, I think, the enigma attached to the taking of one's own life.

When I was nine, a great-uncle of mine killed himself with a double-barreled, 12-gauge shotgun, a gun that sits in my closet today. When I was about ten, I'd position that gun as I thought it must be angled to accomplish a thing so scary, and discovered there is more than one way to carry out such an act.

My great-uncle's wife had died a year or so earlier, about the time he'd sold his ranch up on McLain Flats, and it all kind of made sense that he'd do such a thing. Us kids milled around his house while our dads (and granddads) catalogued the furnishings and divvied up the possessions. After that, we thought we knew about suicide and put it off as something strange to think about later in life when we weren't so busy.

It's one thing for a distant great-uncle to do himself in, but when the deed gets a little closer to home, it is a life-changing event for those who remain. I will never forget the ashen look on my uncle Victor's face when, years later, he came quietly, almost shyly, to my house to deliver a gut-wrenching blow, the effects of which can never be entirely dispelled.

Perhaps to most people, the depression that can precede suicide is an unknown. For many of the others, there is a darkness lurking about, sometimes in plain sight, most of the time locked away, but never completely barred from our minds. Most days, the dark waters swirl, luxuriantly, under our minds-eye, and reflect warm sunshine back at us. We don't fear such darkness, even though we know it. But sometimes, at some point or another in our lives, the black void can swirl up uncharacteristically, as though waking us from sleep, intruding into our consciousness and bathing our minds in its blackness. If we're fortunate, we beat the beast back.

A chance remark, the certain flash in someone's eye, lays open a soul for an instant and you tell them that you fly the same valleys or dance in the same forests and they know of what you speak. A bond, whose strength ebbs and flows with the intensity of the darkness, is formed on some unconscious level that, characteristically, only death can break.

To these people, and as foreign and incredulous as it may seem to those who don't tinker with the idea, suicide is one of life's options. It may be the ultimate issue of control; a choice allowing people on the downside edge to believe they can regain control of a life that appears to have lost its compass. But we can't really know.

As my uncle sat, uncomfortably, on a narrow bench in the house and related how my brother had taken his own life, my heart pounded in a throat parched with dread and the tears stopped just behind my eyes as a dark shroud of miserableness ensconced my being.

This column is dedicated to my brother, Steve, who died in February, 1977.

Disappearing Trail in the West

There was sharpness in the air and we couldn't find anywhere to get comfortable. Waiting on strangers can be tough, especially if it's important. The homestead cabin was cold and it would have taken too long for the wood stove to warm it up and for a while we sat at a table outside until that got unbearable, and finally ended up in the most appealing spot we could find - the pickup truck.

"Those sons-a-bitches don't know where they're goin', ya know that? God-oh-Friday, we coulda had this done, but it ain't our project, so that's that. This ain't my only ranch, not by a longshot, but there's no sense keepin' it - fella couldn't make a living up here on this scrawny ground, no matter how hard he worked."

I took the opening, with Mount Sopris gazing majestically down on us from almost straight above, and offered that probably nobody ever really made much money from cattle ranching anyway, at least not in the United States. He gave a short laugh and offered that I "sure as hell" might be right about that. We talked then about some of the more well-known ranches around North America - the Gang, XIT, 6666, Matador, JA, the King and how we wouldn't mind having a spread comparable in size and activity. Although, if you can't make any money, what's the sense? "The only real money's in real estate, always has been," he quietly said.

But, hell, if you're not strapped for dollars, maybe it's about keeping the myth alive, the knowledge that when you walk out the door, you can survey what's yours and realize the joy of what the West has really always been about - open spaces.

There is an aura that the modern rancher, modern cowboy, if you will, exemplifies - the almost lost identity of our past, galloping through visions that we try so hard in our dreams and fantasies to hang onto, even if for just a little bit. Ranchers are today what ranchers have always been, sophisticated men of the west who give a sensual and artistic bent to the scenes that we conjure up in our minds. Stetson's creased with care and covered in dust, faded blue jeans tucked into the brightly colored tops of cowboy boots, wild rags tied under chins, rustling in the wind, and all assortment of vests, gloves, spurs and chaps adding the finishing touches to the workaday costume of the tall in the saddle, proud cowboy. These men, like the one with whom I batted ranching philosophy around, are rooted in unflinching traditions and are at uncompromising ease with their roles. They are the guardians of a world from our past, the American West of mythic proportions. It is ironic, if you think about it, that today's cowboy, the reality of the cattle rancher's West, is also yesterday's cowboy, the mythical cattleman of the same American West.

We talked horses, some good ones we've had, and as we reminisced, the retired cow dog, Tip, circled the truck and remembered, perhaps, the many reluctant cows he'd put through the corral gate, just a short throw from the front of the truck.

And as we talked, somberness colored the tone, for the rancher realized, I think, that to unburden himself of the land he had nurtured so faithfully over the years was a sign of letting go, the taking of a tentative step into an unknown world where the answers are even fewer and farther apart.

"Well, here they come and I guess we'll have to get out and give 'em a show. Let 'em know who owns the place and who's still calling the shots." Someday, I reckon, they'll have it all, just because we look at land differently, but until then, we'll buck it up and respect the men who, for generations, have traveled the disappearing trail of the West.

French Fete

On July 14, 1789, a band of peasants overtook the Bastille prison in Paris and the beginning of the first French Revolution was born. An odd concept had been fomenting among the underclass, specifically one that believed the king was no longer the representative of God and that all people were equal. Of course, Napoleon Bonaparte mucked it up for a while afterwards, but the idea survived and today the French celebrate Bastille Day much as we celebrate the Fourth of July.

In the 1950s, a woman by the name of Terese David came to Aspen with some unique ideas rumbling around in her head about how she wanted to spend her life. To young boys, she seemed a bit on the edge of insanity with her wild hair and accent of indeterminate origin. We tolerated her occasional attempts at conversation with the illusory patience that curiosity and a smirk can afford. To make ends meet, she opened a clothing, knickknack and whatever store in a tiny Victorian on Main, directly across from today's Main Street Bakery. I was eavesdropping the day in the White Kitchen when she confided to the "chef" that due to legal pressure from some people in New York City, she may have to change the name of her emporium to something other than the "Pied Piper." For years, I wondered (still do) what kind of dark thought process motivates someone in the "Big Apple" to pick on an old lady trying to make a living out of a small miner's cottage in the mountains.

Inevitably, she changed the name to "Terese David of Aspen" and life went on, although she took on a more sophisticated line of clothing and, due to bourgeoning demand (pun intended), hired a general manager by the name of Ferne Spaulding. Always one to encourage attention toward our town, Ms. David came up with the idea of celebrating Bastille Day in Aspen. Being rather young then, I'm not sure I remember why she picked Bastille Day, other than its date was conducive to a midsummer's festival, I suppose. Also, as the signature event in a revolution against oppression, it had a basis in human terms, something that would have been important to her.

For years, it was hugely successful with locals and tourists alike and began to have its own draw, sort of like Winterskol. Unfortunately, and reminiscent of a reverse Bastille Day, aristocratic manipulators in the town of Aspen took some sort of umbrage at the under- and tourist- classes enjoying themselves so much, and declared that henceforth, Bastille Day was, for whatever reasons, politically incorrect and would, in the future, be known as International Day. I would say that was also the year Aspen quit taking a stand on the hard issues, but there are those who would say it happened earlier or later, so I'll let it go. Terese David was justifiably flummoxed, and her participation after such dysfunctional politicking was less than enthusiastic.

The last Bastille Day in Aspen had reached a high level of production and on a warm, romantic evening, well after midnight, on a stage left standing at the deserted confluence of Wagner Park and Cooper Street, I found myself seated at a grand piano. A couple of friends composed the beginnings of a soon-to-grow audience as I took the opportunity to play for the town's "last call" contingent. Well into a quiet ballad, a girl named Gisele (how could I forget?), with a soft touch and looks masked by darkness, took the stage slightly behind me and after a few nervous whispers and giggles, began massaging the back of my neck. I shivered and played with increased intensity. In the heat of this July 2005, the events all fit together in my mind, not neatly, but conveniently, as a tribute to an unconventional Terese David and the enthusiasm she had for making something inimitable happen in a town that occasionally needs an innovator to go against the current.

Front Door to Heaven

If you happened by, it may have been difficult to guess what was happening in the little church on the hill above Carbondale, and unless you had a stake in the man's life or that of his family, it didn't get a second look. For the record, we were saying goodbye to one of Aspen's own, an original, native Joe who for all practical purposes spent his entire life here. More and more old-timers are dying down valley, and that's not so much because they deserted Aspen, it's more about being able to walk down the street in the middle of the day and say "hello" to someone they know.

A man of my dad's generation, one I've known forever and for whom I'd swim the deepest creek, turns around in his church pew to shake my hand, and remarks with a grin that I'm one of the last of the young ranchers (with connections to the original settlers) who's still ranching. There were many like him in the gathering, people who came from pioneer stock and are now staring at the last chapters of their lives, still unwritten adventures ahead if one can judge by the vitality in their flashing eyes. I do claim to be one of the youngsters, but God, it's getting nice to have someone open a gate for my horses and me once-in-a-while.

There's the youngest brother over there, talking to some sweet-sounding woman like it's the only conversation in the world. He was always the good-looking one, the one with a wide smile. Wherever there was music, he'd be there, usually in a light-blue silk shirt, gold chain around his neck, pushing some well-dressed gal around the floor. That kid could dance, flashing big moves and showing off his stuff. And unlike a lot of guys, he didn't drink too much and somehow never let the sweat show through.

We're at the reception and an intriguing woman I grew up with sits across the table from me, her enticing smile and generous attitude slowly mesmerizing me, and I wonder about the nuances that kept us apart instead of bringing us together. Memorial services remind us of our own mortality with an uneasy bluntness, and maybe that's why there is such a great display of reverence toward the deceased and his family. We all want to be remembered in a good way, no matter our protestations; recognized for something, no matter how small.

People like me are no more members of Joe's family than the man in the moon, but at the same time, our destinies are bound in ways that are remarkably similar. Like Joe, we may have buried our ancestors here; certainly we toughed out the bad times and enjoyed the good; earned our keep and raised our children. We've appreciated every day we've ever had in this small valley, each tomorrow an unopened gift.

It's the stories that make a place what it is, give it it's soul, and that's one of the things about Aspen that still remains - you can't buy your way in and be accepted for long, but you can live it in for a lifetime. And it's people like Joe who get the lasting accolades, who become our heroes and who still make up the meaningful core of Aspen, guys and girls who go to work every day and tell the stories late into the night.

And Joe, who had been given a key to the back door of heaven somewhere along the way (why does that seem so appropriate?), couldn't have known, but his oldest son, a priest who serves at the Vatican, brought the full authority of the Catholic church with him to let us know that the clout of Rome was unnecessary, that Joe had carved out his own niche in the land of the gods and had assuredly walked in the front door.

History of Owl Farm

There has been so much written about Hunter S. Thompson and Owl Farm out in Woody Creek lately, maybe it's time a little history gets thrown at the subject.

The road from Highway 82 to Lenado and parts unknown was dirt, mostly red, fertile dirt that was stirred into dust with the passing of every car, horse or buggy that traveled it. Woody Creek was a ranching community and the as-yet-unnamed Owl Farm was owned by Margaret Arlian, a woman who made cheese, wine and brandy, which, according to my cousin Wayne, was not always predictably mild.

It was in the early forties when she sold the place to a man named Otis Smallwood and his wife. Smallwood was a large man who loved the ranching life and had a gentle affinity for a very young (yours truly) neighbor from up the road. His son, Norman, made model railroad engines, a big draw for me and which Otis surreptitiously let me handle during our visits. Norman has since become a good friend of mine and I am pleased to note that he remembers the history of Woody Creek in much the same way that I do. He gives solid credence to stories that likely only he and I remember. Of the two Smallwood kids, the daughter married a bronc rider from Meeker and Norman got a degree from the Colorado School of Mines and went on to a stellar career in the world of business.

The Smallwoods are deserving of their own column, but let me say that one day in 1950, they were gone, replaced by Al and Alma Barbier, a hard-working couple who always had an eye toward a better way to get things done. Early on their watch, the original ranch house that stood along Woody Creek Road burned down, giving the Barbiers the welcome opportunity to build a new house of logs, one more suitable to their style of living. That same house, with the now infamous kitchen, stands there today.

The Barbiers were innovators and willing to try most anything to increase production and sales in their various enterprises. They not only sold eggs, they guaranteed them; their milk barn, now a guest house, was the finest in the valley with an immaculately clean concrete floor and, of course, automatic milking machines. They were also innovators in land development, in a way, and were among the first in Woody Creek to subdivide, long before Pitkin County had heard of zoning.

In the early sixties, the Barbiers sold what remained of the place, still a large ranch by today's standards, and moved to town, opening up the Sweet and Snack Shop, the coolest teen hang out Aspen ever saw, then or now (Freddie Fisher was also a regular). They had sold the ranch to the Sandersens of Aspenhof, Maine, who owned the namesake Aspenhof Lodge on Aspen's Main Street. Of course, this lodge was sold and renamed the Christiania.

The Sandersens were great neighbors, particularly since their oldest son, William, or Billy was in my grade at school and it afforded us both the opportunity to share "guy" stuff with someone. I hadn't seen Billy in a long time and then came the tragic news that he had been killed in Viet Nam. I was in college then, and the true cost of the war was inextricably brought home with his death. Billy was buried on the ranch in Woody Creek, a fitting and proper resting place for a kid who gave everything for his country. Late in her life, his mother called me to reminisce about Billy and we covered some territory that was very important to her. The grief of a mother who loses a child is never gone, its dilution measured in minuscule drops.

Apparently, the ranch was cut up a little more, and Hunter Thompson ended up with part of the land north of the Woody Creek road, including the main log house and dairy barn the Barbiers had built.

There wasn't much fanfare when Thompson hit town, as I recall, and soon the main house seemed to have most of the life sucked out of it. Quiet and uninviting during the day, it didn't have the allure that would make it a neighborhood stop. His writing ability notwithstanding, it appears from this quarter that the continuum of time will judge Thompson's celebratory era in Woody

Creek as a hand-me-down thought unneeded, but tolerated, by a
unique neighborhood.

A Horseman's Dying Dream

One look out the passenger's window and you could tell something wasn't right. Sitting stiffly on the covered porch, posture straight and stern, with lightless eyes staring straight ahead, the man gave off a feeling that we were about as welcome as an insurance salesman, or worse, vultures.

At the pinnacle of a wide and verdant valley, with a name that only those directly descended from Mother Spain could properly pronounce, we found the hidden jewel of the southeastern Colorado mountains. More than a thousand acres of rugged, well-tended ranch land, reached by a dirt road no wider than the truck we drove, it should have been a cow-producing haven, but served instead as home to a small herd of approximately ten horses. They were of many descriptions, but generally had good conformation and were pleasing to the eye - all mares and unweaned foals with the exception of one dorsal-striped buckskin gelding.

We focused on the horses and soon enough, the sick old man from the porch wandered down to share his knowledge of the herd, dragging his lifeline, an oxygen bottle, with him. Such talk put a sparkle in his eyes and you could tell right off that he loved these horses more than most anything else around. "You boys would do yourselves proud to take a couple of those colts home. Make good workin' horses, you know. I'd a caught 'em up for you, but this damned lung cancer keeps me from doing anything but packin' this friggin' oxygen around."

He wanted a decent price for them - $300 - 500 on the colts, and although you could tell it would kill him to turn loose of any of the mares, he figured they were worth about $2500 apiece. Busy trying to stay alive just so he could die honorably, he could be excused for not grooming the burdock and hound's tongue seeds out of their manes and tails. Burdock, in particular, leaves horse's tails reminiscent of wooden clubs and makes manes and foretops totally useless.

Maybe the old man hadn't heard, but the ban on horse slaughter has taken all "speculation" out of the grade horse market, leaving foals such as his worth from $20 - $50 and the aging mares worth around $200 - $500. How are you going to tell a dying man that the value of his herd has been decimated by strangers, mostly mindless zealots suckling at the hind teat of conformity, incognizant of the repercussions their anthropomorphic and misguided actions will have?

As we left, I couldn't shake wondering how perplexing it must be to face slow death, long day after long night, and how difficult it must be to see what you once believed a small legacy for your widow become an almost worthless liability. The tragic realizations of the incurably stricken man and the thundering hoof beats of the unusual herd echoed in my mind, leaving an unsettled feeling deep inside.

The sale barn manager will refuse the horses, saying there are too many "weeds" stuck to their tails and "we don't want horses like that going through here, no way. They just won't sell." There was a time the dying horseman could have fixed it, but that day has passed.

No sooner will the old man be laid out in an inappropriate coffin, beige silk framing his shrunken body and awkwardly wearing the only suit he ever owned, than his son-in-law or best friend will be pushing the gentle horse herd down into a sunken ravine, holding them there with hay and oats while the crack of a 30.06 rifle resounds over the quiet cold of an early winter morning, dropping them one by one.

Legendary Line

If you watched the "skier cross" event at the 2010 Vancouver Games, you can imagine what the girls in this original 1960 photo were up to, airborne off a roll between Buckhorn and Dipsy Doodle. The photograph was taken by Life magazine, documenting Olympic training in Aspen.

Five local girls, side by side in the air (Fleeta Rowland, Judy Marolt, Roine Rowland, Cherie Gerbaz and Sharon Pecjak), they were the best of Aspen's ladies at the time, and it is questionable still whether a couple of them shouldn't have made the Olympic squad. (Pecjak won the Roch Cup in 1962.) For the cover, Life magazine liked the display of the Aspen girls so much they photographed the eventual Olympic team off the same bump, having them attempt to replicate the Aspen girls form. An irony that still stings.

Forward ahead fifty years, and luxuriate in the reputation that Aspen has maintained as a ski racing town. The U. S. Alpine Championships were held here the last week of February, a coup that few places in the country could pull off. If you don't think that's a big deal, ponder this: Eight Olympians, including Alice McKennis, ran their races in Vancouver and then hopped a plane to Aspen, expressly to participate in our NorAm Spring Series and U. S. Alpine Championships. And the Roch Cup, one of America's most prestigious and longest running ski races, shelved since 2001, was once again the focus of America's ski racing world.

Things seldom go according to plan and a few weeks ago, when the race crew got set to make artificial snow at the top of Aztec, a frozen underground water pipe created almost insurmountable problems for them. Take a little Aspen irreverence, coupled with creativity, perseverance and a healthy respect for tradition, and poof! The downhill was run instead on Ruthie's Snowbowl, just like the old days, fully sanctioned by the Federation Internationale de Ski, and the week took on a vibrancy that couldn't have been achieved any other way.

A couple of years ago, Penny Pitou (two silver medals at the 1960 Games) and some other impressive ski racers went with me on a cruise of Ruthie's. Thinking they desired speed, I sadly miscalculated. What they wanted was to mentally re-create the Roch Cup downhill they had run as youngsters, before Aztec was cut. Fortunately, my memory served the purpose and reliving that race clearly meant a lot to them.

For today's kids, it was a chance to compete on a tough and legendary line that has a reputation for frustrating some of the world's best. This year's crop of racers, including local Wiley Maple, figure to be the stars of World Cup and Winter Olympics Games in the future, and their potential can only be further honed from the experience of competing on Aspen's world-renowned "America's Downhill" course of continually changing terrain.

It takes a lot to put on a ski race, not only in terms of money, but volunteers of every stripe are always in demand. Lunches need to be delivered, gates need to be kept, hand timers are critical, even in the electronic age; announcers, scoreboard writers and a ton of other positions are crucial to the success of ski races. Getting up close to competitions of this caliber can be quite exciting.

It's been a lean winter for snow, but with the U.S. Alpine Championships and NorAm Spring Series came the powder many of us had been craving, even though it created havoc on the race course. As Chief of Course Pat Callahan put it, "If you want snow, schedule a downhill." And, so be it.

Old Houses

When I was a kid growing up in Aspen, there were old, abandoned houses everywhere. Men of the lost generation, guys who could remember the turn of the 19th to the 20th century in Aspen, would occasionally be seen surreptitiously ducking into one or another of these houses and I always wondered if they stayed in those old houses because they had an attachment to them, or if they moved around town at will, staying wherever might be convenient that night. The houses had no feel, no heart or soul to them, and generally their exteriors were of a non-descript gray, unbecoming color. As a young boy, I tried to imagine the families that at one time had lived in them, tried to look in an old window and see the bright colors of Christmas, or maybe see a mother and father watching their young children play in the living room. But, they were always dark, always cold, and the imagination could scarcely take away the curiosity of abandonment they represented.

The other day, on a clear, azure-sky day without clouds, brightly hanging in a sun-filled canopy over the valley, I had the opportunity to look at an old, abandoned house on an upscale Aspen street with a bit more personal attachment than I did those houses of old. My uncle had sold his "old" Aspen house and had moved on. The old house stood there, at the top of a rise, almost in the middle of the acre of land that ensconced it, windows dull, no flicker of light coming from within, not a hint of discernible movement inside, no visible pulse of habitation from any quarter.

There was no indication of who had lived there, who had painstakingly planted the trees that now towered over the house; no indication of the joys and sorrows that occurred there on any given day; no clue to the thoughts or lives of any of the five kids who had grown up there, nor of their parents, or of the nephew they unofficially adopted and who forever after called that house his home, regardless of where he lived.

I lived there when I first got out of college, equipped with very little in life other than a ravenous hunger for women, alcohol and powdered ski slopes, maybe in that order, but I have to say that the alcohol was the easiest to come by. Whatever my behavior, I was somehow tolerated, my absences from the dinner table or my room treated with an understanding that could only come from family.

The wedding reception for my first marriage was held there, as was the wake after my brother's death a couple of years later. The promise of the future, the finality of death. My uncle and I had a 100th birthday party there - he turned 60 almost the same day I turned 40.

If we'd gone uptown for dinner and it was a good night, we'd end up at Sunnie's Rendezvous for an after-dinner libation and a round of BS with whoever was there. If it was an even better night, we'd bring Sunnie, Ralph, and 3 or 4 other people home with us for breakfast. The house would rock from the stride piano style of world-famous pianist Ralph Sutton, the billiard table would be racked time and time again for another round of bottle pool or billiards and the clink of ice continued to be heard into the small hours of the morning.

Years later, most of them sober, I was the only person there the day my aunt came home from the doctor's office with the diagnosis of cancer. She was nervous and couldn't wait for my uncle to get home so we sat at the kitchen table, holding hands and crying together about the effects this insidious disease might have on her future and that of her family.

She was soon gone, well before turning 60; my uncle's heart was broken and the business that he and my aunt had headquartered out of the house for the past twenty years was soon sold. The family had suffered a serious breach, but the soul was still there, hanging on and slowly getting better, year after year.

The years rolled by and the sadness lifted, although it really never went away. But it was still a family; the kids got married and started their own families or started careers; we had dinners together when the mood struck us, and the billiard table got more than its fair share of use. A new generation of skiers, the grandkids, young and still growing, with a place to camp in Aspen whenever they wanted, would leave the house on powder mornings with bright eyes and visions of skiing like they'd never skied before.

Sensing the impending crash of the wrecking ball, I put my truck in gear and slowly drove off, the empty windows staring back at me as I rolled away. The memories will never leave, but they will never be all in one place anymore, either.

This was my first column, published 1/8/2004 in the Aspen Times.

Lesson on the Animals among Us

It was an incredulous remark, inappropriately but casually injected into the conversation, not so much as to make a point, but rather to further inculcate the viewpoint of those of an environmental and political persuasion, one apparently not opposed to using slander in its mission. The remark went something like, "It's nice to see wild game returning to the Roaring Fork Valley after the intense predator control practices of the ranchers." What? Others have repeated it several times since.

If you've studied local history, you know that the elk herds in this area were exterminated (probably deer, as well), mostly as a result of feeding hungry miners and railroad crews. There was no refrigeration, few cattle, but still fresh meat had to be provided on a regular basis.

Professional hunters were common in those days, men who followed the gold and silver strikes, selling meat to hotels, boarding houses and general stores. They also supplied a secondary and profitable market with elk teeth and animal hides. Ranchers did not plunder the elk population, and I'd wager that if you ordered a steak in an Aspen eatery back then, you couldn't be sure you weren't getting bear, cougar, horse or coyote instead of elk, deer or beef.

To be sure, the few ranchers and farmers, just like the thousands of town dwellers, had the frontier belief that there was a right to live off the land, and did so. But in those early days, there were no large herds of cattle to protect; milk cows were more common than beef cattle and farming was still the most viable means of making a living for those preferring the country life.

By the time cattle ranching became the leading money maker in Pitkin County, most of the predators such as bear and mountain lion, at least the ones not killed for meat or sport, had disappeared for there were precious few game animals left to feed on.

To give you an idea of the intense predator control conducted by local ranchers, we have to go no further than my great-grandfather, Jeremie, who emigrated to Woody Creek from Val d'Aosta, Italy in the 1880s. He wandered Woody Creek and the mountains surrounding it for more than 60 years, tending his farms and cattle, and in that span saw one mountain lion. It doesn't appear there was much opportunity during his lifetime to desecrate the local pride.

The Woody Creek ranchers, perhaps unlike those in other states who still fear wolves, realized early on that predators generally will, if given a choice, kill wild game before attacking domestic stock. Those ranchers were instrumental in getting elk reintroduced to this area in 1912.

My grandfather, Ben, born in 1891 with both feet firmly planted in the Old West, ranched in Woody Creek along with his father and four brothers. They were among the first in this area to see the advantages of producing large numbers of cattle and early in the twentieth century ran about a thousand head, pasturing them on forest permits in the mountains between Sloan's Peak and Porphyry Mountain.

Predator control wasn't on their agendas, as there were very few predators. On our many journeys through the mountains (1950s), Gramps and I once saw a mountain lion in Collins Creek. He said it was only the second or third he had seen in his entire lifetime.

Bears were appreciated for their proclivity to consume the remains of dead cows on the range and certainly weren't hunted down. According to oral history, from 1940 to 1990, two bears were killed by my family, one when it entered the range rider's cabin at our cow camp. The other, with bad intentions, attacked a string of horses tied up at the hitching rail during lunch break.

Despite the inaccuracies espoused by those less enlightened, coyotes and free-roaming domestic dogs have created the biggest problems for cattle ranchers in this area. And there has always seemed to be a preponderance of both.

A Memorial and a Reunion

It was an odd day, the last of August, as we climbed the stairs to the third floor of the Elks building and entered into an afternoon reception that would indelibly color our minds forever. A certain, long-forgotten electricity could be felt coursing through the crowd, the energy building, with an intertwining of solemnity and festivity that cannot exist without the requisite feelings of deep sorrow.

It all had started earlier at the packed Catholic Church as we participated in a service for our good friend, Judith Fitzpatrick Byrnes, who died August 22, 2005. A rare type of brain cancer had brought her down, long before her time, and we milled around the church before the mass, uncertain what it all meant for any of us, steadfastly there to pay our last respects to a classmate and friend we had respected since the day we met her.

I say good friend, but can honestly say that since high school, I had only seen Judy three or four times. But in that way of really good friends, if we hadn't seen each other for a hundred years, we'd still have been stalwart buddies. We first met back when we were both a couple of gangly twelve-year-olds, the year her family moved to Aspen. My dad was on the school board, her parents were teachers, and between them they cooked up the idea that Judy should spend some time on our Woody Creek ranch, getting acquainted a bit before school started. From then on, we had a solid friendship.

In junior high, Judy tried, without much success, teaching me to dance so I wouldn't be quite such a wallflower, and although she had eyes for someone else, let me tag along on some of her dates, allowing me to think I may have been part of the action. We slogged through swamps, climbed mountains, rode horses, built campfires, and starred in the senior high spring drama together - Judy, the quiet, serious athlete, me the rambunctious, serious athlete - and we made a heck of a team.

I walked around town the other day, one of those warm, blue-sky, no cloud days, impressed that the leaves hadn't left us, and reminisced about our high school days, the friendships we all had together, some of the rivalries, but mostly about how, being in that neighborhood of what used to be the red brick school, it was almost possible to reach out through the sunshine and touch a long-ago afternoon. Walking slowly west, I took in the smell of fall and a profusion of memories.

Just down Hallam is our classmate Katie's house, so familiar on the corner it could have been the 60s, and I reasoned she might actually be there, visiting her mother. There was the strong desire to go back in time, to stop and say hello. The shy person that Judy tried to help on the dance floor kept me from stopping, and it wasn't until I got home an hour later that I finally dialed the number and got the long-remembered voice of a girl who giggled softly as she said we hadn't seen each other for at least thirty-five years, maybe more.

Priceless things happen between people when the paradigm is changed in unforeseen ways. There were more people at Judy's observance than you could ever round up for a class reunion, and bonds were re-established that had gone lacking for many, many years. My soul was soothed by one in particular, and it was satisfying to reintroduce generations of people to each other who had a translucent, but so important connection back then. We let our guards down and there were hugs, kisses, tears, laughs and the holding of hands among friends who probably won't ever see each other all together again. It was a beautiful day, countered by the dark and insurmountable cost, more than any of us could stand, paid by the woman whose memory we honored.

Mentor and a Hero from the Past

The crash of thunder hammered my ears and the lightning lit up the darkness of my granddad's kitchen as, for God only knows what reason, we sat there, my mother, my aunt and I, waiting for the storm to die, or maybe for one of us to die. And then, like an apparition from out of the storm, the image of my grandfather appeared in the rear door window, astride his big, blue roan cow horse. As he slid from the back of the beast, obviously disoriented, my aunt Eileen ran out to help him into the house.

Blood caked his nose and the corners of his mouth and I could see where it had run down the front of his shirt, deep underneath the black rain slicker he wore. I was used to climbing up into his lap after dinners at his house, snuggling with him while he snoozed in his rocker. I'd never seen him at work, I guess, at least not in a slicker, one spur missing from his muddied boots, Stetson hat crushed into a funny shape and distress in his voice. I hadn't thought the man to be mortal.

Blue, the horse, had lost his footing and rolled them both down a slime-covered Collins Creek embankment, landing on Gramps at the bottom. The women got the stove roaring with some dry wood, then Eileen did her best to clean him up, asking about the mishap. He was visibly relieved there didn't seem to be anything debilitating that might hold him up for long. The gals helped him into a dry shirt, tried to straighten up his hat a tad and on the way out the door, he grabbed a dry pair of gloves. On the porch, he wriggled into the well-worn, black oilskin and with the rain still coming down, mounted up and headed back into the storm and Collins Creek, to finish whatever mission had been interrupted by the wreck.

That's the first real memory I have of my grandfather, other than bits and pieces, and it took place when I was five or six. The next summer, he became my mentor in the world of ranching, and we spent most days riding up Collins Creek, checking on the cows and the grass. Mentor, hell, he was my hero and no matter how old I get, that will never change.

The fall I turned eleven, Gramps and I took our last ride together. He no doubt knew the score, but I wasn't sophisticated enough to realize what was going on. We sat under a huge jack-oak, waiting out a horrendous hail storm, and as we sat and talked about school and stuff, Gramps gave me the only hug I can remember sharing with him. On the way home, with the air sharp and alive from the squall, Grandpa let me know he was headed to the hospital for surgery the next day.

That winter, he stayed in my parent's upstairs bedroom, sucking oxygen out of a green bottle, too weak to venture from the bed. Many people came to pay their respects, and he always said the same thing: "I'll be feeling better in a few weeks." I knew he'd be up and around 'cause I'd seen him do it before. A little more TLC, I figured, and Gramps would roll out the door once again, ready to face the storm of life. When you're eleven and your granddad dies, your heart breaks, hard.

Fifty years later, I'm still moving cows up the path and there isn't much, except skiing, that I'd rather be doing. But you know, lately the thought whispers through my mind that maybe I'm still trailing those goddamned cows around the side of a mountain because I'm hoping for one last chance to help Granddad get that final leg up, to ride into one more sunset, help I couldn't give him all those many years ago.

A Range Rider for Forevermore

The first time we met, I was two years old and he'd just arrived at the house, about half-in-the-bag after having had a drink or two down the road at my great-uncle Sullivan's place, with a big smile upon his face, and an Indian Head buckle holding his belt together. Looking for a ranch job he was, having arrived in Glenwood by bus and hitchhiked up to Woody Creek on the rumor that he could probably find work. By using one of today's descriptive phrases, anyone hanging around our front yard that day long ago would have said, "Cowboy, my ass!"

Anyway, I conned him out of the belt buckle that afternoon (with the aid of a little booze and his desire for a job) and for the next 50 years listened to him complain that he'd had to tie his pants up with a piece of rope until he could get to town. My granddad had hired him on that momentous day and he worked until his retirement, usually employed by one Vagneur family or the other, moving cows, breaking horses, irrigating, putting up hay, and doing all the other ranch chores too tedious to mention. To me, he was just a hero, and it didn't matter what he did.

He was 25 or 30 years older than I, but in a sense, we kind of learned the cowboy ways together. He'd arrived here a greenhorn from Vermont, expressly to ride horses in the mountains, and if that meant being a ranch hand, so be it. Early on, he found part-time work for the Red Mountain group of cattlemen, spending summers in a tent up Hunter Creek, learning the ropes. It wasn't long until he hired on as the range rider for the Red Canyon Cattlemen's Association, a job performed mostly from our lonely cow camp in the Sloan's Peak area, watching over twelve hundred head of fattening Hereford cows. The die was cast and Al would cut short anyone who called him a cowboy, letting them know he was a "range rider," first and foremost, and forever more.

We spent a lot of time together during my young years and he taught me a lot. I learned about U. S. military life in the Philippines, malaria and the mosquitoes that carry it, and how it left Al susceptible to tick fever. He had examined almost every discipline under the sun, by virtue of his lonely nights at the cow camp, with little to do but read books. It was entertaining (and educational), listening to him expound on subject after subject, up to and including relativity theory, but what endeared him to a kid like me was his innovative ability to make a positive out of almost any situation. I learned to like onion sandwiches when our cabin supplies would allow nothing else; discovered how to wash coffee cups in the water trough when in a hurry; developed a sense for seeing the humor in an ironic twist of fate; became aware that Al enjoyed baking biscuits as much as anything; got to know the kind of man who would give you the shirt off his back; and surmised that if nothing else in life, I wanted to be a range rider, forever more.

Al and I knocked back a few drinks in Aspen's watering holes after I got old enough and worked together occasionally until the last Vagneur ranch sold. As so often happens, the glue that held us all together dissipated with the sale - Al moved to Grand Junction to live out his retirement and I never caught up with him again. Alfred Franklin Joseph Senna, Jr., III (ask my cousin Wayne), died last week, at 80 or so, and I reckon with a heart as big as his, he might be the one to finally corral the devil's mighty herd.

Sad Reunion

Back in my college days, I got in the habit of patronizing a certain piano bar, simply because the guy on the box was quite proficient and taught me something from time to time. We became friends of sorts, and so it was that he introduced his new girlfriend to me about the same time she came to live with him. Typical of scoundrels, he had enticed a true beauty, an ex-CU cheerleader, to share herself with him, and she and I hit it off right away - same school and stuff, you know.

In the blink of an eye, they were married and then the troubles began. He became bored with her almost as quickly as he'd married her, and began asking me to take her around town, do anything, just get her out of the piano bar and provide her some entertainment. Cramped his style, he said, to have a woman hanging around. Of course, the lady and I became good friends, and without her old-fashioned notions about marriage, the piano player would probably still be wondering where we'd gone.

The raspy voice on the phone the other day announced her presence, saying she'd like to come see me. Soon, a car dropped her off and she was a bit nervous coming up the walk, but I didn't really notice, shaking a little myself as I held the door for her. From a distance, she was the same girl with big, blue eyes, shoulder-length blonde hair and a sexy energy in her step. But closer up, the lines in her face were deep, particularly around the eyes, just a little deeper than they reasonably should have been. Her eyes still had a brightness to them, but it was more of a glaze than a shine.

As she sat close, holding my hand and telling her story, there was a lot I didn't hear. We were mostly two strangers, brought together, in part, by a man who long ago seemed to quit caring about anyone. Did she really tell me that not long after they'd left for Chicago, a baby on the way, his drinking and drugging got fierce and occasionally he'd come home from working a downtown club and slap her around over imagined infidelities she'd committed?

Through rehab and moving frequently, they'd managed to have another child before the inevitable, merciful split came.

But the lines in her face didn't come from divorce - she'd lost nothing there. Perhaps they came later, when her oldest child, a son, was killed by a hit-and-run driver at the age of nine.

Could we walk out to see the horses, she wanted to know, a nervous energy taking hold of her, and we started out that way, a big smile coming over her face. But, no sooner had the horses greeted us than she wanted to get back to the house, unrealistically afraid she might miss her ride.

There had been alcohol rehabilitation for her (whiskey, water back - oh, hell, forget the water), and the past few years had been clean ones, although the temptation was always there, and maybe sometimes there was a small relapse, but she managed to keep it under control. Or so she said. But, like the sun, her eyes were beginning to sink a bit and the look was coming from far away, and where was her ride anyway?

Slow, rubber tires on gravel gave away her daughter's arrival, followed by the slamming of a car door; then suddenly, the quick clitter-clatter of little feet on the concrete walk and an undersized knock on the open door. Standing there, almost a carbon copy of my friend, was the cutest little granddaughter you could see anywhere, looking as delightful as my friend must have looked at that age. A glance toward my old-time confidant revealed eyes that were, for the briefest of moments, alive and twinkling, the wrinkles and worry gone. Somehow, I know it's okay.

A Seriously Flawed Chain of Events

He was just a little kid, about five years old, skinny as a rail and smart as a whip. It seemed like every time I turned around, he was looking up at me with big, curious blue eyes that always seemed to say, "Please take me along." A real pain in the ass, if you looked at things in that sort of way, or so it might have seemed all those years ago.

It was some sort of a half-baked, daytime Christmas vacation party, one of those affairs that start out with good thoughts and progress downhill from there. Family friends were visiting from out of town and to further the confusion, I'd had a friend spend the night, all in an effort to ensure that everyone had a memorable and festive respite from the real world. The head count before our ill-fated expedition left the house was four, until my little brother made a compelling case that was hard for anyone to turn down, including my mother, so five of us ended up heading out into an overcast day that hovered around 20 degrees below zero.

Before we returned home, one of us would be in a life threatening situation and the rest of the group in serious angst over a seriously flawed chain of events. How hard could it be for a group of kids (all ten or eleven, with one five-year-old) to get in trouble in the middle of 1200 acres of ranch land? Our adventure went exceedingly well, with yours truly breaking trail through about two feet of soft, fluffy snow, until we got to the edge of Woody Creek, about a half-mile from the house.

Still waters run deep say the poets, but the fast-moving currents of mountain streams can be dangerously deceptive, as well, and with the flair of unthinking kids who should have known better, we decided to cross the ice-covered creek. My brother's apprehension before we began our crossing should have been apparent, and maybe it was, but got ignored in my own focused euphoria. In his attempt to fit in with the older kids, he had no hesitation in bravely stepping onto the ice and joining us in the dangerous crossing. In a rare display of intelligence, we put him between two of us older kids, just to be on the safe side.

Preordained misfortune didn't strike, naturally, until we had reached the ugliest section of water, and even then, the ice couldn't suddenly break under anyone except my little brother Steve. It happened very quickly, and I'll never forget turning around to see him, in almost instantaneous slow motion, begin to slide below the ice and disappear into the fast moving, dark water.

A quick grab with our arms pulled him from under the crystallized water just as all but his head disappeared beneath the deadly covering. Had we missed, there would have been no second chance. In my desperation to save him, I got my upper body soaked pulling him out, as did the other kid nearest him, but there was no time to worry about our individual predicaments as my brother's face exemplified the seriousness of this emergency situation. It was of paramount importance to get him (and us) back to the house as quickly as possible.

Almost immediately, his clothes were frozen solid, his legs unable to propel his small body through the deep snow, and as we carried him near the house, Steve became semi-conscious from the cold. Upon our arrival, the adults took over with their life-saving procedures, while the rest of us wondered how something so deadly could happen so quickly.

My little brother died about thirty years ago, a young man in his prime, not from falling through the newly-formed ice on a mountain creek, but from the eccentricities of life that can sometimes consume those of us most vulnerable. And even though he's dead and it's an impossible thought, ironic at best, I'd sure like to apologize for almost killing him that day, long ago.

A Shot Too Hard to Bear

We'd just settled into our sleeping bags when the horses began making a ruckus, snorting, pulling back, and stomping the ground. After a bit, they seemed to calm down, but we should have known it wasn't over.

My head was near the tent wall when suddenly, heavy breathing could be heard, right next to my ear; not of the human kind, but of something outside which, whatever it was, occasionally rubbed its nose against the scratchy fabric. Unlike a horse, its tread was silent.

As you might have guessed, the possibilities weren't endless, and even though we had strung our food (including a hindquarter of venison) up a tree, the thought of a bear (what else?) in the tent posed problems of a kind we weren't used to dealing with. It was the 1960s and bears, unlike today, were still wild, unpredictable animals.

My buddy, Roy Holloway, and I were about 14 and 15, by the memory of it and were, we suspected, quite capable of taking care of ourselves. A plan, worthy of at least "B" Hollywood, with incredible potential for bloody resolve on either side, was soon put into action.

I knew this 4-man tent well, a large, green canvas behemoth made before the days of lightweight synthetic fiber and aluminum frames. It had been my summer home for the past 3 or 4 years, mostly set up in the backyard, but several times a season packed into the forest by horse, for a camping trip alone or with friends.

In the softest of whispers, I detailed the plan to Roy, as it was, after all, my tent. He was to hit the zippered door of the tent solidly with his shoulder (I'd done this before), busting out in a flash of exuberance, and then drop directly to his knees. Almost in the same instance, he'd pan the scene, right to left (the noise was on our right) with his flashlight, poking a hole in the almost opaque darkness.

Following immediately behind would be yours truly, only as we exited the tent, I would stand upright and swing my 30-.06, semiautomatic rifle to the right, catching Roy's beam of brilliance and follow it around to the left, zeroing in on whatever we spooked in the dark. We were purists of a sort and didn't have much use for magnifying scopes, so this wasn't as technical as you might think.

The plan went off with magnificent, unyielding perfection. Roy was without error in his part and I caught the beam of radiance from his handheld light just as he began the predetermined arc. We instinctively knew that we had two, maybe three seconds to pull this off, so there wasn't a lot of time to contemplate the exact nature of what our actions might accomplish.

With trigger finger at the ready, the first creatures of consequence to come into my view were the horses, which I fully expected, and almost before that even registered, Roy's light was moving rapidly leftward, following the rustle of something large leaving the area.

Not more than ten feet away, we caught up to the tail-end of a large black bear, scooting for the safety of darkness as fast as he could. There was almost time for one shot, and that might have done it, but there's something intrinsically wrong about shooting an animal in the ass, particularly one as large and dangerous as a bear.

If the most ferocious thing a bear can show you is a rapidly disappearing backside, you're going to create bad karma by taking the shot. When you least expect it, out on the trail next year, or maybe the one after that, something bad's gonna happen, just 'cause you asked for it.

We stayed two more nights, without changing our modus operandi, and never saw or heard the bear again. The poor bastard.

Stolen Romance

It was time to sift through an accumulated pile of communications populating a portion of my bookcase, and as I gathered up the boxes of cards, newspaper clippings, and letters that documented certain triumphs and sorrows of my life, an unusual envelope with a faraway post mark fell innocently to the floor. Simply by glimpsing the distinctive penmanship, my mind relived a night of tender lovemaking with a tantalizing woman who came quickly into my heart and left again almost as suddenly. The enclosed card was telling; a photo of three polar bears caught on an ice floe in the middle of nowhere and inside, a quickly scrawled, "I love you," followed only by her first initial.

She lay half facing me, head on my shoulder. The great quilt comforted us as we watched the dying firelight dance on the old cabin walls. Tentatively, I reached down and grasped her hand, drawing it up to my chest. We must not move and alert others sleeping in the small space. Our touch was soft at first, but quickly became hard and firm, caressing each other urgently through this outwardly innocent connection. Our desire became more intense for each other, and our hands pressed together as hard as humanly possible.

It was a passion that longed for release, a passion stronger than either of us had felt before. We were one as our feelings for each other coursed through our bodies, the impending climax that would never come imminent nonetheless, and as our souls orgasmed on a plane beyond the physical, our lovemaking became less urgent and more tender. Her breath was deliriously hot on my neck as she whispered an almost inaudible caution of "shh." I carefully moved her hand to my mouth, slowly and delicately loving each curvature, each single nuance, the very uniqueness of her, reveling in her taste. It was a dance of syncopation, her hand responding to my mind and tongue as I sought the most tender and vulnerable areas. She, in turn, caressed and stroked my hand, the wetness of her mouth creating audible and profound pleasure for us both. Slowly and quietly, the passion ebbed, its urgency spent, and as our entwined hands relaxed, we drifted off into tortured sleep, knowing this brief and futile interlude was our only allowance, made by a monogamous world sleeping nearby that, if it knew, would judge us for the tenderness we felt for each other.

What is this about? Stolen moments, forbidden love, infidelity, or natural desire? What sparks the sudden connection, at a perfectly innocent, week-long holiday get-together, which drives us to reckless behavior that might better remain unrealized? It is about love, that is true, but one cannot have such without beauty, and beautiful thoughts are what remain long after the assignation is no longer real.

During her remaining days in town, we managed a couple of hurried and private interludes behind closed doors, delicately and deviously trying to hide our feelings from friends and family, thinking we were buying time, but it was an impossible situation to maintain. In an unusual fashion, I would have risked destroying her marriage and perhaps both our lives for the chance to pursue such a unique dalliance to the ends of the earth, but an unspoken tremor of common sense echoed in our thoughts, not in any concrete or decided manner, but more in the way we just painfully, and eventually, let it dissolve. Until she boarded the plane for home, we nimbly jockeyed around each other, fully cognizant that large families seem unerringly designed to keep everyone out of trouble. And in the end, it simply became a mystical romance that might have been more in another time.

With a wondering smile, I placed the card back in the envelope, thinking that life is but an accumulation of small moments, the most precious of which come together to create an unbreakable, priceless thread of reflection upon our existence.

Those Events We Can't Forget

They come around, those events we can't forget, and even though they're not life-shattering, they'll stick with us forever. For every season, it seems, something comes around that I haven't thought about in years, but maybe due to the particular lean of the sun or the reflection of the moon across a ribbon of water, it creeps into my mind and holds me prisoner until I've used it up. And maybe it isn't the event itself but more the atmosphere around the happening that grips my allegiance.

As I was growing up, the mountain behind our house was called many things, but certainly not Vagneur Mountain — that came later. My cousins down the road called it Gobbler's Knob, an assessment I found rather intriguing, but my father or his father never really had a preferred name. Sometimes my granddad referred to it as Wild Horse Mountain, as in, "Let's go round up the wild horses on the mountain," and I would jump at the chance. There were two evergreens prominently displayed high on the otherwise mostly bare face, and I took to calling it Two Pines or, as we most commonly referred to it, either "the mountain behind the house" or "where we elk hunt."

Snow had fallen a few days before, and many leaves were still golden, hanging on for — what? Our amusement or cover for the elk? A certain amount of planning had gone into the mission, as I found out just the day before we left, but it didn't matter because I had been included in the plan. Unlike the previous year, when I'd broken my maiden as a first-time hunter by bringing down a nice five-point bull and when we'd left the house well before daylight to reach the top of the mountain by dawn, this year we were going to camp on the mountain the night before, an attempt to lessen the early-morning stress.

At 13 years old, it's one of those remarkable things to put your trust in your dad and go with the flow, not worrying about every little detail and not asking a million questions. And so it was that we came upon a deserted cabin in the middle of a dark pine forest on that mountain behind our house, one of those surprises in your backyard that have been there for eons, completely unknown to you. My great-grandfather had used it, keeping a crew up there in the summer to cut timber for his sawmill down at the main ranch, a sideline continued by my granddad up until the 1920s.

It wasn't much to look at as we pulled up, what with a caved-in roof. Only about six logs high remained, staggered around the perimeter, the rest having fallen by the wayside over the years, but toward the back, enough roof remained to keep most of any precipitation off.

Whatever it was, it was a part of us, part of our lineage, our history, and my dad, who had used the cabin innumerable times as a youth, had not forgotten it. Part of the magnificence of the memory, I reckon, is that he was sharing this with me, not that he even mentioned it, but it came out in conversations I overheard, little bits and pieces, and a kid who tried to keep his mouth shut could learn a lot.

There were six of us in the party, but we all took care of ourselves pretty much. My dad and I, we cut pine boughs for mattresses and laid our sleeping bags out next to each other under the shaky roof, warm and content. He had a new bag, not so much a sleeping bag as we think of it today but more a bedroll from the Old West, a comfort that a man with horses could afford. He gave that bag to me a few years later, and I enjoyed it a long time not only for camping in the mountains while working cows but also for Lake Powell expeditions, and it was a reliable friend on long road trips.

There was something about that hunting excursion, a closeness we had; he was treating me as an equal and not a son, and it probably was because I wasn't screwing up and testing his patience. I held up my end of the bargain, taking care of the horses and making sure everything was picked up, just like one of the crew.

We hunted up there a few more years, never using the old cabin again but sometimes pitching tents or leaving the ranch well before daylight, and somehow it just seemed easier that way. We never talked about it, and I'd pretty much forgotten about that outing until just the other day. And like my memory, which is hauntingly clear, visible remnants of that old cabin still remain.

Sunday is for Reminiscing

It's hard to say how some conversations get started, but once ignited, they take on a life of their own, sometimes going for days and sometimes never ending in our own minds. It was a simple remark, something about no matter how tough the ranching got, we weren't going anywhere, not in this lifetime.

We sat at the kitchen table, a couple of ol' boys, swapping stories as old as the time our families have been in the valley, stories that we each understood before they began, but they had to be told, nonetheless. If you don't have the anecdotes, and certainly if you don't understand them, you'll never be accepted for what you claim to be, if a rancher is what you claim. Irrigation water that won't run, cows that won't fatten, horses that "suck up" and "help" that is clearly misdefined are typical subjects.

And then it took a turn, as Billy let slip that his mother had traveled to Glenwood Springs with my great-grandmother, "Grandma Vagneur," so that the elder Vagneur could have some eye surgery done. In a situation not that unusual for "new" Americans, Grandma Vagneur needed an interpreter as she only spoke the French patois of northern Italy, in the Aosta valley. Billy's mom was probably no more than twenty or so, and it was an adventure for her, as attested by her telling of the story to her children.

Billy was born in the house we were using for our conversation (he's about my age), and the big thing about houses, we both concurred, was that they needed to keep you warm and dry. Beyond that, we didn't much care about fancy or square footage. We generally agreed that, no matter the house, neither one of us was going to be very far from our roots when we hung up our saddles for the last time.

"There might be better places to ranch," I offered, but then, "Where would we go, at our age," he asked, clearly referring to the fact that it would be difficult to garner and absorb more than a hundred years of history into the new spread, in the time we have left. "I can tell you things about this place that would mean nothing to anyone else, but mean everything to me," he said. "I can stand in the middle of the hayfield and feel at home." But what got us melancholy was the fact that if we stood in the center of it, like tomorrow, without knowledge of the history, without our participation in that history, it would be nothing, if not meaningless.

We talked briefly about how my widowed grandfather, Ben, was a "character" at dances up and down the valley, and how neither of us ever got to town enough as kids. "Basalt was close by, "Billy said, "but it was more or less as lively as the ranch." "At least Aspen had a movie theater," I explained, "or else we would have been about like Basalt." "Oh, my." Billy liked the movies, you could tell, watching him relive the memories.

And the dreams began to interject themselves and we talked on. "I'd like to have a ranch in Arizona, maybe, just to winter the cows," says Billy, "and get out of here when it's cold. But you'd stay for the skiing, wouldn't you?" "Yeah, I like winter. Gawd, don't you wish we could harness up a team of big horses and spend a snowy morning feeding cows from the hay sled?" "I remember that," said Billy, "not like today, with the enclosed tractor cabs and heaters. It used to be rough."

It was 6:00 PM and I stood up. "See ya later. I got irrigation water to move." We were both in our work clothes, dried sweat and dirt on our faces from a long day already. Billy says "yes," he has "to milk the cows, anyway," but he can't resist a parting shot. "It's Sunday, isn't it?"

41

Uncle Jim's Trunkful of War Mysteries

References to World War I in recent editions of the paper have brought back memories of an old soldier from those days, a man, possibly heroic, who still manages to confound me.

The old, brown steamer trunk at the foot of my brass bed isn't much to look at, but it serves quite well as a prop for a coyote's tanned winter hide and as a reminder of days when such pelts were a prize, a time long ago when such things didn't make people squeamish. I hadn't opened the chest (which mysteriously became mine many years ago) since childhood, and with a sudden, burning curiosity, reached for the latches with trembling hand.

The mundane minutiae of life that is saved by some can be very revealing at times - quite boring at others. Every check that the Stapleton Brothers ranching company wrote from 1931 to 1944 is still in that trunk, and there are glimmers of a family life from the past that jump up at one with remarkable clarity, although clouded with uncertainty around the edges. There are deeds to land, bookkeeping journals, bills from livestock companies, and other things pertaining to ranching life in those days.

Also, of course, are letters home to Aspen from my great-uncle, Jim Stapleton, stationed in World War I France, offering very little other than confirmation that he was OK. Of particular interest were the contents of the paper bag I found, a bag made of the finest and smoothest paper imaginable, of a pale pink shade, and had it not been carefully folded and placed in the middle of a World War I pamphlet containing the names and addresses of all in Jim's unit, I might not have been curious enough to open it. Inside was a picture of Jim as a young man, and enclosed within the edge of the frame was a very small envelope, containing a generous lock of golden curls, signed, "Love, Marion E. Smith, September 23, 1912". Jim would have been 17 that year, and perhaps this was his first, and last great love affair.

Jim was, in the words of several family members, "a mean son-of-a-bitch," a remark made without kindness or remorse. I remember well his final homecoming, shortly before his death at 58, convalescing from a heart attack while apprehensively awaiting the final convulsion. What glimmer of susceptibility, what chink in the gruff and seemingly impenetrable exterior did I see that made me (at age five) run across the dining room and jump excitedly into the big, leather chair with him, telling him I loved him? It could have been the exuberance of a young child caught up in the machinations around a serious illness, but I don't think so.

Further down in the trunk, buried beneath WWI uniforms, including a government issue hat, sat an intriguing box, tightly wrapped and tied, containing exquisite linen kerchiefs, tucked inside of which were further, romantic notes from Marion E. Smith, written during the war. Also inside was a container surrounded by very fine, delicate paper. Carefully opening the fragile, skillfully wrapped package, a powerful, deep lilac fragrance of the Italian countryside, almost 100 years ago, touched my senses in a way that was nearly overwhelming. A present brought back from the "War Across the Sea," for a sweetheart of years running, carelessly tossed into the bottom of this trunk when he learned of her perceived desertion? Had she possibly grown tired of waiting for his return, or had he, stuck in Europe, become withdrawn and unresponsive to her questions from home.

If the relationship was ever consummated, we shall never know, but I am more drawn to wonder when the boyish smile he was once known for (as the youngest son), faded away, never to reappear. Perhaps it was when he got off the train in Aspen.

Tony Vagneur admits to changing the last name of the woman in this story - out of respect for her family.

Abstaining From Traditional Love

There it sits on the table, my grandfather's death certificate. Not much information contained therein - born in Woody Creek, 1891, and died in Woody Creek, 1958, with both events occurring about 1/4 mile apart. There was a lot of living in those 67 years, I reckon, but how would we ever know unless we knew him. He died in the middle of the night while the rest of my parent's house slept, his breath stilled by the insidious spread of terminal cancer.

An acquaintance and I stood in the cool breeze of an autumn evening, talking on the deserted porch of an old ranch house. His wife of twenty-some years came to check on us and one could feel the electricity between them, even in that brief moment. "Do you love your wife," I asked, rather boldly? "Yes, I love her deeply," was the reply as he stared out over the fading hayfields and pondered the richness of what he'd just said. "I wish I could empathize," was my foremost thought, as I turned and walked inside.

Granddad and his wife Grace were a hot item back in the day, and from old pictures, it is reasonably clear they were very much in love. My grandmother died a very young woman, leaving my grandfather with four kids to finish raising and an insistent depression that was difficult for him to manage.

When we're very young, our existence seems to parallel eternity, but soon enough, we must acknowledge our mortality. We sat on a large rock, holding hands and watching the clear, rippling waters of the Arkansas dance around us, wanting to encircle each other with the passions of a lifetime and make our connection irreversible, but we held back. First, we needed to relive the intervening years, decades spent apart. My divorces and her own challenges. Where did we leave off - in our 20s - so young and passionately in love, yet determined to travel our own paths, eventually to see them converge here in a strange town, on a batholith of impressive proportions. "Do you think, with just a bit of luck, we could have made a go of it," she asked? "I don't know, but right now, I wish we'd tried," was the reply. "You're the one who broke it off," she offered. Of course it was, I always do.

As a young boy, my summers were spent with Gramps, learning to rope and ride, to drive tractors, and how to get along in a man's world. He had a girlfriend in town he spent Saturday nights with, and my tender and unseasoned friend Norma and I would sometimes spend a portion of our weekend with them, drinking Cokes to their mixed drinks and dancing it up at the old Eagles Club.

A friend says, "Why don't you get off the younger women and find someone you can at least talk to?" "Do you have meaningful conversations with your wife," I ask? "Not much anymore, but you know what I mean." "No, I don't know what you mean. I can have conversations with almost anyone, regardless of age," adding, "I may be single, but even married, you appear lonely."

For Granddad, his wife's death was a loss that ran very deep, but it was not the end of romance. Divorce and heartbreak hurt too, whether you welcome or fight them, but the mind's ability to heal, to overcome the disappointment, is incredible and nothing can put an end to the romance in me, either. I have come to realize, with some relief, that I will never have the traditional home and family, simply because I do not find that to be a necessity. But, yes, I have also come to understand that I can love very deeply. And, I suppose in the end, my death certificate won't read much differently from my grandfather's.

Ah, Those Luscious Lips

Harried might have been my feeling, as a couple of buddies, who at the time owned the Woody Creek Tavern, talked me into delaying a coveted trip into the mountains to become an accordion-playing polka meister at a long-awaited Oktoberfest party.

I forwent the lederhosen and stuck with my usual attire, which may have put me somewhat out of sync with the main group, a loose-knit affiliation of disparate motorcycle mavens and lumberjacks from the valley whose forte was rock 'n roll. My accordion and I filled our niche with fervored festivity and gave the scene some Bavarian flavor, even though most of the polkas were Polish. We didn't see it coming at the time, but this particular party set the stage for the following New Year's Eve extravaganza that soon enough turned bloody and ugly, but that's another column.

Basically, I finished my gig early, bowing out to let the principal band take the music wherever it pulled them. My main memory of the evening was of a very tall and buxom biker babe with a large, intricate tattoo covering most of her back, right down to the top of her low-slung leather pants. Her soft, silky, black hair fell below her hips, forcing her to coax it aside to display the artful design. For whatever reason, she kept her eyes on me and covered my mouth with a delicious lip-lock whenever the opportunity presented itself. She had full, sensuous lips that were impossible to ignore and the sweet, wet kisses lasted for long and pleasurable interludes. Never did we exchange so much as a word between us.

Despite my good intentions, all of that fooling around kept me out too late and I drank far more than reasonable, which considerably delayed my departure for the mountains the next day. A nasty hangover had parked itself over my being like a veil of deep depression and I moved slowly.

Overnight, a winter storm had blown into the valley, and it was with a bit of trepidation that my good mount Willie and I, leading a sure-footed pack horse, left from the ranch around four o'clock in the afternoon. It's a steep climb in altitude to our cow camp, and the farther up the mountain we traveled, the more intense the storm became. Just as twilight turned to dusk, we entered a meadow close above the cabin, where the low clouds and blowing snow howled around and under the horses, making it impossible to see the trail ahead.

There was the familiar sting of excitement burning in my chest as I bucked the elements, traveling alone and feeling the danger. Pulling up in front of the lonely, dark cabin, opaque shadows were the only discernible shapes, and I was beyond caring that I might fall over when dismounting, simply from the cold in my bones. Then, just as my right foot touched down, a group of nearby coyotes let out their mournful, quavering wails, and the hair on the back of my neck stood up. "Please, let this moment last," was my thought as I hung tight to the saddle, but it was over almost as soon as it began.

With focused energy, I managed to take care of my horses, got a nice, warm fire going and cooked a little dinner, making my pallet up as I worked. Fitfully, sleep came and went, and I looked out into the stygian abyss often, gauging the depth of the snow, which eventually topped three feet.

I'd wander back to bed and slowly drift off, caressing the memory of a beautiful woman who draped her legs around a different breed of horse and whose tattooed trunk and voluptuous lips had become a peaceful, sleep-inducing enigma in the midst of a raging storm and throbbing hangover.

Aspen Mountain Trail Crew

From the time I was about six years old, I wanted to be a ski patrolman on Aspen Mountain, but being a kid from the small town at its base, figured I'd never have a chance at such a high-level skiing job. Later, my cousin, Leroy Vagneur, worked there a winter or two after graduating from college, so I thought that perhaps it may not be a total impossibility.

For me, college graduation opened no doors (by choice) and coming home to Aspen, I skirted the issue of ski patrolling, not thinking it possible, until one autumn night in the Red Onion, someone mentioned that it might happen if I'd call Charlie Maddalone, the Aspen Mountain manager. Charlie was a basketball referee when I played for Aspen High and didn't put up with any nonsense. He told me he thought he could get me on the trail crew, something I'd never heard of, but said the patrol was a more complicated matter. Take it or leave it was the terse offer. I took it.

Ken Lindsey was the trail crew leader (Lindsey's Loop, skier's left of Lower Corkscrew), a man whose distrust for authority was even larger than mine, and my name having come from management, I had an uphill battle to fight, not only with Ken, but with the entire crew, which numbered 5 or 6 and included guys like Jons Milnor, Tom Canning, Gary Krubsack, Jim "Sully" Sullivan, and Ted Bachle. There was an attempt to freeze me out, but as Jons later said, "You could ski, so we had to take you on."

And ski we did. Our job, of course, was trail maintenance, in the days when snow cats couldn't do nearly as much as they do today. We'd shovel the tops off of moguls on runs such as Percy's and FIS, ski-pack Silver Queen, Little Corkscrew, Corkscrew Gully, etc., - and on powder days, we'd take the ticket packers out for a couple of hours so they could garner a same-day lift ticket for their efforts. Lindsey made sure his crew got a lot of fresh tracks.

How hard was all that? Not very, and when we weren't working at our assigned jobs, which was a large portion of the time, we were an elite group of hard core skiers. Of course, we had to stay out of sight as much as possible, so we learned to ski tight trees without blinking, huck over big rocks and around old mine shafts, and knew every spot on the mountain that could afford at least one good powder turn before the pine boughs would take your head off. We grew to like socked-in, snowy days when the crowds stayed home, because we could ski more of the mountain. Flat light was our friend and the more miserable the snow conditions, the bigger our playground.

Pernod, the grand French elixir, was having an American promotion that winter, along with a now-defunct winemaker, so our variety of after work libations was enhanced considerably, and we were forever being entertained by a rash of ski and surfing movies, made the previous year by every jamoke who could afford a camera. We partied a lot, but kept ourselves reasonably well-kept for the next day's skiing.

Back in those casual times, Aspen Mountain seemed much bigger, simply because there wasn't a gondola nor any high speed lifts. Everything on cables was closer to the ground and most of the trails were narrower, including the lines cut for the lifts. Skiing was more of a journey, rather than a quick rip to the bottom.

Late one winter, ski corporation management decided we were unneeded and unceremoniously discharged us. Truly, the end of an era and I am forever grateful for the education it gave my skiing. Most of us were fortunate enough to be offered ski patrol jobs the next year, which of course, we accepted. Then, the real stories began.

All-Star Aspen

We keep reading in the local papers how celebrities aren't a big deal in Aspen, but then every time one sticks his/her head out from under a rock, some reporter or columnist oohs and aahs, making the rest of us queasy. Before you think I'm antisocial, I'd like to add my two cents regarding said lackluster brouhaha.

The celebrity thing got off to an early start in my life with the presence of Gary Cooper in Aspen. My great-aunt, Julia Stapleton, somehow got invited over there to the Lower Red Mountain address for lunch, and she took my mother and me along, just for the heck of it, I guess. The Coopers had a wild squirrel on the back patio that was reasonably well trained to beg for food, and tossing him nuts was the highlight of my visit with the legendary film star.

In elementary school, it didn't take us long to figure out that star-studded celebrities seemed to stay at the Hotel Jerome, and we knew which door to knock on if we wanted to see 'em, because one particular suite was always reserved for big shots. If a face we recognized answered the door, we asked for an autograph - if not, we'd say something about "sorry, wrong room" and buzz on down the hall. Obviously, it was a hit and miss system, and sometimes we'd get autographs from people whose signatures didn't match up with the faces we thought we'd seen, and that prompted arguments about what had gone wrong, until the next week, when we'd beat on the door once again.

It seems like a big deal to a lot of people nowadays to see splendiferous people here and there in town, but it used to be more commonplace and a non-event. Going down to my uncle's house on Red Butte Drive one winter night, I helped a woman get her car unstuck from the driveway across the street. I later said something to my aunt about the neighbor lady looking a lot like Cher and was informed that Cher was indeed the neighbor. It wasn't uncommon for Buddy Hackett, another neighbor, to poke his head in the door with the latest of what he thought were good jokes. Please, knock first, was the sentiment.

One day, as I performed dispatch duties for the Aspen Mountain ski patrol, a caller asked if I'd go over to the Sundeck and tell Michael Douglas that the film crew wasn't coming up the mountain that day. "Sure," I said, wondering how screwed up that poor guy on the other end of the phone must be. Besides, we were the ski patrol, not a messenger service. As I was buttoning up my morning shift, Robin Perry, the patrol director, called me over to the Sundeck, saying there was someone he wanted me to meet. Yeah, it was Michael Douglas, letting me know he would have rather made a few runs than wait around for that elusive film crew. Oops.

Of course, there was the time I became the stunt-double for the Marlboro Man during the filming of some commercials around Aspen. Per the script, I was to rope a black stallion who had escaped from a corral just moments before, and save the day, for whomever. After a couple of days filming my unique attempts at roping this "runaway" horse, the big star was brought in for the close-ups. Someone eventually noticed that I had been doing the roping with my left hand - the "face" was right-handed. Two days of filming costs a lot of money, so the "talent" was told to do the best he could with his left hand. Another "Oops" which still makes me smile.

What makes a celebrity, anyway? If any of them who come to town put their pants on any differently than the rest of us, be sure to let me know; otherwise, I'll call you.

The Passing of an Outlaw

We gathered around the casket a little nervously, taking a polite last look without wanting to. What you see doesn't mean a thing, except if you haven't seen one before, you suddenly know what a corpse looks like.

What you don't see is what makes a life; small nuances like a glint in the eye or maybe how a guy held his coffee mug in the mornings or danced the two-step at the old Eagles Club. A guy I never liked shuffled up alongside me and whispered, as though I might agree, "There lies one worthless prick."

He was younger than me, freckled face and a tight upper lip that always held a smile. Despite his prepubescent age, words rasped over his tongue like that of a much older boy. Football was his dream and his folks had bought him a pair of shoulder pads, a helmet and a pale yellow uniform with the number "1". He ran the sidelines of every home game the Aspen Skiers played, conducting his own imaginary game in the distance, but careful to copy every long run I made. He'd proudly stride up to me after the game, telling me how he'd re-created the competition in his mind and I'd pull him in with an arm and a smile.

After college, I asked about him, thinking he'd have made a fine athlete, but there weren't any words of support. His dad died in a nasty car wreck, just about the time the kid could have really used a father, and his mother had trouble keeping the family together, what with little money and trying to self-medicate the pain.

He was darker, like his Cherokee-blooded mom, and maybe that ancestry was why alcohol made him a little crazy. Where the anger came from, it was hard to say because life is never that simple, but losing his immediate family in the formative years was a likely suspect. Maybe it was watching Aspen rapidly change, shutting him out, even as he struggled to grow into a history of horses, lumber jacking and ranching.

"Don't take any crap off that kid," were my instructions as I tended bar at the Eagles Club. "Throw him out before he hurts you." Being a hero carries some responsibility, even if it was in the past, and I asked him politely a couple times to "straighten up or get out." His eyes were hard, his face without expression as the whiskey spoke, "Don't mess with me - you'll regret it."

We went to the alley at my invitation, where I longed to give him the thrashing I thought he'd earned, knowing full-well it could backfire. We faced off and a smile crossed his face, "Tony, for Christ's sake, I can't fight you. We've been through it, man. I'm goin' home."

He was a bad outlaw who couldn't smile for the cops though, and after years of getting their asses kicked, they finally nailed him on trumped up charges and sent him to prison. That was the end of him, but still it took time.

Out of jail, he sometimes worked on a neighboring ranch and we'd occasionally pass each other by in the mountains, always riding alone and looking for cows. He was a free spirit with little need for talk. He'd take my cow camp whiskey without asking, but would split a cord of firewood for the cabin without being asked.

At 50, weight had piled on his medium frame, his eyes had slicked over, and one morning as he mounted up in the horse corral, his heart stopped, ending a journey that never really took off. If there was time to think about it, he likely went down with relief that it was finally over.

Whatever he was, besides my friend, it's hard to say.

Bottled Demons Unleashed

The gray of early dawn greeted my eyes as a woman's shrill voice echoed through my mind, rapidly becoming reality. "Tony, Tony, where's Horace?" the sound fairly screamed at me, a woman desperate to find her husband and who, out of some sort of deference, had waited for first light to bother me. I tried to lie to her, to buy myself a little time to figure out just exactly what she was talking about, but she saw through it and offered no resistance as she closed the door and walked away.

The last time I'd seen Horace had been at lunch the previous day. My parents were gone somewhere and I was, even though only 16, the "boss" out on Woody Creek's Elkhorn Ranch. We had two hired men that summer, Horace being one of them and he and I had, out of coincidence, arrived at the ranch house about the same time. I was heading to the post office to check the mail (letters from a sexy Texan) and offered to take Horace along for the ride.

Being a kid and unaware of unknown adult repercussions, I asked Horace if maybe he wouldn't like to have a beer with lunch, as in "let's get a six-pack," and he readily concurred. We headed up the road to the ranch, going slowly, and by the time I had downed a beer, Horace had killed four and was working on his fifth (beer). Driving by what is now Hunter Thompson's old place, about halfway home, he asked me if maybe we shouldn't go back and get another six-pack. It was my opinion that we needed to get back to work, but Horace said if I'd let him out, he'd walk back to the store and get some more beer. "I'm just real thirsty," he said.

There was not an inkling in my mind of the kind of demon I was helping to unleash, even though this was a strange turn of events, and so stopped the car and let Horace out. To be perfectly honest, I didn't think much about him the rest of the day. We were on a twelve-hundred acre ranch, doing different things, so it wasn't unusual to not see another person for most of the day. If I did miss him, it was no doubt with the thought that he had gone home, giving himself the day off, a phenomenon I knew little about at the time.

However, his wife, in an adenoidal instant, had pointed out something far more serious than an afternoon off, and my heart pounded in my chest and ears as I tried to put the pieces together and figure it out. As the sun came up, I relayed my story to her, and she settled in for the wait, something she had obviously been through before.

My dad got a call from Horace, in Cheyenne, about two weeks later, wondering if he could get bus fare home and a little money for food. Dad, of course, sent the money and as he figured might happen, Horace didn't show. "He'll call again, when he's ready," said my father.

It only took about a week the second time, but that was the call that stuck and as my dad and Horace came back from the bus station, it seemed like everyone was out to watch them pull in and curious to see if Horace had anything to say. He was grinning from ear to ear, glad to see some familiar faces, but boy, he didn't look too good. About as white as the chalk on a blackboard and shaking like an aspen leaf in a windstorm.

Despite it all, it's hard to know how a man and woman put things back together after a rift like that, but they did, and Horace finished out the summer with us, as sober as the day my dad hired him. I'll just never forget his wife hollering up the stairs that morning.

Another Ranch Bites the Dust

The ranch is gone and it's hard to describe how the soul gets sucked out of something, but if you're not careful, a part of yours can disappear, too, if you're standing too close.

I'd been feeding these cows and calves fairly regularly for the last couple of months and had grown to know them in that way one gets attached to animals. There was the flat-backed, brindle faced momma we called "Hippo" after a big-chested girl somewhere; sporadic black steers, with just enough nuance between them to make identification possible; #0224, a heifer with a blue tag in her left ear who, every morning gave me a look of curiosity as though there might be something between us. I'll never forget the two "dinks," a couple of wasted two-year-olds who had lived through diphtheria, pneumonia, harsh winters and should have died or been put down, but through the miracle of antibiotics and a kindhearted owner, they were still treading the earth, minding their own business.

Yesterday, we loaded four silver livestock trailers, pulled by gleaming red Peterbilt trucks, with cows and sent them either to the sale yard or the new ranch down in southern Colorado. None of the cows had been in a trailer before and weren't too keen on the idea of taking a seemingly impromptu ride. Born on the ranch, they had done their jobs well by throwing good calves, and were more than a little recalcitrant to load, knowing that boarding the glossy aluminum "pots" meant trouble, somehow. In the long shadows of the fading afternoon, a last glance revealed the feeding ground to be a wasteland, empty of life and striated by cold, windblown snow that only added to the loneliness of the flat agriculture land.

Today, my friend Sara and I got to the corral feed mangers just before daylight, ready to throw hay for the last of the herd, around 100 head of calves and get them ready for their first ride as well, in a sleek truck. It was about zero degrees and my well-gloved fingers, wrapped around the wood of a pitchfork handle, were soon numb. Deep inside, there was an ache, knowing that once the corrals were cleared, the cattle ranch, like a puff of smoke, would no longer exist. There might be new cows and calves someday, but they won't have the genealogical history of this last bunch, nor will they add the dynamic personality these cows and their owners have laid down over the last forty-five years. The heart of the place left with the cows, and the soul was hanging by a thread, held by the munching of the calves, heads buried deep in the hay bunks.

When my family sold our last ranch out on Woody Creek, a variable couple of individuals took over the reins, soon giving up the cows for being too much work. A cerebral decision, as was the one to clean out the generations-old cow camp, erroneously thinking they owned the cattlemen's association accumulation of over 100 years of cowboying. But, in the tradition of greenhorns trying to be "one of the boys" by using their heads instead of their hearts, they overlooked the "cow camp diaries" stashed in a hollowed log in one of the walls. In their greed to round up the wash basins, steel cabinets and various knives and lanterns, they failed to see, or even dream that there could be a true heart to the operation.

And so, after the last load of calves pulled out, Ed, Dick, Brad and I turned to catch a glimpse of the empty corrals, and the change was as sudden as the fall of a black curtain across the stage whose best has already been played. The feeling, the myth, the very soul was gone, and we worked as fast as possible to get the last details picked up and begin our healing. The previous owners will live a part of each day here, if only in their minds.

Anthropomorphism

We are, by our own unfettered admission, at the top of the world's food chain, and by that thought alone, we also unwittingly admit that we have serious limitations as human beings. These limitations keep us from seeing the world around us as it actually is, and many times we go to our deaths over the minutiae that consume us, minutiae that most likely have no basis in fact.

In case you think I've finally eaten the last chocolate, I'm talking about anthropomorphism, a word which basically means the suggesting of human characteristics for animals or inanimate things. We somehow have this arrogant attitude that anything other than us on the evolutionary or creationist scale finds us a species worth imitating. A repugnant thought, really, if you think about it. We even think our gods look similar to us!

Anthropomorphism is not a novel concept, thought up by new-age devotees to political correctness. We have no doubt been doing this since before recorded history and certainly since then. The Greek gods were, no matter their individual talents, full of human attributes including love, lust, jealously and hatred. Check out the poem "Beowulf" (9th century) and tell me if the monsters, elves and giants therein don't have human characteristics.

If you've done much reading, you know also that the book of Genesis in the Bible's Old Testament proclaims that God made humans "in His own image." Very heady stuff for a bunch of wandering earth creatures. Can you imagine a god with electricity-like hands and a black tongue breathing slime and bile all over you in the next life? Most likely not, because we have an extremely difficult, if not impossible time imagining "God" to be endowed with anything other than human attributes.

The gods (Gods) aside, we are quite adept at giving human characteristics to everything in existence, including our pets. Dogs are "man's best friends," even though dogs may have a far different philosophy toward life than we do. Some people talk baby-talk to their pets, or dress them up as people, or include them in their wills, and we accept this as harmless "anthropomorphism" and let it go.

This misappropriation of gray matter is what keeps us from fully understanding wild, and even domestic animals. We grow up with companion dogs and cats, thinking all animals must be similar to the warm cuddlies lying on our laps. Most of us have no conception of the difference between these household pets and working animals. It is unfortunate that our knowledge of the working animal's world is so scant as to be nonexistent. If we offer our hand to a sled dog and he responds with a snarl or a show of teeth, it is not the result we expect and we begin to wonder what is "wrong" with the dog to react that way. Maybe we're not in his circle of importance, that's all.

Unless you have personally employed working animals, it would be nearly impossible to have any knowledge of their thought processes, particularly as to what makes them joyous or comfortable. Krabloonik could put up 250 heated dog shelters and find them unused 24/7 in the winter. It may be more cruel to adopt an adult sled dog out to a new home than it is to euthanize it. It's kind of like forcing an ol' grizzled, worn-out cowboy to sell men's suits at Macy's - no good.

As humans, and realizing our limitations and the parameters of our imaginations, perhaps we should look inward for the source of our discomfort before we direct it toward Dan MacEachen and his pack of sled dogs. The behavior of some of us toward him may be far more cruel than anything you may imagine he has done to the animals he loves.

As a last thought; if you think you have a better way, volunteer to work at Krabloonik or some other sledding operation for a month or so, and test the strength of your ideas. You will be respected for attempting to find truth rather than putting forth unsubstantiated or untenable claims without the experience to back them up.

Aspen's Ageless Questions

"Oh," she said, "the good ol' days when we all blended together." There's some truth to that statement, at least if you came here in the 1960s or 70s, but for some of us, those who arrived in Aspen during those years stuck out like sore thumbs.

Two things happened early on that began this airless posturing of a classless society. The first, of course, was the continual reference to Aspen as a "ghost town," before the Aspen Ski Corporation, but more specifically Walter Paepcke, thought they pulled it out of the doldrums in 1945 and '46. The "ghost town" designation merely meant that when the "elites" hit town, such as the Paepcke's and other big-city folks, there weren't any of their peers to greet them. Never mind the hospital, schools, fraternal organizations, restaurants, and the already long-established Aspen Ski Club that existed. It's more glamorous to define yourself as the "savior" of a ghost town rather than being just another "new resident."

After World War II ended, there was a tendency on the part of many of the nation's privileged to "get away" from it all, to escape drab, middle-class conformity and go West, to make one's mark upon the world, so to speak. What better place than Aspen, located on the "frontier," a town on the cutting-edge of a new way of life as conjured up by those "brave" enough to move here.

For those who had struggled through the Depression and other quiet times in Aspen and had wholeheartedly supported skiing and tourism (but who couldn't recognize their own demise), their town was quickly changing from being one that supported skiing into one that was now a bona fide ski town. Money came from outside, businesses were primarily owned by newcomers, the cost of living was going up and the old-timers, increasingly marginalized, were being forced out.

By the 1960s and 70s, a quick glance at the footwear along the brass foot rails in the Onion or other watering holes would tell the tale of a quickly changing population. Beefy hiking boots, the rage (and badge) of new arrivals, held the majority, while cowboy boots, at least those with genuine cow shit on them, were in the minority. You might have been sitting next to some celebrity or rich person, not because they (or you) were so willing to rub elbows with riff-raff, but because the collective ideas of "manifest destiny, saving ghost towns and settling the frontier" were what got most of those boots under the bar to start with, no matter class distinctions. The majority of the hiking boots felt like they were breaking new ground while the cowboy boots felt as though the break was a little closer to their own necks.

Many of the people who moved here in the 70s proclaim that they can't really remember much of the time period, due to the prevalence of drugs and alcohol, but maybe they just weren't paying attention. William S. Burroughs, cult hero and junkie might have put it best in the "Yage Letters," when he said: "In the U.S. you have to be a deviant or die of boredom." Plug in "Aspen" for "U.S." and the 70s begin to come alive.

In the early 70s, the fifty or so ranchers who owned 90 per cent of the private property in Pitkin County were steamrolled by a groundswell of public sentiment for downzoning (engineered by memory-challenged newcomers) that fairly well redefined the playing field for anyone who wished to live here. That's when property values began their whirling, skyward spiral and the middle-class limped it's down valley exodus. The stage was now set for the marginalization of Aspen's history as there were precious few left who understood it.

Those from the 60s and 70s bemoan the changes that have happened to "their" town; those who survived the 90s and 00s are getting nervous about the community they thought they knew; those of us who grew up here in the 1940s and 50s, if we still care, are pondering the same questions.

Aspen's Ladies of Reminiscence

You won't find these women on the glossy pages of shmooze magazines, nor will they be included in musty tomes put together by pale-faced, clinch-butted scholars. But they were some of the women who made Aspen what it is, vibrant people who deserve a second chance at immortality. Unique, they passed just under the radar and are riding a slim rail in anyone's memory today.

I couldn't start this assignment without mentioning the Stapleton women who lived at 233 West Bleeker. My maternal grandmother, Nellie Stapleton Sloss and her sisters, Marie and Julia Stapleton, were three schoolteachers who were all born in Aspen in the 1880s. They grew up just outside of town on the ranch that is, in large part, Sardy Field today. In particular, Nellie and Julia were in demand throughout the state as "icons" of various rural, mostly one-room schoolhouses from Brighton, Black Hawk and Central City to Minturn, Avon, Edwards, Emma, Basalt, Brush Creek, Owl Creek and Aspen. All three were in their 60s and 70s when I was a young boy.

Julia was also a large landowner around the Buttermilk area with couple of her brothers, and was tough as nails. She broke horses, took working "vacations" on Wyoming cattle ranches, was usually the first one into Snowmass Lake in the summer, and taught school for a couple of years in Alaska, just to see how rough it could get up there.

The Bleeker house seemed to be the focal point of a lot of visiting when the ladies were home, with visitors such as Lily Reed. Lily lived her life in the brick house now on the corner of Monarch & Hopkins, unfathomably called the Katie Reed house. (Katie built it, but Lily kept it together for many decades.) A tall, imposing, imperious woman, Lily drove a purple Ford, always seemed to wear a purple or lavender dress, and wore her white hair high on her head in a beehive sort of arrangement. I swear, it had a purple tinge to it, as well. Her piercing eyes kept a young boy from asking impertinent questions. In spite of it all, there was a sense of fragility about her that always made me wonder how she was doing.

There was the woman with an Italian accent, who lived at the corner of 3rd and Main, a Gina Lollobrigida look-a-like who, without knocking, stormed into the Bleeker house one day and erroneously accused me of stealing a Bible from the Community Church Sunday School. My shy, quiet grandma took after her with a house broom, telling her on the way out the door that she could borrow the broom to get home, if she needed it.

Right next door to my grandmother, lived Mrs. Robert Coe, not particularly remarkable in her own right, other than she was mostly Native American with long, black and silky, braided hair. She taught me to tie my own shoes (OK, she was remarkable) and to eat butter and sugar on a slice of bread. Her major contributions to the town were three gorgeous daughters, Susan, Nancy and Judy Coe, still talked about by boys (now men) who knew them, when. Playmates of mine, they were affectionate, earthy girls, who moved away around the time it could have gotten truly sweet and dangerous between us.

On the northeast corner of Main and Garmisch lived Mabel Beckerman, a slight, 70-ish woman, in a yellow dress who sat out on her porch most every afternoon, with her short, brown hair tied up in a knot on top of her head. Taking in the last vestiges of the day, she would be smoking a cigarette and sipping a glass of whiskey. Mabel had a 3-story Victorian, the perfect mini-hotel for seasonal ski bums, right where the Orthopaedic Associates building sits now. From her perch, she could throw a colorful epithet at anyone who passed by, and usually did. Sometimes, if she was feeling good, she'd share her afternoon libations with a scrawny kid of 9 or 10. Once her house was gone, Mabel wasn't far behind.

I love ya, Ladies!

Aspen's Siren

Accolades to the snow gods are rolling in, people are smiling more than usual, and skiing is, as ever, absolutely fantastic. I've been away from the "big mountain" for a while, feeding cows and helping ranchers move their operations, but was back in time for Monday's "official" ten inches of powder. A stroke of good fortune, I'd say, but have to admit I was a little off my game. A friend, standing at the top of an untracked Summit, hollered "Go for it," and without hesitation or stopping, I launched off the road, grabbed air and hit the soft snow, skiing the top portion as badly as I ever have. It came together about halfway down and the rest of the day became the stuff of history, filed away with all the other unforgettable days on Aspen Mountain.

When I was a kid, Aspen Mountain was it, at least if you wanted one with a ski lift. Hopes, dreams, fears, nightmares - all could be imagined - as a young boy looked at the mountain, bathed in the light of a full moon. Unchanged since, she can thrill you to the outer limits when you're enjoying her charms and spit you out when you're spent, but from a distance, the siren song beckons, the allure of her ivory skin tantalizing in a way that can prove fatal to fools and ski bums, alike. Once in her clutches, as in a romance of the kind that can drive you crazy, there is naught to do but to see it to the end, even though it may take a lifetime to do so.

It may be possible that Carbondale, in a different way, could exist without Mount Sopris, but it's highly unlikely that Aspen could manage without her namesake mountain. It's a one-sided, but symbiotic relationship that has been forged over the years, born of necessity, and certainly it's true that if Aspen ceased to exist, Aspen Mountain would remain, metamorphosizing into something other than what she is today.

Forget the misnomer, Ajax. It's Aspen Mountain, her seductive views first raped and plundered by the hard rock miners seeking treasure within her depths, then pillaged again by the ski enthusiasts, who in that weird way we do, thought they were helping her recover by adding further insult. But, like a strong, indomitable woman, she has survived the revilement, still gives us more than she receives, and has reached the apex of her beauty in this role, becoming our friend, our confidant and our encouragement.

Loving women come and go, mostly go, but some stay and marry mad dashing skiers, becoming the more dedicated and better skier of the two, perhaps born of greater motivation, or put together successful businesses and never leave, not of their own volition. Men who could have risen to the top of esoteric and interesting professions in another world have anchored themselves and their dreams to the success or failure of this town, grateful to have the precious days they do to ski the mountain. As my good friend Bob says, "There are a lot worse addictions in this world."

And then, Tuesday, the light was flat, without snowflakes in the air; there was a suspicion that the powder had been skied out, and most people stayed home, or so it seemed. It felt to me, however, that the skiing was better on Tuesday than on Monday; just perspective, I suppose, or could it be the whisper of the enticing song, calling me back, keeping me on the hill the rest of the week (which wasn't bad) and enforcing the knowledge that the decision to not ski is one that must be made on the mountain, not in the comfort of a warm bed.

Back Where I've Really Always Been

Riding the bottomland, looking for cows, my horse Drifter and I are slowly coming upon a gnarled cottonwood, yellow leaves rippling in the soft breeze, its trunk worn smooth by generations of cattle rubbing themselves against the rough bark. There's a big, red-tailed hawk loafing on a particularly distraught limb, giving his eyes a rest, it appears.

Over and over, Merle Haggard's words roll through my consciousness, unattached to any particular time period but, nonetheless creasing a pattern in my brain that can't be ignored: "Well, today I started loving you again and I'm right back where I've really always been." Rather droll without musical accompaniment, but still powerful thoughts if they catch one in the proper frame of mind.

When I was in college, I pictured myself with three or four wives, living on a large, secluded ranch with ten or twelve kids, all of us sleeping in one big heap in the huge living room, intricately embroidered pillows and thick down comforters by the dozens all over, around and under us. First thing in the morning, I'd dash out the door and gallop into the rising sun on my favorite mount, the clear, cold air setting me up for a delicious day.

Such fantasies convinced me I had already missed whatever it takes to be a true family man and in the time since, there have been a couple of broken marriages and a string of encounters that might be impressive if anyone kept track of such nonsense. Dreams of - whatever it is - have constantly woven themselves in and out of my life, and it seems I've chased the elusive exoticisms in a stumbling, but sincere way. Or maybe I've failed to recognize the dream?

Am I the college professor, the politician, or the composer? Oh, wait, those are your previous husbands. I am the scribe who tastes your love, the elixir of a life passionately lived, all affairs brief, but serious dalliances along the way. We were made for each other, you and I, as it will never last.

Does our first love set the tone, if it is a serious affair? Is that the foundation upon which we build the future, even though that inescapable eventuality may not contain the woman who gave us our first experiences with the delicacies of love? Or is it the infatuation, that indescribably good feeling toward someone that gives our hormones free rein, that which is so enjoyably delectable? I still feel that way about lady friends, so whatever it is, don't turn it off. But maybe our first love's indelibility cannot be denied? Is that back where I've really always been?

Was it the way she opened her coat for me on a cold winter's night, in front of the gymnasium after a losing game, inviting me into her warmth? Or the glimpse of her white neck, open and alive and sensuous in the dim light?

Perhaps it's like a riddle, a question with an answer we can't quite discern, and even if we guess the solution, it's all completely open to interpretation. Does it matter, anyway?

Up ahead, the raptor, who has dallied longer than he should, fidgets his wings to prepare for flight, drawing Drifter's ears forward in an unalterable quest for the source. Then, with an almost impalpable flutter and a cursory glance over his shoulder, the hawk is quickly into a fast rising thermal, almost straight up, leaving us to our own way.

Bastardized Names

The other day I mentioned that there was a good photo of past mayor, A. E. Robison in Guenin and Daily's book, "Aspen: The Quiet Years," to which a compadre responded, "His name was Robison, not Robinson." My reply might have been, "I know what I said," having grown up just down the street from him and his wife, Honey, but I bit my tongue.

Robison's sister-in-law, Mona Frost, was my sixth-grade teacher; one of his brothers-in-law, Dr. Ligon Price, mounted the head of my first elk kill, and the story could go on if I'd let it, including the fact that real estate magnate Eric Strickland is his grandson. The point being, however, is that we should be thankful for those who verbalize accuracy, even redundantly to those of us who believe we know the score.

Essentially, nobody called the mayor A. E., but more often referred to him as "Gene," unless they were trying to put a finer point on a political disagreement, in which case SOB might have been uttered a time or two. Quite appropriately, this illustrates the point that it is all too easy for us to bastardize important historical names.

The next time you head to the Back of Bell via the dark side and pass Seibert's, think about it for a moment. Is it really "see-berts" or could it be "sigh-berts?" The latter is the correct pronunciation, and the seemingly more common former no doubt causes Vail founder and ex-Aspen Mountain ski patrolman Pete Seibert, namesake of the trail, to roll over in his grave.

You'd think a simple name like McLean would be hard to screw up, and when an entire parcel of the valley is named McLean Flats, it should be impossible. However, "McLain Flats," just west of town, somehow came into vogue and now we're stuck with it, no matter how incorrect. Originally, that area was called Poverty Flats (not to be confused with Horseshit Flats, close to Hunter Creek) due to the scarcity of irrigation water, although a hardy few tried to eke a living out of the soil, including settlers Gavin, Gray (today's W/J) and Goodwin.

In 1904, my great-grandfather Jeremie Vagneur, with the backing of local investors, built the Salvation Ditch which to this day supplies water to McLain Flats and Woody Creek. With the abundance that water could now afford, Poverty Flats was renamed McLean Flats in honor of original pioneer Donald McLean. Not McLain.

The ghost town of Ashcroft is not quite what it seems, either, and its route a bit convoluted. First civilized as "Castle Forks City" in 1880 by the likes of Calvin Miller and buffalo hunter Amos "Panhandle" Kindt, its name was changed in 1881 to "Ashcraft," in honor of one of the founders, T. E. Ashcraft. If you wanted to argue it, that'd still be the correct name, although you'd be hard pressed to find much support.

If you take a drive up to the preferred parking lot for the Capitol Creek trailhead, at the old guard station, you'll pass an elegant sign on the left announcing the imminent locale of the Nickelson Creek Ranch. Only problem is, Nickelson Creek was named in honor of the Nicholson family, who settled that area and lived there for generations. It's clearly not the present owner's doing, but what Washington map maker should be shot for such reckless abandonment of honest intent?

And, once again, I would be entirely remiss not to mention Aspen's embarrassing snafu over at Dean Street. Actually, it's Deane Street, named after early settler and first Pitkin County Judge, Josiah W. Deane.

This is the kind of historical insensitivity that insults our forefathers and reminds us that bureaucrats and others in our community have no conception of important events previous to their arrival here.

Bear Encounters of Many Kinds

It's common knowledge that there are lots of bears roaming around the valley during the summer and fall, and the secrets, if there are any, may be found in how each of us deals with whatever encounters we face. I chastised one of my uncles a couple of years ago for calling the cops on a bear he found raiding his refrigerator, telling him the bear really didn't need to get any strikes for trying to eat. My uncle replied with good advice, "Do anything you want with the bears you find in your kitchen."

My most egregious lack of common sense regarding bears was to bolt (at age nine) from the family car in Yellowstone to play with a couple of supposed grizzly cubs, seemingly abandoned by their mother. About the time we got friendly, I heard the loud cracking of branches deep in the woods and witnessed the pines shudder from being grazed by one angry momma bear. My own mother, unable to move, was quietly but desperately, ordering me to get back in the car. It all seemed friendly with the bears, and I remember the cubs milling around my feet as the sow charged across the meadow at a good run. Slinging slobber from side to side, she went around to my left and as she did so, I ran my hand down her back, feeling the coarseness of her silver-tipped hair. She did a 180 around my backside, and with a loud grunt, sent her cubs fleeing toward the forest. I suppose she never even looked back to see if I was chasing her, because on some level she realized someone so dense couldn't possibly be a danger to her family. I think my mother set the record for paleness about then, and I got one of those major lectures.

Last fall, my cousin, Ken, warned me about a particularly big and surly black bear that was hanging out around our summer horse pasture and his house. Other neighbors gave me the same admonition, so I kept my eyes open for trouble. One evening, just at dark, I went to check on my horses. Not seeing them, I began to cruise through the rather large forest of Gambel oak that the horses use for shade and hanging out. The bear was at the front of my thoughts as this particular stand of oaks has been very enticing to bears and is, without the benefit of sunshine, a tad spooky. I walked through the scrub oak on trails well suited to bears, having to bend over and duck my head under branches as I traveled, making me unable to see very much further ahead than the front of my boots. Coming out of the oak brush, satisfied that the horses weren't in there, I immediately forgot about the bear and was thinking instead about where I might find my elusive equines.

Continuing the search, I had to pass a small, bushed-up cottonwood on my right. It didn't evoke thoughts of hiding bears and besides, any bear worth his salt should have heard my footfall by then, so I didn't even consider a bear encounter. As I got within 30 feet of the tree, one of the biggest black bears I've ever seen ambled out in front of me, giving me a look similar to, "This trail isn't big enough for both of us."

I have to tell you, after being so careful to avoid running into him in the oak, I wasn't scared, but more like ticked off. "You SOB, get the hell out of here!" was the start of my tirade, deteriorating into further denigrations and slurs as I ran toward him, thinking I might kick my boot halfway up his posterior, with a little luck. Fortunately for me, I scared him pretty good and he took off up the trail, disappearing into the darkness. That's about the time I realized my heart was pounding and the familiar adrenalin rush was coursing through my veins.

My offensive behavior may have been the preferred alternative in either instance, and I've since wondered what might have transpired if I had approached these incidents with a weak heart.

Bears in the Wild and in My Memory

When I get up in the morning, one of the first things I see is a painting of a grizzly bear's wrinkled snout, large, white fangs framing a man-eating mouth, and unavoidable, dully-crazed, menacing eyes looking back at me from the bedroom wall. He is ferocious, appearing out of the blackest night, and would be quite fearsome if I didn't know it was a painting. Maybe it isn't truly a grizzly and represents pent-up anger instead, lurking on the edges of my consciousness. But when the wind blows the first snows of winter around my yard, I can smell his breath. Artist Doug Franklin, a guy I grew up with in Aspen, created that canvas years ago.

There were the grizzly cubs in Yellowstone, the year I was nine, and the sow that spared my life must have told the story a thousand times of how some innocent kid nearly took her patience to the limit by ignoring her mad charge and how he ran his hand down her back as she circled around him. That was a long time ago, and it's still a compelling memory in my mind.

To tell the truth, I've seen so many bears around here that I lost track of the number many years ago. Oh, they come and go, and there might be a long spell where I don't see any, and then all of a sudden, maybe I'll see 6 or 7 in one week. Some stand out in my mind with majestic clarity; others look old and near the end of their time; but for the most part, they seem to be adolescents or young adults, although a few cubs can always be seen dancing around their mothers.

A couple of weeks ago, there was a confrontation with an unusually large black bear, with hair of the darkest hue. I was walking up a very deep and slippery irrigation ditch, which was overgrown with vision-blocking willows, and I thought the splashing sounds I heard ahead were caused by my dog, Topper. The bear no doubt thought my splashing sounds were coming from more floundering fish like the one he was toying with in the recently drained channel.

In a heartbeat, we were upon each other and the inevitable lock of our eyes occurred at about the same time we both realized we had made incorrect assumptions. To the bear's credit, his look was more of the "I think you're in the wrong sandbox, kid," rather than any type of fear. I couldn't crawl out of the canal without making myself totally vulnerable, so I breathlessly stood my ground, feigning an air of total nonchalance. After thinking about it, the bear awkwardly left the ditch, casting me a disbelieving glance over his shoulder as he ambled away.

The first thing you see when you walk into my living room is a painting of two grizzly bears, a male and a female, their marauding activities exposed by soft glowing light, perhaps from a campfire. It was painted by a woman who, in the course of my life, has been one of the great loves but also the other half of a friendship of the most enduring kind. Created at a time when we both were going through some wrenching changes in our lives, it depicts (in a spontaneous, synaptic brush of oil on canvas) the years of intimacy we shared, two imaginative lives intertwined but separate, sometimes going in the same direction, navigating myriad longitudes and latitudes of dreams and excitement, dashed hopes and dead-ends, at different speeds and at different levels of emotion. It was partially in response to a short story I wrote for her about metaphorical, bullying grizzlies in the mountains surrounding a spectral valley of never-ending challenges.

When it's all said and done, the bears are important, but it really isn't about them, not really, or is it?

Boom – From Winter to Spring

The change from winter to spring comes without subtlety, something like getting hit from behind with a two-by-four. One day, you're skiing dynamite snow on the Ridge of Bell, no one else around, and the next, your butt is affixed to a tractor seat, dragging the awakening spring pasture grass into greening alertness. My friend, Erik, offered to hide my ski boots so I wouldn't be tempted by the extended ski season hysteria, but I think I'm over skiing for this year.

When you're in the ranching game, spring is one of the busiest times of the year. There are hayfields to be plowed, oat fields to be prepared and replanted with grass; horses to be ridden out; horse tack to be cleaned and repaired; calves to be branded, machinery to be oiled, greased and coaxed back into operation; irrigation ditches to be burned, cleaned and repaired, and last but not least, dreams of summer expeditions and adventures to be dreamt.

When I was a kid, I spent more hours on a tractor than I wanted, even though I loved it, and spent countless hours circling the agricultural fields, looking forward to the day F.M. Light would show up at the ranch. Actually, it was always one of F.M. Light's sons that showed, driving an old-time van full of western clothes, boots and equipment. Based on the good credit I had with my dad (my employer), I'd order a pair of cowboy boots, a couple of shirts and maybe a new hat. A week later, my purchase would show up at the Woody Creek post office, almost as good as Christmas. I bought my first brand-new saddle from F.M. Light & Sons of Steamboat Springs, a roper with a 15-inch seat, back in the days when you couldn't buy stuff like that around here.

About the biggest spring activity is the branding of the calves, a labor intensive project that always involves outside help. I'd invite my buddies from town to come out and we'd spend the weekend getting the job done. By May, the ravaging late-winter and spring storms, which so easily seem to decimate calf yields, have fairly well ceased, and the rancher has a good idea how his current calf crop turned out. He'll undoubtedly lose a couple more calves, but the odds are against it, and there is a lot more optimism about the upcoming summer than there was earlier, particularly during a winter like this last one.

Drifter, the blue roan that was so faithful last fall, the one that carried me from the valleys to the tops of the mountains, through draws strewn with deadfall and around narrow, cliff-side trails without giving me any trouble, is now the horse trying to buck me off in the small corral I've chosen for the first ride of spring. "Come on, ol' buddy, give me a break, you S.O.B." No time to worry about it, for as soon as I get him rode out, there's Billy, the agile paint, impatiently pawing the fence as he waits his turn. It was exciting when I was younger, but all I know for sure is that the ground gets a lot harder the older you get. However, in that way Mother Nature sometimes has, I'm better at staying on now, probably 'cause I'm more patient.

I've got a new border collie this spring, one I'm reluctant to call a cow dog, at least not until I get a chance to see if he has any "cow sense." Nonetheless, I have all the faith in the world in Topper, just from the way he tries to herd me around the place.

It's gonna be a good summer, I reckon.

Bovines and True Brand Recognition

By the time we get the herd sorted through the serpentine of alleyways and corrals, the dew's been burned off the grass and Randall, connoisseur that he is, has the branding area organized and the irons hot as fire. Jobs are handed out with as few words as possible. "Johnny, you'll need two syringes," means Johnny has just been given the job of vaccinating the young calves, and so it goes, until all the procedures are covered. Usually the owner sizzles the hides himself, thus eliminating any argument if a brand happens to look like hell instead of the Mill-Iron Slash or Lazy-V C it's supposed to be. Explain it to a hanging judge as the rustler spits a wad at the wall and says "ain't nobody could read that caricature of a brand."

The horse's ears are up in anticipation of the day's activities and before we've even started there's a lot of action taking place in the midst of the swirling dust, bawling calves, and riders and horses, true professionals both, waiting for the call. We spin a loop or two to warm up when suddenly, the boss hollers, "Bring some calves in, dammit."

It's a methodical game we play, time after time, urging our horses up near the backside of a calf, usually at an awkwardly slow pace. The challenge is to get the timing just right, to pitch that coiled and twisted twine with the accuracy of a pirate sniper's bullet and send it true, lassoing up the hind legs of a suspecting calf. When you can do that without thinking about it, time after time, odds are you'll get invited back.

But you're not there yet, cowboy. Quickly, pull the slack out of the rope and dally it around your saddle horn, giving it a wrap or two, depending on your preference, and head your horse for the gate, pulling the calf behind you. After you've done this a couple of times, your horse knows more about getting to the fire than you do, so you've mostly just got to pay attention to your squirming little dogie, making sure he doesn't get hurt in the process.

Timing is critical here, for you can't place your cargo at the branding area until the one in front of you is done, and you can't stop your forward movement, or the calf, without a taut rope, will kick that string off his legs faster than a banker calls in a bad loan.

It's about cadence and skill and the boys doing the branding work on the ground are a jovial bunch, but make them walk too far to throw your calf or run them over with your horse, and you'll find out just how fast you can become a marked man. Mostly, they're young and tough and have arms as big around as thighs on a guy like me. If you're good, you and your horse can make life much easier for these guys, but if you're not very good, the boss will soon be asking you to go close a gate or something at the far end of the ranch, just to get you out of the way.

It's a dead serious game, doing everything you can to protect these little bovines from theft and disease, and even though a lot of banter gets tossed around, there is no room for error. Miss a vaccination and a calf may die. Screw up a brand and you'll either look like a damned fool or spend the rest of your life trying to live it down.

With an obtuse remark about how your girlfriend might look better in the shirt you're wearing than you do, the boys on the ground let the calf up and it's up to you to bring 'em another one. Time after time. It gets in your blood, like fresh powder snow.

There may be more efficient methods to get the job done, but I can't imagine what they are and besides, the old, original ways make more sense and soothe the soul the best.

Breaking in a Friendship

It was hot and dusty and we'd already ridden a couple of ornery ones. Harold spit in the dirt at his feet and said maybe since we were on a roll, we ought to do one more. Why not? But first, we drove over to the Woody Creek Store, precursor of the Tavern, and got a six-pack to ease the heat and our tired muscles.

We'd been breaking a few horses for Art Pfister, some that weren't quite good enough to put with his regular string, and after keeping them way too long, he'd finally sent them out to Harold's place - four- and five-year-old geldings that hadn't been touched since they were gelded.

The last to go that day was a big-boned, blood-red bay that we'd done some ground work on but hadn't yet ridden. We were good at minimizing the uncertainty of the first ride, but these were mature horses who'd had time to develop attitude and could suck-up and swap directions quicker than a dog on a dropped sandwich, so it sometimes seemed as though we might never get them to see things our way.

Harold Hall, a well-respected horse trainer, fairly well had one speed - determined calm. We stashed the beer in the shade and went to work on the bay. We usually left big broncs like that tied up and hobbled while I got on and let them have their first attempts at escaping civilization. Harold, a man of my dad's generation, never said much while we worked, and it was usually a nod of his head or a soft voice telling me to mount up, or that he thought it was time to unbuckle the hobbles, free the lead rope and let the horse test my resolve.

We'd had some rough ones to ride, but this gory-colored SOB was givin' me more fits than I really wanted, and I'm sure if you were watching, it was ugly, but I stayed with him. Got the "vinegar and mustard" out of him after a while, and he calmed down enough to where Harold popped a beer and sat on the fence, watchin' me work the horse, turning him back against the wooden rails and making him stop once in a while.

Harold offered me a beer while I circled the corral cooling the horse down, and as I went for a dust-killing guzzle, Harold tossed his hat under the horse's belly, with the predictable result - the beer went flying, my hat right behind, and it was lucky I stayed on. Mostly what I remember, though, was Harold's quiet laugh, telling me I'd done a good job or he wouldn't have taken the chance of messin' with me.

We broke a lot of horses that summer, including a few from Texas, but somewhere along the way, we had a falling out. It wasn't anybody's fault, I reckon, other than mine, for keeping too much of my life under my belt and not explaining some of my craziness to Harold. But, like a couple of ol' cowboys, we got it back together to finish the season, knowing we'd spent our final summer of working together.

The last time I saw him, he was coming out of Magnifico Liquors with a pint of Jack in his hand and he invited me to get in his ol' white Chevrolet pickup truck. We had a taste, and then after I hurried back with a six-pack, we proceeded to drain the booze along with the beer, relived some good times, and nearly headed up to the old Eagles Club to do it up right.

We'd begun to patch the rift that afternoon sitting in the truck, drinking beer and whiskey, laughing and watching the cold autumn rain come down. We parted friends. It seemed about a week later when Harold's heart unexpectedly quit him, and my hurt ran deep.

Built For Comfort

It was a genuine, old-time barn, built out of hand-hewn logs with a hay mow on the top and feed bunks lining one wall of the ground floor, an oat box conspicuous in the corner of each stall. Thick, wide, mountain-grown pine floorboards had been rubbed smooth by years of clomping horse's hooves.

When we used large barns for tacking up horses, not for keeping them inside all night, it was a display of nature's finest choreography every morning. The first person into the breaking dawn would throw hay down into each cubicle, enough for breakfast, measure out oats for each cayuse and then quickly open the barn door to the waiting herd.

In the horses would clamber, like kids into a movie house, snorting, snuffling, dancing excitedly on wood and proudly lining up in "their" stall. If one got in the wrong space, someone would holler the horse's name and without further instruction, the horse would get in the proper spot. Those days are very rare in this part of the country, anymore.

At the end of the alleyway stood the tack room, its walls lined high with team harness for the large horses that once pulled the feed sleds and maybe a hay rake or two. Lower down jutted out the saddle racks, structured of local pine, and a person could almost guess which saddle belonged to which member of the family.

On this day, a shiny, new saddle was slung proudly over the rack nearest the tack room door, its newness in stark contrast to the well-worn leather of the other occupants silently standing vigil there. It was a Fallis Balanced Ride, with a black, padded seat, the rest displaying lightly tooled brown leather with the name "Bill" engraved on the roll of the cantle.

I gave him a little grief, the "Old Man," as I sometimes called him, the guy who told me on our first meeting that most people in the neighborhood thought he was a son-of-a-bitch and he'd appreciate it if I didn't try to dispel what he considered an advantageous reputation. Not that he'd given me any reason to.

My spiel went something like, "A new rig like that is gonna bust your ass, big boy," to which he replied, "Someday sonny, if you don't wise-off too much, you'll be as old as me and you'll see the advantage of spending a little money for comfort." He went on to say that riding horseback all day didn't really hurt his bones until he turned sixty, like that was some kind of milestone.

That character, Bill, a genuine article of the West, had twenty-some years on me and I pretended not to hear, but I've never been able to get that statement out of my mind either, not for the past twenty-some years or so.

It wasn't long after, sneaking up on my fiftieth birthday, that my hips began to hurt like hell after a couple of hours in the saddle, and I complained to my cousin Wayne, ranching icon of the Woody Creek Canyon, who gently explained that riding a Fallis saddle had been a family tradition for the last forty years and how did I miss that nuance of life. "Geezus, I'm still riding a good saddle I bought during my high school days," was my well-reasoned reply.

Wayne loaned me an old, beat-up Fallis he had stashed in the barn and I began to feel reborn. I rode that saddle hard, never felt the pain again, and late in the summer, ordered my own Fallis rig. I can say now, with certainty, that I feel more at ease sitting my saddle all day than anywhere else.

I passed Bill's elucidated pain threshold of "60" without missing a beat, and if pressed, would have to confess that I now own two custom-made Fallis saddles, one of them engraved with Colorado columbines and my cattle brand.

It's not a small thing, a cowboy's saddle, and it's as personal and important to your comfort as the shoes you wear or the women you hang out with.

Calving Season

My dad and I had 'em halfway surrounded, a herd of registered Hereford cattle, at the top of what we called the Big Hollow. Dished into the topography of our southwestern mesa, roughly a mile long and half-a-mile wide, it made a great spot to feed the cows in late winter, what with the sides of the hollow at least partially blocking the wind.

We were on a mission of grave importance, making certain that any cow ready to give birth in the next couple of days would be taken down to the lower ranch and sequestered in what we jokingly referred to as the "maternity ward."

Imagine the plight of a newborn calf, slithering from the womb and hitting the ground on a cold, dark night, with only its mother to soothe the sudden harshness of a new reality. It might be 20 below, or the wind might be howling without repentance, swirling across a barren winter feed ground without regard for the calf's quiet entry into the world.

Like all animals, a calf is hard-wired for survival, but obstacles abound. After making an inelegant drop from the womb, its mom licks the afterbirth from its rapidly cooling body, drying it off and trying to keep it warm at the same time. There's only one thing of importance on a calf's mind - get up and suckle. There's no conception of death, only a strong and tenacious craving for survival. In nature, you either exist or you don't and you're only privy to one of those concepts. For a newborn calf, or its mother, there is no time for esoteric thoughts about hypothermia, more blankets or last rites.

My dad, riding his big buckskin mare and easily visible in a red, wool coat, had me hold the herd from dispersing while he rode through the cows, about 300 strong, checking for those that looked ready to calve. It was, even with the sky a deep lazuline blue, bitterly cold, well-below zero, and the forecast was calling for even colder temperatures.

The sprawling mesa was about a mile from the ranch headquarters, totally out of sight of all civilization, and there's always something exhilarating about that. Early in the morning, my dad and the hired hand, feeding the cattle with a team of horses and a big sled, checked carefully for "ready to deliver" cows. Dad would go back later and round them up with his horse, and me, if I was around. We couldn't quit because we were bone-cold; there were cows we had to find and take home with us.

It didn't seem I could take much more, but still we worked on. "Come on, mama, head this way, away from the herd and over the top and down the hill, where things will be good for you."

Close to the house, a three-sided shed, back to the wind, held numerous stalls, each one fluffed deep with fresh, clean straw, ready for newly arrived babies. At one end was the enclosed "intensive care ward," containing heat lamps, a ready row of medicines and syringes, and the calf-pulling mechanism, sometimes needed to help first-calf heifers finish the job.

On bitter nights, like the one we were about to experience, a tragically cold and sick calf might end up in the house, sprawled across the warm kitchen floor; a serious case might be curled up in the bath tub. My dad, in addition to being up all day, would spend the night checking, checking, and rechecking, unwilling to leave anything to chance.

There were nights I stood next to Dad, observing him smile at the first kicking signs of life, or watching him do everything possible to save one that, no matter my dad's wishes, couldn't hang on. Seeing the tears in my father's eyes, either from joy or sadness, always clouded my own, mostly in homage to the depth of passion and commitment my dad carried for his role in life.

Choking on Humble Pie

As I swung my leg over my big blue roan Drifter and screwed my ass down tight, strangers eyed me for the wild ride that never came. Their big boss, lined up in the middle of his mounted crew, pulled his unshaven cheeks in, sucking tobacco juice together over his tongue, getting ready to launch an ugly one. And out it came with a thwacking squirt of expelled air, a long, glorious, globulus gob of saliva and chew, thoroughly mixed and utilized, headed for a big rock about five yards distant.

Most guys spit without caring where it lands, but this fella wanted to put particular emphasis on his share of the conversation, so with a deadpan face he watched it fly, tiny eyes glued to its trajectory, lips still pursed from the effects of the effort, until it splattered against its obvious target. Quick as a flea, he turned those pig eyes on me, just to make sure I'd witnessed his skill with spit, and then asked the question he'd wanted to say all along. "That the Hancock horse you paid big bucks for? Them dirty bastards is mean sons-a-bitches."

Mr. Tobacco and his bunch had shown up uninvited, looking like marauders out of the Old West with their broad, cape-shouldered Aussie slickers in full display, thinking we might have corralled some wild cows they'd lost from another valley and wanted to make sure they got their beef back. The unsaid accusation floated the air like scum on a pond.

We weren't on a ranch you could drive to, even though it had most of a road in place - you either rode your horse in, or walked, and when somebody talked badly about your horse, or cows, it could piss you off. I was thinking a sucker punch to his swollen gut might even the score.

We'd overnighted 200 pair of cows and calves in the middle of almost 400 acres and a day's work of separating them out for market lay ahead of us. The rain was intermittent as we began the gather, and there was something about the cold that spelled snow.

There's an old cowboy saying that goes something like, "Don't try to impress everybody with how good you are, because over the course of the day, folks'll figure it out." It saves people from getting on your butt not if, but when, you make a fool out of yourself.

Sometimes it's the luck of the draw, I reckon, and the tobacco-stained horse expert and I ended up side by side on a hummock overlooking the corrals, agreeing that none of his wild cows had come our way. While we were stopped, he couldn't resist laying a long line of self-righteous BS on our ramrod and without waiting, his crew busted on down the trail, tired of the empty chase and looking for some relief.

In my mind, at least as near as I could write it, I had him pegged for a moron, mostly because he couldn't let go of that "tough-guy" image he was trying to project. "You better hurry on down there and catch your boys," I finally said. With that and a nasty expletive, he turned and laid the spurs to his big sorrel gelding, with unwanted results.

The horse, already distressed at being left behind, deserted the ground in a big high-dive, maybe throwing in a little "sunfish" just for flair. Mr. Big, unseated at the beginning, finally left the saddle just before the horse touched down. Nothing but legs and slicker flying through the air did I see.

He landed with a nauseating thud and the sounds he made trying to catch his breath weren't pretty. His eyes pleaded with me for a little help as he looked around to see who else was watching. I caught his spooked horse and helped him up and he rode off, still occasionally sucking pathetically for air. He never said a word - not "Thanks" or even "Go to hell."

Christmas Gives a Second Chance

This column, against my better judgment, is about Christmas, but to get there, we have to go back to the spring of my freshman year in college. I'd decided to stay on for the summer semester and toil away in the library basement, reading from tomes of poetry so aged they smelled of mold and as though they had been handed to me by the decaying hands of those who had so eloquently written there, in stingy ink.

To finance such an extravagant idea as summer school, I took on a school bus driving job which consisted of locating the children of migrant farm workers and bringing them to school each day for breakfast, a shower, clean clothes, and a day's worth of instruction in the three R's. It was a government sponsored "Head Start" program and was, for me, the antithesis of studying in the library. I was working in northern Colorado, trying to drum up business with people who spoke Spanish.

As this yellow-bused gringo pulled into driveways in front of gray, wasted, old clapboard farmhouses without running water, filled with three or four working families each, everyone inside strolled out, the young eyes bright with curiosity and all hearts overflowing with generosity. By dark, I'd have 15 or 20 kids lined up for the next day, located around an area covering many more square miles than I'd care to remember, and with the coming of daylight, would find at least half of them timidly awaiting my approach.

Each day, a very striking girl, no more than ten, would sit in the very back of the bus and stare wistfully out the window in a way that belied her tender years. All of these kids behaved in an immaculate fashion, but whenever there was a question or concern among the troops, she immediately became the leader and resolved whatever the issue may have been. She very seldom smiled, but her demeanor, as she got on and off the bus, indicated she was genuinely pleased with her ability to go to school each day.

Soon, however, her father determined that she was too valuable in the fields and she was unceremoniously forbidden to go to school anymore. This caused some other problems, as well, since some of the younger children missed her steadying influence and began to drop out of the program. Being young and foolish, I interfered in the father's vision of his responsibilities, insisting that the young girl be allowed to continue with school, she being perhaps the best chance his family had of anything but back-breaking labor ahead of them. Reluctantly, the father acquiesced, for a couple more days, and then through an English-speaking friend, informed me in no-uncertain terms that his daughter was going to work in the fields - no more school.

We all survived the summer and life went on. I continued driving a school bus for college money and at the end of the fall semester, was invited to a Christmas celebration being conducted by a fellow driver, who was also a lay preacher. His flock was small, he said, but passionate and would welcome a derelict such as myself without reservation. I questioned it, though, but finally agreed on the condition that he not make a big deal out of my presence.

Thus, was I singing at the back of the small church when a young lady from the side of the room noticed and came my direction. With a shy, silent smile, eyes toward the floor, the girl from the summer head start program put her hand in mine and waited with me until the hymn was over. She then went quickly back and sat down with what turned out to be extended family, a school girl at last. I never saw her again, but she made Christmas a little lighter that year.

Christmas in Aspen

It comes around every year, like clockwork, and I've been a Grinch about it ever since we quit celebrating it on the old home place. That's Christmas I'm talking about, and the last time I had much enthusiasm for it was almost fifty years ago.

It was a big deal, Christmas Day on the Woody Creek ranch, a family gathering of large proportions which left most everyone in a festive mood, the climax to a celebration that began weeks before in town.

Christmas was more diverse in Aspen, with a different family (my mother's), but it also was a much longer holiday. First there was the school play, in which everyone through the sixth grade participated. It never was religious, and instead of wise men there were court jesters and no one was born in a manger, but there might have been horses or donkeys (or reasonable facsimiles thereof), but never any chickens or goats. Most of the whole town turned out, even people without kids, because there wasn't all that much to do in the 1950s and 60s.

No sooner was that play over than we moved across the street to the Community Church to begin practicing for its Christmas play. That was our one time of the year to have a little relaxed fun in the sanctuary, taking over the minister's podium for narration and a crèche being set up immediately in front of the pews. There were angels in the balcony, trumpets high along the walls and the always-present Mona Frost on the organ. The ever-tireless Mary Eshbaugh Hayes would write the script, different and more interesting each year. Last winter, she sent me a photo of a young Tony V, all decked out in finery of the most exalted sort, the tallest of the wise men, readying to ascend to the upstairs performance.

My maternal grandmother's house hummed on Christmas Eve. Stapleton's, my other family, filled the place with warmth, people I usually didn't see very often, and it was powerful to mix it up with them for a change. Bill Stapleton (you might remember the Wm. C. Stapleton Agency) would team up with Sam Stapleton (namesake of Sam's Smokehouse at Snowmass, although we sometimes called him Pete) and make the best eggnog around, called Tom n' Jerry's. Uncle Bill wasn't opposed to a high school kid having fun and he'd load me up with as much eggnog as he thought I could stand. A couple of times, it was a woozy walk to midnight services at the Community Church.

People started dying, like my grandmother and paternal grandfather, the ranch I grew up on got sold, college beckoned, Dad got sick, and the roots of my life were clipped from my being. Don Stapleton, my hero and best friend, went to Vietnam; Billy Sandersen, a good friend and classmate, got killed over there, and the ugliest of reality began to nose itself into my life with an unsettling persistence.

I've kept my distance from Christmas for a long time, always volunteering to be the one who worked those two days (Eve and Day), even when I owned the company. But I've missed something over the years, the understanding that a holiday such as Christmas delivers, the reliance on family that is self-nurturing. My personal life has been a roller-coaster and although I'm not complaining, I wonder which has been the disease and which the symptom, which the event or the reaction?

For the first time in my life, I've been practicing Christmas carols on the piano, thinking I might be able to contribute to the overall essence, rather than be a bystander. There are people in my life that I love and value, individuals from a lifetime in this valley and, of course, my family.

It's not so much about Christmas, I don't think, as it is about this spirit of renewal and closeness with friends and family. But what better time to have such a holiday, during winter in the magic of the mountains.

Clean To the Bone

There was something surreal about the way it was laid out, the bones still in one place (unlike a cougar or coyote scavenge), trimmed of all fat and muscle, not a scrap of nourishment left, as though boiled to the bone by a hungry, fastidious monster.

I've grown up with bears and ranch cows and this death scene was different than any I've come across in the past. Usually, a bear will eat portions of a dead cow, explicitly the entrails and maybe a hindquarter and/or one of the back straps, but that's about it.

The Black Angus hide was meticulously placed to one side, stripped of all sinew and adiposity, carcass side down. It was still pliable and had a warm softness to it, as though licked clean by a much larger beast, sucking the last bits of nourishment from it before gently spreading it on the ground.

The stomach contents (grass) were strangely undisturbed, left bonded together in a clump where the predator had slipped the rumen from around them. Their still-sweet, still digesting, acidic smell could be distinguished in the clear mountain air. Unlike a sick one, this cow had eaten a prodigious last meal.

Three piles of bear scat were evident in the immediate area, and it appeared the brute went through his phantasmagorical meal in a relaxed and leisurely fashion.

There was very little smell of death and no ravens called out the way; nor had any coyotes been seen or heard, giggling and yipping amongst themselves. Whatever occurred there had happened since last I rode by that spot, four days earlier.

Overall, such scenes create a mood of cool, deliberate thought, for one has witnessed an occurrence of something immense but basic in the natural world, and sometimes in a situation like that, there is a tendency to think that Mother Nature is perhaps making a voulu attempt to offer more to the story than actually exists.

Methodically, I looked for the ear tag, an indispensable, record-keeping item of cattle identification in our modern world, and could find none. The skull was bare of ears, no remaining cartilage to even suggest a lifelike form and a gentle nudge with my boot turned up nothing but the underside of the bony apparition.

With a squeeze of my legs and a cluck of my tongue, my horse Drifter and I headed into a steep hill, grappling our way up a narrow trail to a flat expanse of pasture high above. In this rain-soaked summer, vegetation is dense and tall, making it difficult to see the trail and sometimes we spook animals that haven't seen us, or vice-versa.

The clues are subtle, especially when you don't know exactly what you're looking for, but between Drifter and me, we wanted to go a certain direction and eventually ended up on the brush-covered edge of a substantial cliff with a grand expose of flat, smooth rocks. I'd been there before, eating lunch on those same rocks, and remembered it as a great sentinel over thousands of acres of land, with Capitol Peak and others on the horizon.

But on this day, there was an urgency, a feeling we were on to something so we didn't admire the view, but rather reconnoitered the area, riding back and forth, looking for this sign or that.

And then, there it was, the nest. Not the lair, nor the den, but the nest of a sizeable, carrion-eating bear, if one could believe the large paw prints. This refuge was obviously well-used, with a perfect view of the dead zone.

Who's to know what really happened? But as I traveled back by the now-devoured smorgasbord of dead beef, I spotted the ear tag, clearly visible, lying next to the skull.

Close Calls but Not Curtain Calls

With some hikers having a run-in with lightning around Marble this week, thoughts of close calls have been searing through my mind, much as a lightning bolt would. The stuff doesn't really scare me, but then again, I have a healthy respect for it.

A few years ago, when my sorrel horse Donald was not much more than a colt, we took off from the cow camp with a pack load of salt on Reid, a crooked-legged quarter mare of excellent breeding, our first-line packhorse for the day. It was drizzling cold rain out of a steel gray sky, and the temperature, for July, was in the 40s, maybe less. We had about a 10-15 mile journey ahead of us, and lacking the diversion of a female campmate, took off at an early hour.

Donald was skittish, dancing around and spooking at all kinds of imaginary goblins, almost to the point of being tedious. As we passed the neighbor's cabin, my friend Wyland saw the performance and implored me to be careful. "Don't worry," was the reply.

We rode for a couple of hours, me being challenged almost every step by my enthusiastic mount, and found little change in the weather. There was absolutely no thunder or lightning, giving me the sense that the clouds would be with us for a long time. We'd crossed maybe 5 or 6 ridge lines, passed an equal number of water holes and finally, after a slow slide through the dicey mud underneath Indian Playground, topped out at our first stop, the lick at Twin Oaks.

I'd just realigned the pack after throwing off a salt block and was still on the ground when all hell broke loose. Out of the corner of my right eye I saw, not ten yards away, the dirt behind Reid explode out of the ground and an eye-burning flash from the sky above meet the yearning dirt at the same time. Reid was instantaneously knocked down, dead, I thought for an instant, but back on her feet almost as quickly as she went down.

Donald pulled me high with his first jump, catching me up in an awkward position. Reid's lead rope had been loosely dallied around my saddle horn, my left hand casually on both. When the explosion hit, the rope was inextricably stretched tight over the ring finger of my left hand, breaking it as I later learned. Somehow, I managed to get hold of Donald's reins with my right hand as the desperate attempt of the horses to escape continued, jump after jump. At first I was afraid that I'd get more tangled up in all that mess and maybe killed, but then the reassuring thought struck me that, with my hand strapped to the saddle as it was, those horses weren't going to leave me anywhere without a ride.

Thankfully, it was over in a hurry, and we headed for an aspen-filled draw at a pretty fast lope, jumping over downed trees and sliding and slanting around others. The top of my head felt really weird, and I wasn't too keen on finding out its disposition for a long time. My finger hurt very badly, and in a quick stop to regroup, splinted it with some cardboard and duct tape, and kept going. After traveling all that way, we weren't going to throw in the towel just because of a little lightning.

It was about dark, hours later, as we rode by Wyland and Judy's cabin on our way home, the drizzling sky still draining down, and Wy said something about being worried and was glad we were okay. "Yeah," I said, without stopping, "just another day on the mountain."

Much later that night, after waking with the shakes, I pulled on the whiskey bottle for its calming effects and wondered what a sight we might have made, two dead horses and a rider, without visible explanation, lying on a lonely ridge, high above the valley floor.

Coming Home to Rest in Peace

It had been years since she'd seen him, and as they approached the Emma railroad siding, her heart felt as though it might rise in her throat. There was a touch of new snow on the platform, making it slippery underfoot, while the overcast, gray sky threatened more precipitation. Her sister accompanied her, and there was a hesitancy, a hand-wringing of sorts that telegraphed their identities as they climbed the stairs.

The hisses and clanks of the steam locomotive were strangely comforting and as the engineer pushed the throttle forward, the slack snapped out of the steel couplings between the cars, one at a time, and the black, belching cauldron of fire chuffed out of the station, headed up the line to Woody Creek, eventually Aspen. Left behind, a casket all alone in the cold blustery air, was the one thing they dreaded seeing, but what they had come to witness nonetheless. Who knows what might have gone through my grandmother's mind that day in 1946, a tall, thin woman, stooped at the shoulders and forever worried about everything, as she welcomed her dead husband home to his birthplace.

"Shouldn't someone make sure that's him," her sister said, even though the tag had John Bates Sloss clearly written across it? Bitterly, and the only time she ever was, my grandmother wondered what did it matter, really, he was dead (at 49) and "we don't have to worry anymore about if or when he's coming home."

He meant to come home, he really did, the previous Christmas, to see my mother and to try and make amends with his other daughter, the one who didn't understand his wanderlust ways. But despite his best intentions, with his pockets full of money from tending the sheep camps all summer and a burning thirst in his belly, he never got out of Livingston, Montana. A man can't go home broke, not after that long a time. "O Lord, forgive me, but I'll just take one more drink in this buzzed-up bar and bunk at the ranch if I have to." My mother saved the letters, written on what appears to be Old Chief notebook paper, in a tin box. When he wrote, he was sober, and his loneliness and remorse fairly jumps off the page.

"Oh, Tony, your grandfather was a wonderful man," my mother used to say, and she'd go on about how he'd entertain everyone in the valley with stories about his travels and how she thought he could have been president of the country had he so wished. But along with that, a blackness always crept in, an untold part of the narrative, an almost unmentionable, whispered reference to drunkenness and lack of support. To my mother, his goodness transcended his failings as a husband and father.

No sooner had the train embarked on its up valley run than the folks from Burdge Funeral Home in Glenwood Springs arrived to transport my grandfather's flag-draped coffin to Basalt for the funeral. He was a WWI veteran. True to my mother's words, Bates Sloss (John was never associated with his name) proved to be a popular man and a sizable crowd gathered to pay their last respects. Or so I heard, anyway, as I was just a little over a month old at the time. He is buried in Basalt's Fairview Cemetery.

My grandmother, Nellie Sloss, raised her two daughters admirably well on her own, with little help from Bates, and in later years, whenever I chanced to ask about him, she would dismiss the subject as irrelevant to any rational conversation. Her heartache must have been immense, but the love never went away. On her deathbed in the old Aspen hospital, Grandmother insisted that she be buried next to her husband, Bates.

Every spring, I venture over that way, brushing dust off the headstones and sometimes placing lilac blossoms on their graves. I wish I knew the stories of when times were good between them.

The Gear of Cowboys

As the first taste of light began to give shape to the unknown night shadows, the move was on to get the day rolling. My old man slammed the frying pan onto the stove and the smell of coffee made its way up the staircase to my room.

I tucked a snap-button green shirt into my Levi's (always Levi's - those Wranglers were for the rodeo boys who worked in town or on the construction crews), threw a bandana around my neck and headed for the kitchen. Two eggs over with 3 or 4 pancakes, a mug of steaming Joe and before we had much to say, I was pulling on my boots.

Boots don't have to be fancy, as long as they cover your calves, have a heel tall enough to keep your foot from slipping through the stirrup and a strong ridge above to keep your spurs from falling off. I loved strapping those spurs on, made of engraved blue steel with silver acorns inlaid along the sides; long-shanked with ten sharp points on each rowel and a chap guard just to put your mind at ease. (They're sitting on top of my desk as I write this and remind me of the time I wore them in the Cheyenne Frontier Days parade when I was 17 and some older guy with whiskey breath and ill-practiced legerdemain tried to talk me out of them. "Hell no," I'd said. "These belonged to my granddad.")

If the kitchen is the heart of the house, the tack room surely must be the hub of the outfit. The first man in gets the benefit of its soothing grace, its quiet and unmoving parts. Like fixtures in a wax museum, each saddle sits on its rack, the creative and proud spirit of each man displayed, either in the way he ties his slicker on or by the quirt hung over the horn or a wild rag carelessly tucked into one of the saddle bags. Even when unoccupied, men and horses are evident in a tack room just by the hanging aroma; sweat-dried saddle pads, brushes, combs; empty snoose tins and a few dead beer cans or empty Bull Durham bags in the trash. Tack rooms are built and maintained by men but owned by horses, an inescapable fact of life made clear to those who linger there.

"Ride for the brand," has been attributed to the cowboy life, and who could quibble, but it came a little late for my attitude about it all. "Live the life," was my motto, and I don't think I've missed much. Riding rank horses, spitting tobacco, walking to the pay window at the W/J Rodeo arena after a wild horse race, covered in dust and smiling ear-to-ear: slinging every cuss word you ever heard at some wily cow who thought she knew a better way to lead the herd; branding calves and pregnancy checking cows; and lying in the shade of a big cottonwood with a long-haired waitress from Pinocchio's while a six-pack of Coors cooled in the ice-cold water trough. It hasn't changed much over the years, only today's long-haired gal doesn't work at Pinocchio's and there's soda in the trough instead of beer.

"Where'd you get the hat, cowboy?" someone said. "Oh, man, I've gotten 'em everywhere," I replied, "but it's hard to find a quality hat anymore, people don't seem to give it much thought." Once, I bought a nice hat in Grand Junction but they didn't have time to shape it, so I took it to a hat shop in Las Vegas for finishing and before long I told the inept clerk to just put it back in the box and forget about it. If you want a good Stetson with a personality that incorporates your own, one that'll stick with you and won't go to hell like a three dollar suit in a rainstorm, go to Kemo Sabe on Galena Street.

Where do cowboys come from? Hard to say. It's all of the above plus a lot more. Most cowboys couldn't tell you, because they're too busy beings cowboys. It comes from the heart, I reckon.

About Being a Cowboy

What is a cowboy, exactly? I reckon nobody really knows for certain, although the definition might be similar to that of pornography - you know a cowboy when you see one. A girlfriend of mine refers to cowboys as people with expensive trucks and trailers and no visible means of support. Another friend says she never met a cowboy who wasn't hurt, broke, or both. Still another says she gets a special thrill in finding a pair of dusty cowboy boots parked under her bed in the morning.

When I was a kid, there wasn't much difference between a cowboy, a rancher, or any of the folks who ranched for a living or worked for those who did. Guys like Roy Rogers and Gene Autry were "cowboys," made to order for the imaginations of kids, but because they sang and dressed really nice, we always considered them to be "city cowboys." Then of course, there were the real cowboys, the ranchers, like those folks out in Woody Creek who were our neighbors.

You can buy a hat uptown that'll brand you a cowboy to most folks, one with sweat and dirt painted on its crunched-up facade, and a pair of boots to match, with artificial scuffs in the leather. But being a cowboy isn't about how you look - pretty is not the gist - it's about whether a guy or gal will pick you up from the mud after your horse has dumped your sorry ass in it. Looks take up space at the bar and provide a backdrop for wishful stories, but they can't rope a wild cow or doctor a sick calf.

The life of a cowboy takes the good with the bad. Almost every day, I saddle up a horse or two and head to the high country, either packing salt, clearing trails, or moving cattle from one grazing ground to another. Along the way, I'm graced with looking at Capitol or Daly or other majestic peaks in the Elk Mountain range, take in a lot of fresh air, and see more beauty than many people glimpse in a lifetime. I usually ride alone (which some consider folly), with the exception of my dog Topper, and could die up there as easy as not. According to James P. Owen, Wall Street financier and author, "The code of the west is based not on myth, but on the reality of life on the open range."

There used to be an Aspen City councilman who, from time to time, denigrated the wearing of cowboy hats. Those of us who considered ourselves cowboys and deserving of the right to wear whatever type of chapeau we chose, always felt the councilman dressed reminiscently of a shirt-tailed, poor cousin of Oscar Wilde and who, on his best night, was no better than envy paying tribute to genius.

We take issue with the imagination-challenged, pseudo-intellectual, journalism professionals on both coasts who, in a fit of laziness befitting skid row bums, took to calling George W. Bush "the 'cowboy' president." That's a crock, and a damned insult to every man who ever fancied himself a cowboy, as Dubya fairly well represents just the opposite of everything a cowboy stands for. In Texas, roaming cattle defecate once about every sixteen-hundred acres, so I don't know if that makes Bush a one-cow "rancher" on his 1600 acres near Crawford, or just a guy who's "all hat and no cattle." But, any way you cut it, he ain't no cowboy.

Those who bemoan the loss of our western heritage are the same people who have always used the West as a fantasy destination, a place they'd be if they could honestly live their lives as they wished. Better they not know how tough it is to scrounge an almost impossible living from land that can be so beautiful to the naive eye.

There are still cowboys around, even a few in the Roaring Fork Valley. And like good skiing, you have to get off the road to find them.

Coyotes

Ginger, the Labradoodle, was killed on Smuggler Mountain last week (may her wait at the Rainbow Bridge be without sorrow), and suddenly the coyotes are being excoriated for being coyotes.

Many years ago, Mary Eshbaugh Hayes took a wonderful photograph of children watching a herd of sheep move past her house on Bleeker Street. It evokes memories of idyllic times in Aspen, an era most of us claim to desperately miss. What's not shown in the photograph is the untold back story, the tragedy that followed the sheep through the surrounding mountainsides.

He was a retired government trapper, slight of frame with the intense, lustrous eyes of a man who knows his way around wildness. We sat transfixed in the living room as he entrusted us with his story, even though we'd only come to look at an accordion his wife had for sale. "It wasn't that long ago, it doesn't seem," he offered as he rolled a smoke. "I'd lead a couple horses up to Little Annie Basin, shoot one, cut its belly open and lace it with strychnine. Kill the other one somewhere up Hunter Creek and doctor it with strychnine, too. The U. S. Government tried hard to kill those damned sheep-eatin' coyotes."

It's difficult to judge men like that, but it is incumbent upon each of us to question the hysteria, irrational fear and ignorance that prompt our own government to create such programs.

Last week's blathering bleat, from a man over in Eagle who removes "nuisance-animals," is typical of the illogical fear tactics used by the less-enlightened to justify eradication of wolves and coyotes - "Is a child next?" As if any right-minded person could possibly ignore that ignorant and painful peal.

Speaking of nuisance animals, let's look at the reality of the situation. Dogs off-leash compete with the coyotes for field mice, voles and other goodies in the Smuggler area. What clear-thinking coyote wouldn't call the steady stream of free-roaming dogs on Smuggler a "damned nuisance?" Or, a convenient meal?

In spite of an attempt by some in the media (and even some who live here) to paint Aspen as another Disneyland, it's still a town in the middle of wilderness. The rides here aren't necessarily sterile, safe or guaranteed, and a walk with your dog is to take a chance on interaction with whatever's out there on any given day. If you want, use no leash or let him/her drag the leash behind, but be prepared for the consequences.

The implication that coyotes are somehow "bad actors" is to miss the point. According to quotes in the Aspen Times: "These coyotes were working together. They clearly had a plan." "But these coyotes are wild, they're dangerous, and they hunt and kill so they can eat." ". . . dangerous to the community at large." Kudos to the coyotes. They survived the government trappers.

Don't get me wrong, I have absolute sympathy for Ginger's owners. My daughter's dog, Earl, was killed by one of my horses several weeks ago, and I clearly know the heartache. But, so far I have not felt emboldened to call out the American Quarter Horse or American Paint Horse Associations, bemoaning the plethora of "dangerous" kicking and stomping horses in our valley. To what end?

As someone said, "You could have kept Earl out of the pasture," to which the only reasonable response is, "You could keep your dogs off Smuggler Mountain."

It all boils down to personal responsibility. The coyote takes care of himself, despite some depressing odds. In turn, we can take care of our pets or let them fend for themselves, but we shouldn't complain when it doesn't always come out in our favor.

Uncle Victor's Passing

My uncle Victor died last week, and I'm reminded once again of how complicated death is. I'm not talking about the wills and the property divisions, nor is it the personal relief that his suffering has ceased, or that at last you don't have to worry about when it's going to happen.

When someone dies, it's usually a huge event for the family, as though it's never happened before, even though in the end, we all must eventually go that way. In a religious sense, I reckon we could rejoice in death, for it may mean access to the eternity of the after-life, but from some of the sadness I see at church-held funerals, I'm not so sure everyone in those rows of wood is on the same page concerning the promise of ever-lasting life.

For the survivors, death is an energy-burning affair that even if celebrated, still must be endured. There's a new reckoning in our lives, even if we anticipated the end for weeks, or months. With a finality that is deafening, our loved one inescapably leaves us and we are expected to continue the game of life, even though we're now short a playing piece.

And maybe that's where the celebration comes in – the regrouping of family, far-flung members from all parts of the globe, reuniting not only to mourn the loss but to reinforce the connections that have held us together for generations and reaffirm to each other that between us, we have something special, no matter the winding road ahead.

We are fortunate to live in this area, for even in the midst of power-money and egos the size of barren wastelands, there is an enduring sense of community, long held together by and tied to the history of Aspen, a communal bond that soothes the pain and brings rejoicing to the gathering of friends and family.

The officiant at St. Mary's, Aspen native Albert Loushin, took us down a quiet road, presenting deep reflections on Aspen's past, a time period to which the dwindling few of Aspen's old timers are unimaginatively and perfunctorily relegated, the dust bin of the "Quiet Years."

"No," says Albert, "those were the Golden Years," precursor to the growth explosion of people and money we've seen in recent history. Days when a gentle breeze rustling through the cottonwoods could be heard over the din of Main Street traffic. He continued, "People say the soul of Aspen has changed, but when I look out over the congregation and see folks sitting in the same pew they've occupied for 50, 60 years, I think there's a continuity here that can't be denied."

Red Butte Cemetery, run by an all-volunteer board of long-time Aspenites, is an unsurpassed refuge of beauty, a green, tree-lined expanse of peacefulness that might help make eternity bearable. It was a military burial with the Elk's Lodge in attendance. People always talk quietly in cemeteries.

Towards evening, the curtain opened on the final scene, a small family dinner at Uncle Vic's Blue Lake house, his last refuge from the storm while free will began to leave him. His memory pervaded our conversations, and we all learned a little more about the man we all thought we knew so well.

I climbed in my Jeep and headed for home, and then the tears came. Oh, Victor, I loved you and will miss you, but it is not for you I cry. I long for the crunch of gravel under my tires at your old Red Butte house, the powerful center of family life for so many, many years, long-gone to bulldozers, and with trepidation, I fear we will never again all be in the same place, with the same closeness between us.

And that is the complication, the tragedy, unforeseen and unexpected but as guaranteed as death itself.

Death, At Home on the Range

She was lying in a shallow depression, just below the line of sight, but the stench of her rotting corpse was unmistakable. Usually, ravens put me onto such remains, but on this day, there was an eerie quiet surrounding the scene, as though we had ridden through the gossamer sheen that separates our reality from that of the unknown.

I have seen a lot of death in my travels, and it never fails to set me back a bit. My horse Billy and I rode near the carcass and stopped, giving a silent salute to the once dynamic creature. Fortunately, I can think like a dog on occasion and managed to call Topper off the scent before he had a chance to roll in the midst of such canine delight.

After our voiceless soliloquy, the three of us set to work. I dismounted and approached what was left of the rotting beast; Billy kept his head close to my right shoulder, ears cocked forward, as if making sure this wasn't a dead horse he'd have to worry about all day; and Topper lay off to my left, eyes never leaving me, hoping for a distraction on my end that would give him just the sliver of opportunity he needed to revel in the dog-enticing smell that originally drew us there.

First thing the big boss will ask is, "Didja get the tag number?" meaning from the ear tag, which has all the pertinent information such as year born, lineage and ownership. I usually cut the tags off and take them home, just so there is no chance for misinterpretation, but in this case there didn't seem to be any tags. As I lifted the now unnatural, eyeless head and turned it over, looking through the carnage of the scavenger feast, I felt an empathy with this cow that was hard to shake.

Instinct had no doubt taken her to the fence she lay along, an ancient attempt to get home before she died. There's no rule about where bovines should perish, but many times it seems like it's beside a fence line, near a gate. But maybe that's just my imagination. Most cows die in a slaughterhouse, which may be more precise and preferable to death on the range. What can it be like, if you're an instinctual animal, to not understand why your body no longer functions as it used to and why your legs are too weak to bear your weight? It doesn't help that your lungs are filling with fluid and your body temperature soars in the hot August sun.

Just before she lay down to die, the Black Angus no doubt tried to let her calf suckle one last time, taking care of business to the tragic end. Her labored breathing called in the coyotes, never far from cows and calves, and their yapping song went through the tree tops, signaling winged scavengers that a veritable plethora of vittles was inevitable. The cow had no choices left as the coyotes began to tear at her milk-laced udder and soft underbelly, long before she was dead, nor could she close her eyes tight enough or long enough to keep the birds from plucking at the tender orbs. One final attempt to locate her calf and a raven harvested the last of her vision. It's not about intestinal fortitude or big, mean and dumb cows - it's about mercy and dying.

As I count her legs and study the misshapen, cloven hoof of her left hind, it's hard to envision the infinite miles this old mother cow has put on those hooves, up and down rocky, steep trails, her last year perhaps in pain from the foot injury. But no matter her physical limitations, never did she shirk her responsibilities of ruminating diligently and caring for her calf, nor did she refuse to go to the mountains by remaining bushed up along some cool, live-water creek bottom.

No, she wasn't a wild creature, but neither was it her fault we insisted she be dependent upon man for her survival. We share in her death.

Déjà vu in the West

It's hard to say when it first hit me, having grown up here, but there was a slow, deliberate, realization that something was terribly wrong with the management of the West, something that could most likely never be fixed, but that even in its crippling state of permanent purgatory, things would move along and continue to get done as they have for the last couple of hundred years. Unfortunately, things are even worse than I could have ever imagined.

History is a strange thing - it sometimes makes good reading, as in Catherine the Great, and of course, we all know the old adage that "history sometimes repeats itself." That truism has gotten us into some terrible jams and unbelievably, we're in a devastating wreck here in the West right now. Shortly after the Louisiana Purchase, myopic thinkers like Thomas Jefferson and those of his ilk in the Congress, overseers of a cash-strapped government, thought the best thing to do with all our land west of the Mississippi was to sell it and raise a little money for the treasury. Doesn't that sound a lot like George W. Bush and his wry-smiled hump, Dick Cheney?

The Homestead Act of 1862, allowed by Abraham Lincoln, furthered this idea of somehow making the West "useful" and the land rush was on, creating the "frontier" mentality that was just about the destruction of the then-existing west. 160-acre homesteads might have worked well in Illinois, but splitting up the Great Plains into such small plots and encouraging farming was a travesty of the largest kind in American government. I guess we could say no one knew any better - that might be the polite way to deal with such a debacle - neither the government nor the people, hastily plowing up the short prairie grass of the plains and setting up the history-changing dilemma known as the Dust Bowl.

This was a disdainful and insulting way to manage the Great Plains and the Rocky Mountain West, and the few dissenting voices, such as John Wesley Powell, were ignored. If the plains were suited to the grazing of millions of buffalo, wouldn't it have made sense to open the same area up to cattle grazing in large tracts and thus preserve the integrity of the land? A veritable similitude. No amount of common sense would have saved the bison, anyway. Indian eradication as a priority and 160-acre plots (later 640's) took care of them.

Today, the onslaught of gas drilling rigs covering the western slope of Colorado is being allowed by the same type of thinking that created the earlier problems in the West. Of course, just as before, it is politicians and people ignorant of the region doing the thinking, and like before, those of the frontier, those with an understanding of the land, are not being listened to. As Mark Harvey, producer of *A Land Out of Time* (a film documentary of immense proportions that should be seen by everyone who cares about the future of the West), says about the Federal Government: "They (Feds) hold the public hearings mandated by law, take tens of thousands of public comments favoring conservation, and then proceed with energy development as if the hearing never took place."

Bush and his administration have mandated that "cheap" energy be developed at all costs. That's oxymoronic thinking, if not outright ridiculous B.S. It can't be cheap if it's developed at all costs. Land irretrievably destroyed by the actions of a few large corporations (in concert with our government, under the guise of providing for us) is a loss too great for this nation to bear, no matter the need.

If we look at history, it is an understatement that those in Washington, D.C., are not good land managers. We (you and I) must stand in front of the bulldozers and be counted, at all costs.

Dirt Streets and Mud Puddles

It's happened to all of us at one time or another; someone says the streets of Aspen were still dirt in 1965, or dirt in 1975, or maybe are still dirt. I've heard that Main Street was paved with silver, and also that the moon is made of green cheese. No doubt as you listen, your personal knowledge doesn't quite agree with what you're being told, but it makes a good story, so why interrupt. And if you weren't here back then, the first story you hear is most likely the one you remember, so that becomes the truth of the matter, no matter.

The most historically accurate story goes something like this: Main Street was dirt, not silver or gold, until the Colorado State Highway Department paved it in 1938, starting in Carbondale and going through Aspen. This also completed the paving of the entire stretch between Glenwood Springs and Aspen. (It is possible that the rumor about Main Street being paved with silver got started because mine tailings from some of the silver mines were used as gravel on the street, although that remains anecdotal and non-confirmable.) Just for your information, paving on Independence Pass was finally completed in 1969.

Almost all of the remaining streets in Aspen were dirt, until 1952, at least. That's the year the town fathers decided it would be a good idea to oil most of the streets in town and make things a little more "cosmopolitan." After 1952, it would be somewhat of a misnomer to say the streets were "dirt," as the oiling actually worked quite well and after a few years, layers of oil and gravel built up that certainly resembled asphalt pavement, with the exception that the edges of the streets were still mostly dirt, and there were a tremendous number of potholes.

Negotiating these streets was somewhat hazardous for the youth of the town, particularly after a rainstorm. In the spring, recess was a good time to have a game of marbles out on Hallam Street, in front of the school. If you "lagged" a bit hard, or were forced to play too close to a mud puddle by a group of older kids, your chances of losing a marble to the brown waters standing over unknown depths were greatly enhanced. Not only that, if the teacher was a little late in ringing the bell, many kids had an innate ability to end up with wet gravel and mud all over themselves.

There were on some occasions huge pot-holes, or even bigger mud puddles that got reputations of heroic proportions, and it usually became a mission of some young boys to see if they could dump another kid, or two, into one of these leviathan pools. Of course, a fight had to be started at school first, just argumentative in the beginning, and as the final bell rang, the kids involved (usually followed by fans on both sides) would wend their way down the street to a certain puddle that had been, by now, expectantly mentioned a time or two. Of course, the ploy was clear to everyone and the bets were on. Girlfriends could be won or lost in a single evening around a mud puddle, and as we learned the hard way, the winners didn't always win.

Around 1962, Aspen started slowly paving the downtown core area, and by 1963, almost all of the downtown had been paved. Sort of a harbinger of things to come.

After that, no one seemed to care much as to when the rest of the streets got paved, but it slowly got done over the next few years. It mostly happened while I was away at college, or at least when I wasn't looking, and not only did the rest of the streets get paved, but the changing of the town started in earnest. The Tomkins Hardware building caved in under the weight of spring snow, Ed Tiedeman closed his general store and coal delivery business, and almost overnight we were slammed to the backs of our seats by the sudden acceleration of growth in Aspen.

Divide and Conquer

It must have been wild back then; open, unspoiled vistas in every direction, wild game behind every ridge, stars bright enough to hurt your eyes, and not much above us in the food chain. Oh, the occasional, cranky Indian band might thwart your idea of a good day, and it would be impossible, even in this day and age, to dismiss the dangers posed by an unsociable grizzly bear.

The words of long-dead authors give us a clue as to how western pioneers viewed the world, and it's not always attractive. The area from the Missouri River to the Pacific Ocean was once thought of as a vast, unexplored region, forbidding and inhospitable to all but the most stalwart of mountain men. Native Americans weren't even referred to generically as "Indians," but called instead savages, no matter their view of the world.

We have a tendency to look on past ages with a somewhat pitiful stance, wondering how people back then could possibly have navigated through life without our modern equipment, inventions and technological advances. No one can say for certain, but I'd bet those pioneers of the early 1800s would take one look at today's world and say, "No thanks."

Our western attitude has been one of "conquering" Nature, starting with the Lewis & Clark Expedition and continuing onward until the moment you read these words. We drill into the dank, dark world underneath the Gulf of Mexico to extract ancient oil, and then when technology fails us we naively demand a better system of fail-safe oversight, as though we really can control everything. The cumulative effect of our inwardly-focused thinking seldom enters the equation.

If we look closely at Lewis and Clark, we find a tough but misbegotten band of explorers, sent out to do the impossible by an egocentric president, Thomas Jefferson. It took this group three years to travel to the Pacific Coast and back, and they'd still no doubt be somewhere along the Lolo Trail, trying to find lost horses and men if it had not been for the help of the Native Americans who had long before settled this country.

In 1806, barely three months into their winter stay at Fort Clatsop on the coast of the Pacific Northwest, the Lewis & Clark expedition had completely exterminated the once-plentiful area elk herds. It was just one of many egregious errors. The Chinook and Clatsop Indians, who had lived there for generations in relative comfort, were no doubt horrified. Such early, bad behavior had ugly forebodings: Look to Aspen in the 1880s and we witness the same disregard for the local environment with the obliteration of native elk & deer populations.

Many mistakes were made along the path of federal land management, not the least of which was the Homestead Act of 1862. This contrived scheme to settle the West was in reality a method of doling out stolen Native American land to taxpaying "Americans." The key word, just like today, is "taxpaying," as in property. Soon to follow the treatment of the "Indians," of course, was a cry for the extermination of natural predators such as the wolf, coyote and eagle. We killed off the buffalo, plowed up the prairies and wondered where the apocalyptic Dust Bowl of the 1930s came from.

Today, we build hugely visible towers on mountain tops to direct air traffic; we build taller and uglier antennae for the transmission of cell phone signals; throw darts at each other over the now-contrasting philosophies of "wilderness" and "public land"; we still fear wolves and in Aspen, talk about neutering crab apple trees because we don't know how to coexist with black bears.

Just like those who came before us, we predictably forge ahead, intent on "conquering" Mother Nature, actually arguing about what kinds of mechanized and motorized travel should be allowed in our last remaining pristine areas. I'm not sure we'll ever get it, for like old dogs, we seem incapable of learning new tricks.

Speaking to Dogs, and Horses

It has been said that certain breeds of dogs, such as border collies, can recognize up to 160 different words, as though that would somehow be a measure of intelligence. That's not many words, if you think about it, considering what these dogs are capable of in the area of stock handling. It would literally take thousands upon thousands of human words to adequately describe what simple commands to a dog can initiate, setting in motion complex routines that a dog understands through instinct, body language and sound from a single command or whistle.

If there's one thing that makes us feel superior in intelligence to other species, it's our ability to speak and comprehend languages. Animals thus are looked at disparagingly when the subject comes up, even trying as hard as we might to erroneously infer language capabilities upon chimpanzees. Consequently, we walk away from the subject too soon, failing to make the distinction between "animal language" and "animal communication," selling the intelligence of our natural world companions far short.

Horses, too, have an ability to understand certain words, particularly their own names and certain other communications, such as "Whoa," "Back," "Gee" and "Haw." A skilled teamster can work a well-trained horse or team of horses from a distance without having hands-on contact with them, strictly using voice commands.

Dogs and horses are better at understanding us than we are at understanding them, which in the context of reality, makes their lives much more difficult. Most of our meaningful communication with dogs and horses is of the non-verbal kind and body stance, facial expression, eye contact and posture generally have far more meaning than words ever could. Many times we give the wrong impression of what we expect; for instance, comforting a dog aggressive toward others. Giving such comfort tells the dog we appreciate his ferociousness and we wonder why the hell he keeps it up.

But, think of the poor horse that gets an inexperienced rider on its back. It can be the difference between dead weight and blissfulness. From the horse's perspective, is the weight of the person in the proper place or is it too far back, too far forward, is there enough weight in the stirrups, enthusiasm in the pose? "A horse can sense your fear," is a knowing statement, for he can immediately become suspicious of your tightening grip on the reins, the petrified feel of your muscles against his body, and the saliva-starved sound of your voice.

"This horse has a mind of its own," is the most common complaint heard from neophytes after a riding experience with a horse more knowledgeable than they. The only answer is, "Of course he does, and it appears you underestimated it."

It's easy for most people to understand that getting and taking care of a horse might require some prior knowledge, or at least a wholehearted willingness to quickly learn. Not always so with dogs, as people take them home from cardboard boxes in front of the grocery store or from a pet store without any idea of what they're getting into. The Aspen Animal Shelter diligently tries to steer people in the proper direction with adoptions but still, many of us think our loving anthropomorphism will compensate for any communication deficiencies we have.

Unfortunately, without some wisdom concerning the process, we make mindless movements toward our animals that they consider with mindful absorption, giving them counter-intuitive impressions of what good behavior might be, and before you know it, our pets have developed bad habits or obsessive behaviors that we can't correct. Sometimes, in a sorry attempt to explain away such deficiencies, we vindicate aberrant compulsiveness as "cute."

Thousands of years ago, we entered into a solemn bond with those animals we domesticated, to forever take care of them and it remains our obligation to do so in an intelligent and caring manner.

Dogs in Our Midst

You can imagine it, the last of the fires burning low, giving off just enough light to make visible the eyes of the surrounding wolves, hungry, patiently waiting and inching inward, ever so stealthily. Given the intricacies of the human mind, it's easy to understand how one might be tempted to toss a left-over bone toward those inquisitive, intelligent eyes, if for no other reason than to witness the excitement with which it was received.

And so began the domestication of the "dog," about ten- to fifteen-thousand years ago. Most likely we tamed and cultivated canines from the packs of gray wolves roaming the earth back then, an excellent evolutionary theory and a seemingly brilliant human idea, given what dogs contribute to our lives.

Historically, it all seems to make sense, but as a kid growing up, it was sometimes scary and usually confusing. Our dogs on the Woody Creek ranch were for work and there really wasn't much interaction with them other than that. When "off the clock," they lived on the porch or in their doghouses and usually minded their own business. Naturally, we always glommed onto one or two as our favorites, but they were the exceptions.

When I was pre-school age, I'd wander a block east on Bleeker to play with my friend Doug Franklin. He and I got along fine, but it always seemed like when it was time to go home, Lou Wille's Russian wolfhounds would be out enjoying the afternoon sun and it was a challenge to get by them on the way back to my grandmother's house.

They were SOB's, a nightmare for a kid to deal with. They'd knock me down in the middle of the street, dirt in those days, and if I tried to stand my ground, they'd attack from different angles. My face and my hands always seemed to be healing up from the scrapes. Complaints came from other quarters, as well, and Lou, being the honorable man he was, eventually took care of the problem.

Fred Iselin's big, drooling St. Bernard, Bingo, would make the rounds on a rather meticulous schedule, usually coming toward my grandmother's house from the alley that ran behind the Elisha's garage. He always seemed unimpressed with the antics of kids and generally ignored us, but I clearly remember waiting and watching out the kitchen window for his expected arrival. He seldom missed his rounds and sometimes my grandmother and her sister Julia would leverage his appearance into stories about European St. Bernard's and their daring rescues in the Italian and Swiss Alps.

Today it might be hard to visualize, but in the 1950s, early 60s, there were bands of ungrateful curs roaming the streets, irresponsibly turned loose by their owners, and we all kept an eye out for them. They'd knock you down and sniff you over, looking for food and more than one kid lost his bag lunch to the brutes on his way to school. Generally speaking, they were incredibly unfriendly, snarling and growling if anyone tried to get them to move along. A cry of, "The dogs are coming," was usually enough to get us all inside someone's house or fenced yard. No one ever proved it, mostly for lack of motivation, but the cure for these errant packs was believed to be poison.

If you look at the last 10,000 years, it's clear not much has changed. Dogs are still being used as pack animals along mountain trails, although their participation today is not central to our survival as it was to the Utes before they began looting horses from the "yellow-eyed" European palefaces.

Dogs still turn around several times before they lie down, mark their territory with obsessive consistency and seem to be our "best friends," although no one really knows what they think.

And we, the great masters of our universe, just as we were ten-thousand years ago, still believe we are smarter than our dogs.

Dumb They Are Not

We were in "foreplay" before the start of a commissioner's public hearing, everyone sizing up the crowd and looking for a good place to sit. Bob Child, popular Pitkin County commissioner and Capitol Creek cattle rancher, was sitting in the front row, making himself available for "pre-show" questions when some mustachioed lackey from God-knows-where, in an ambiguous attempt to ingratiate himself with Child, said, "Man, aren't cows the dumbest creatures on the face of the earth? They have nothing going on."

Child, ever the gentleman, was clearly taken aback by such a rude observation, the ignorance of which deserved no answer, but he smiled and offered a quick defense of the bovine personality.

Cows, or cattle if you prefer, are hard-wired with everything they need to get through their world with dignity, and an inadequate assessment of their intelligence by an unknowing outsider isn't something they're going to worry about. Naturally, any creature that doesn't genuflect, in some way, to our superiority, is easy to call stupid, but if you know cows, it soon becomes clear that most of them are quite confident they occupy the top rung of the food chain.

On the open range, we make an auspicious quartet; cows, dogs, and horses that interact in a most remarkable way. Throw in some humans and the problems start, but then again, the group wouldn't be very cohesive without human intervention.

There isn't much that scares us, being the individuals we are, for most of the mammal kingdom shies away when they catch our smell, but cattle and other cloven-hoofed animals face a dilemma of a different sort. They spend the night in thousands of acres of wildness, without protection other than their own wits. Their immature calves are bait for any number of wilderness predators and protecting their young is of paramount importance. We seldom see the manner of creature that sneaks up on them in the night, but sometimes we find the remains of unsuccessful defenses.

A Black Angus, with a black calf, is hard to see, but when a band of coyotes, or an angry, starving bear, or whatever other night monster you might imagine, makes its stealthy attack in the darkness, it must be difficult for the cow to fend off the fast moving intruder(s) and keep track of her young in the lightning fast attack. Does a cow feel panic? Does adrenalin keep her focused?

Normally, cows see the dogs jogging alongside our horses and instinctively know it's time to move on up the path. But this fall, the livestock are particularly sensitized to the cow dogs, and one wonders what may have prompted such behavior. Cows that normally trail along without complaint are prone to turn on the dogs and chase them with bawling, hoof-flailing, vicious candor.

It's a dance of life-and-death, for if the dog misses his step, there won't be a second chance, not with these cows. My dog, Topper, goes for the left hock, the cow turns on him that direction, and then in a move that is blindingly fast, Topper goes for the right hock, but the cow is already threatening that way, taking away Topper's remaining opportunity for success. It's a frustrating job for a dog, and he has to be ready to turn and run for his life the split-second the cow decides to pursue him down the steep mountainside.

One day, my buddy Dan brought his dog Sam over to help, but these are what we call "three dog" cows, and we only had two. Inexplicably, in a reversal of lingo, three cows took after Topper at once, their bellering attack a tad frightening, for we were not more than inches from the dog. If a cow, as has happened, decides to take out your horse, it can be deadly for the rider or the horse.

Topper and Sam refused to quit, my horse Drifter did his best to keep the angry beasts off Topper, and we got the herd where we wanted them. Call these cows what you want, but they aren't dumb.

Earl Was Always Up For a Challenge

This isn't going to be one of those tear-jerkers about how sad it all was. That's not the way Earl operated and there's no sense to compromise him now. He wouldn't like it.

Earl came from Rangely, a dot of a town in Northwestern Colorado, as a gift to my daughter from her then-future-husband, Ty. Earl was supposed to be a Chihuahua, and was said to be a purebred, but the kennel lady lied to Ty, and hell, you can't tell too much about a small pup at weaning time, anyway.

We got lucky, it seems, for Earl was something bigger than his advertised breeding, but we were never sure what. Oh, he had a few of those "small dog" mannerisms, like a shrill bark, but I can't recall a thing that intimidated him, even though I doubt he ever topped fifteen pounds on the scale.

Earl spent the summer of 2006 with me, and we learned a lot from each other. I refused the oft-used moniker of Grandpa, and instead became Uncle Tony, a name Earl recognized as readily as his own.

My daughter, Lauren, was doing a college internship at the McCabe Ranch and much to my early reluctance, I found myself Earl's daytime chaperone. I refused to coddle him and he went irrigating with me every morning and afternoon, running alongside as I trudged the fields, moving the water and checking the cows that shared the pasture with my horses.

If the cows seemed too close, Earl would come to my "rescue," jumping high and snapping at their noses, keeping after them until they moved off at a run. Then, he'd trot along, not looking for approval, just resuming his pasture patrol, long, thin tail darting from side to side.

Earl wouldn't come if he thought you were going to lift him up into a vehicle, but if you opened the door and asked him, he'd fly in with the greatest of pride. That's how big dogs do it, I reckon. He taught me the joy (again) of having a dog and made it possible for Topper to come into my life. Earl loved to hug your neck, if he liked you.

Earl seldom saw a stranger he didn't challenge and it was with trepidation I looked back one day to see a mother skunk about ten yards behind me in the grass. Earl was jogging my way, head moving side to side and I fully expected a confrontation, but the two just stopped and looked at each other for a second, and went their separate ways.

We could have insisted Earl be a lap dog, but no one would have been happy about it, especially Earl. He thrived in the horse barn at Chaparral, darting around the big hunters and jumpers, keeping watch over his kingdom. Facing down coyotes was not uncommon for him and once Ty had to pull him from the clutching jaws of one heading into the dark abyss, with Earl loudly insisting upon his superiority.

And last Thursday night, as I came home late from a meeting, Earl gave me a playful look of "Let's go, Uncle Tony," and away we went with Topper to feed the horses. Earl ducked between my legs as he usually did, and I watched him notify each horse, letting them know he was staying at my house.

He'd done this hundreds of times. Walking toward the hay shed, I looked up just in time to see Earl, nose down in the grass, get snuck up on and slammed by a curious front hoof. It wasn't fair by any means, but it was animal-to-animal, in God's world, not a speeding car or some such thing.

There wasn't a scratch on him and his legs worked fine, but something wasn't right and you could tell he was leaving us, even as he ran to the gate. I carried him into the house and laid him on the couch, where the impenetrable wall of death washed gently over him and Earl became the stuff of legend.

Early Education

It seems like a lot of good packages come in three's. You may recall that a couple of months ago, this column paid tribute to some of Aspen's ladies of reminiscence. We mentioned the Coe girls, Susan, Nancy and Judy, a trio of earthy beauties who piqued the developing hormones of young men around town, myself included. About a week after that piece ran, my friend Doug Franklin, who had lived in the same neighborhood, sent me three pictures from that time of Nancy Coe herself, a dashing young sweetheart with a very shy, but beguiling smile. As she got older, I'm sure the smile became less uncertain and more enticing. She was, just as my memory told me, a beautiful girl.

After the Coe's moved away, our hearts were heavy and it became clear that life without them was going to be a lot less intriguing, our further education most likely limited to that which we gleaned from books. A sad state of affairs, so to speak, until the fateful day when we got hooked up with the Just girls. My good friend and knockout in her own right, Pamela, introduced me to these young ladies, and in an instant, the whirlwind of life was cranked up several notches.

The three girls, Carla, Joella (Dodi) and Norma, lived just across Hunter Street from the Catholic Church in a single-family house. Tall, long-legged and with fine features, they were basically three different shades of blonde and triple the persuasion for any normal young guy in town paying attention. Norma, who always seemed to be called Nomi, was in my class at school and was, for a couple of exciting years, my on-again, off-again girlfriend.

It must have been that their mother worked at night, because we seemed to spend a lot of nights playing over at their house. There was one of those dim, single-bulb street lamps hanging over the corner of Main and Hunter (home base for many kick-the-can games), which lit the way to the fascinating world of the Just girls. As we neared the house, the code was revealed, saying, almost unfalteringly, that if the porch light was on, it was OK to stop in. If the light was off, it meant that Mom was home - stay away.

Carla and Dodi were older than we were by a couple of years or so, but it was a better-than-good night when all three girls would sit down with one or two of us guys to play a few rounds of spin-the-bottle. There was an interesting, unspoken ethic at play, one that said we all could have fun and explore each other's sexuality, but in ways that were acceptable to the group. Pairing off was not allowed outside this close-knit interaction of youths with desires on the brink of explosion. It all seemed to work reasonably well, and kept things from getting too serious on any level, but there may have been exceptions.

It's easy to conjure up images of kids gone amok, having sex in pantries or behind couches under the shadow of the ever-watchful eye of the Catholic church but, in reality, we were a bit more innocent than that, probably because we were still a little young. We were learning to engage, physically and mentally, with these girls and others that hung out at their house, learning how to interact with those of the opposite sex. But make no mistake about it, these were, at least in our minds, no mere schoolgirls. They were high-powered women, the likes of which I doubt have been surpassed in Aspen since, and who, of course, will remain in the memories of more than just this writer for the rest of our lives.

Aspen, as we all know, is home to more than its fair share of alluring women. The proof of this can be found in a glance around, right or left. Those of us who grew up here have known it all along, and we are forever thankful to the wondrous women who gave us the early education between the sexes that could have happened only within the confines of youth.

Lasting Legacy in Emma

Imagine the big, heavy Concord stagecoach, rumbling along somewhere between a trot and a gallop, six gleaming horses up, two-by-two-by-two abreast, the driver leaning into every turn, nervously spitting tobacco juice, his able assistant ready at a moment's notice to brake the wheels, if coaxed.

The pace was brutal, every hillock to be negotiated, each turn to be skillfully navigated, being continually cognizant of the up-and-down, forward-and-back swing of the passenger-carrying coach, an exercise in understanding and utilizing gravity. In those days before rail, blowing and sweating horses needed to be changed about every ten miles, with stage stops in Woody Creek, Emma, Yellow Dog (now Satank), and then on to Defiance (Glenwood Springs).

Emma, a collection of deteriorating brick buildings alongside Hwy 82, just west of Basalt, was originally located slightly further West, on what was the Vasten farm. There was strong impetus for a stage stop there, with accommodations, based on the needs of the horses and mules.

Wait, the mules? Jerome B. Wheeler, well-known Aspen pioneer, had established coke ovens in Jerome Park, well-above Marion and Sunshine, and prior to the existence of rail, hauled the coke to Aspen for its use in the smelting of silver ore.

Large freighters, similar to the one seen in "Dances with Wolves," could not make the trip to Aspen in one day, and thus a stable was built to house and feed the overnighted mules. The ringing of the resident blacksmith's hammer could be heard over the roar of the still-wild Roaring Fork and naturally, a saloon was built adjacent to the barn.

Strangely, there's a lot of conjecture about how Emma got its name, but quite simply, it was named after Emma Shehi, the woman who ran the eating house at the stage stop. Some people wanted to call it Garrison, an early name, but Emma won out by popular vote.

There was no Aspen Junction (Basalt) until 1887, so a trip down valley by stagecoach would not have passed that burg of gurgling, hissing and huffing steam engines, clawing their way through the mountains. No, Emma was the mainstay of the mid-valley, an agricultural community that held the only area post office for miles around.

The Denver & Rio Grande Railroad came through town in 1887, and Emma began to take on a new appearance. Sprawling stockyards were built to contain the cattle being shipped to distant markets and the local farmers could now compete in the town of Aspen, then in its mining heyday.

The French-Italian farmers and ranchers arrived in the 1880s, bought out the original homesteaders and acquired additional lands. The flat, sagebrush covered terrain gave way to larger, more productive ranches. As a sure sign of the nationality of the settlers, the D & RG railroad would occasionally drop several carloads of grapes off on the local siding, to be used by the wine-making immigrants.

The Emma schoolhouse, the one presently seen on the south side of 82, was built between 1910 and 1912. There was a continuing, lively chorus of tough school marms over the years, my maternal grandmother, Nellie Stapleton Sloss and her sister, Julia Stapleton, included. I have a photo of my great-aunt Julia standing in front of the building with her students.

And why am I talking about Emma, for God's sake? For one thing, Pitkin County has fortuitously decided to save the old buildings from further deterioration; Emma's importance to valley history has long been understated, but it's more personal than that.

My maternal great-grandfather, John W. Sloss, owned ranches nearby in the early 1880s and one of his brothers owned the Emma Store for several years. My grandmother Nellie married John W.'s son Bates, and when I'm irrigating neighboring hayfields, my mind's eye can sometimes see my lonely grandmother behind the windows of the empty schoolhouse, waiting for her husband to take her home.

Exodus

For almost anyone who has lived here, now or in the past, there's a part of Aspen deep inside that will never die. You can hate her today for the lovely past she's let slip away, or love her in the present, not knowing what fate befalls either of you.

Aspen's history is full of big names, very few whose descendants still live here. There was a ton of mining money to be made, but it took a lot of people, living in small Victorian cottages and boarding houses, to carry water for the big boys. We hear of Jerome B. Wheeler and the rest going belly up after the silver crash of 1893, but it's hard to sympathize, for they already lived somewhere else, eh? It didn't happen overnight, not like Exxon's Black Sunday, but happen it did.

Soon, wind whistled through the windowless clapboards where children once played and dry, blowing snow built up around the lonely, second-floor cotton mattresses where some of the last of the old miners took refuge. Like horses out the gate, the town had left for better pastures. Except for a few.

It took a while, but insult finally followed injury in the 1950s and early 60s. Widows of men who had played the silver boom and bust to the bitter end or ranched their lives away, remained, with little other than their tiny Victorian houses and grand gardens to show for a lifetime in Aspen. City water and sewer lines needed to be upgraded to assuage burgeoning growth and between special utility assessments and the rising tide of real estate taxes, these frail, bewildered women with nowhere to go were driven from town. We barely noticed.

The 1970s saw the great exodus, still talked about, of longtime, hard-working folks from town, many of them unremarkable natives who had lived through the "quiet years." Firemen, cops, plumbers, hospital workers and business owners left for less-expensive lives down valley or from whence they'd come. For some, it was difficult to resist the spiraling real estate prices; others soured on the prolific new breed of people who had arrived;

and still others found it hard to live in a town that was getting more expensive every time they looked around. A low mill-levy doesn't mean much to a working man when the value of his house increases exponentially every two years.

Countering that, in the 1970s and 80s, many free-market condominiums and houses were built in an attempt to soak up an abundance of young workers who had arrived on the wings of the wind, reaching for the Aspen dream. The Pitkin County Housing Authority was still finding its legs and people needed shelter of all types. There was also an influx of women who, as time has shown, were smarter than the men they married or had relationships with.

These folks gambled their years in Aspen, figuring they'd never lose, but life shuffles the deck with blinding fury. Many of them single men and women, living in houses and condominiums 25 - 30 years old, are facing expensive upgrades and tough choices. Unlike the 50s and 60s, times today are much different. Real estate prices are tumbling, making the decision to leave a difficult one, for after a lifetime of work, you only get one shot to leave this town whole.

Uncertainty clouds the skies of common sense and prosperity has become a threadbare hope, but yet the taxing districts are still on full-throttle, what with the airport and hospital expansions unfolding, not to mention interest due on existing debt. The school district is ringing its bell for more, too. What taxes?

The miners and widows who got pushed out many years ago were fairly obvious. Those in the path of today's game-changing wrecking ball are quiet players, the last threads of our inherent local vitality. If we lose them, it'll be a tragedy. Don't kid yourself.

Facing Death in the Woods

I'd just gone out to feed the horses some oats when a group of high-powered rifle shots could be heard up the creek from the cabin; within seconds, another gun fired off a couple of rounds in rapid succession, and then all was quiet. The sun had just risen into a cloudless, blue sky and I wondered what it was like to die on a bright, sunny morning, with blown up lungs and a fading glint in your eye, looking at your own blood in the freshly fallen snow.

I left the cabin for the last time that day, my gear loaded on two pack horses stringing behind me. Somewhere along the trail, there is a giant rockslide from thousands of years ago, probably created when a small geologic fault juxtaposed itself side to side, slimming and slamming those rocks to the top of the earth. At the bottom of the slide, near the edge of a fast-flowing stream, is a small opening in the pines, about 30 by 50 feet, which is well shielded on all sides, except from the trail high above. I've been in a few wrecks there moving cows, mostly because of the rock slide, and I always look that way, as if acknowledging a curmudgeonly old friend.

Studying the opening, I spied a large bull elk pulling some grass out from under the side of an evergreen tree, in an uncharacteristically nonchalant manner. Whether he had lost his cows or they were a little farther back in the pines, I couldn't tell, but I stopped to watch this magnificent animal, figuring he would bolt at any moment. When it was clear he wasn't going to run, I swiftly and quietly pulled my lever-action, .30-.30 out of its scabbard and dismounted, all at the same time, a maneuver practiced hundreds of times as a youth. Very cautiously and stealthily, I eased up ahead of the horse, giving him a little breathing room if he needed it when I fired the gun. I squatted down in the rocks and took careful aim, fixing the great bull in the cross hairs of a powerful scope.

Most guns in my family have a history, it seems, and the rifle I held was manufactured by Winchester in 1899, the year my grandfather turned eight. Undoubtedly, he bagged his first big-game with it, and the year after his death, when I was twelve, I took my first bull elk using the same gun. There I was, holding a ton of tradition and emotion in my hands, the shooting iron pressed tightly into my shoulder, contemplating a shot that most elk hunters can only dream about in a lifetime of hunting. Less than fifty yards off the trail stood a trophy-quality elk, six symmetrically grown points on each antler, almost a gift from the powers that be. I had pack horses at the ready, and was only a couple of miles from the horse trailer. But there was a hesitancy in my desire, no rush to send the distinctive, deadly crack of rifle fire into the air, accompanied by the instantaneous thwack of bullet entering mass, the sound that would signal the absolute end of this majestic beast.

And then he acknowledged me, but rather than jump and run off, he examined my intrusion out of the corner of his eye, slowly raising his head. I had the scope on him and could see the interest in his eyes, but no disdain, nor fear. As I lowered the gun, he and I locked eyes for the briefest of moments and then, almost casually, he trotted off into the dark timber. I slowly slung the weapon back in its sheath and leaned against my horse for the longest time, arms crossed atop the saddle, feeling a sense of great satisfaction.

Whiskey and killing must be alike, I reckon, in the sense that after a time, some men just walk away from either or both of them without really knowing why. But most remember when.

Fall

Autumn hangs in the air like the last full globe of seasonal sunlight before it slinks into its own splendid setting. Gorgeous days soothe our souls while our breaths are held in anticipation of the first stinging snow. The crisp, falling leaves, dead to another year, fill the irregularities of the earth beneath us.

Overhead, a gaggle of Canada geese, coal black against a steel-gray sky, sway and honk their way across the valley, looking for the perfect refuge from falling darkness just as they've done for thousands of years.

Behind my house, green, lush grass awaits the arrival of my horses, coming home from their summer pasture. The change of the seasons is upon them, too, and a mouthful of hay seems more enticing at this stage of the game. Through my office window, I spy rows of hay bales, stacked with finesse and covered with a billowing tarp, ready for the taking, but all good things in time.

Still in their summer home, these equine beauties are far more interested in me now than earlier in the year, when succulent spring grass provided them the punch of a nutrient high and they raced and bucked their way around the perimeter, oblivious of my desire to catch them.

The corral, nuanced under huge cottonwoods along a live stream, provides welcome shade in the summer, but by this time of year has become more of an habitual place for the horses to gather and patiently pass the time, rather than a necessity. Their winter coats are beginning to show, ever so minutely, and they look to me with interest in their eyes, knowing I hold the secret to how we'll treat the change in seasons. Hearing the clang of the metal gate, they run to the corral to wait for me, as though they don't want to miss anything.

The high country becomes colder at night and the cattle, used to living without fences, turn their thoughts more toward home rather than climbing higher and through some primordial link, seem to gather in hard to find locations. Ranchers spend more of these days in the hills, gauging the location of the cows and preparing for the fall roundup.

It all moves with a beat of steady syncopation, man and animal alike, clearly in tune with Mother Nature, for it cannot be any other way and remain successful. By now, the cow dogs, like professional athletes, are in top shape and can go, and go, all day without a backwards glance. They know which direction the cattle need to move and require little guidance from the cowboys.

The dogs, the horses, the cattle, the people, are all aware that the high-primed glory of summer is heading toward short, cold days under a fast-moving sun. Dusk becomes a time to hurry up rather than a time to bask in a days' work well done.

Like the wildlife that must depend on its own wits to survive, the domestic world gently prepares itself for the inevitable change, relying on a hard-wired instinct of the ages that strives to protect them from foolhardy paroxysms that may spell disaster.

And although it may be anathema for a writer to say so, the changes come and go without the need of verbal support or human philosophizing. The thread of life, of which we have so little understanding, continues its inexorable march toward the infinity of tomorrow.

Soon the chill winds of winter will succor at the stark, silent bleakness of the mountainsides, warming us from the inside and without being told to do so, we'll feed our horses and cattle, protect our dogs and begin rummaging around for our skis and boots.

Fast Lane Fallout

Last week and like an apparition, she stood before me. Young and attractive, with an incredible smile, her energy emanated with an infectious vibrancy. We'd hardly gotten to know each other when an unpleasant breakup with her boyfriend took her from the usual circles and I hadn't seen her all summer. In reply to my question of what she'd been up to, she answered that she was "living the Aspen lifestyle."

"That can be good and bad," I offered, mentally wishing her only the best in life. It was great to see her, someone clearly enjoying her young life, but however auspicious, that event triggered an encroaching shadow that soon had me contemplating a darkness from long ago.

Aspen was a smaller town back then, in population and in directions to go. My ever-wandering high school eye picked up on an exceptional woman, four or five years older than I, particularly obvious even in a town already filled with glamorous ladies, and it seemed as though I saw her around with a dedicated regularity that defied logic. Naturally, I didn't see her every night, but whenever she did cross my vision, it was either entering or exiting some nightclub or bar, off-limits to kids like myself, and she always seemed to be exhibiting a new fur or some other exquisite garment of sophisticated dress. Her escorts seemed to change with the wind and on a certain level, I believed that they were living the "Aspen story" in a manner consistent with the way it was presented.

Where can you go on sleepless nights to fight the loneliness and get a little numb, hoping for eventual, elusive slumber and still remain almost anonymous? A quiet bar is good to find, especially in a town known for its rowdiness, and the Red Onion was her attraction, back in the early seventies.

She still appeared beautiful, at least when viewed from the swinging doors, with a naturally enticing posture and waist-length, light brown hair. Fresh out of college, my heart skipped a beat, realizing it was the tantalizing woman of my high school dreams, apparently all alone at the bar. She didn't want to talk at first, but soon recognized me for what I was (something I refused to realize), another lonely person looking for an anchor in the night. Her vitality that had years earlier seemed so evident, so captivating, even from a distance, had been shredded, and there was a subdued tone to our conversation that was devoid of passion, but incredibly warm.

It can be a brutal stint, life in Aspen's fast lane, especially if you're young, willing and unsuspecting. Illusions are the stuff of reality and riding a wild time is not something to be built upon, not in the long run. A reserved smile is really cover for deteriorating teeth and make-up is for those that have something to look forward to.

Perhaps as she stared into the mirror behind the back bar, there was a suspicion that her future had already been lived, that she'd spent her best, and maybe alone at night, in her cramped room, she yearned for an unknown fork in the road, just so she'd at least have a choice.

We met occasionally, late at night, sharing beers and quiet discourse. Whatever had transpired previously hadn't stolen her dignity and I've always been flattered by the fact that she liked me, despite the past that should have left her distrustful. We had a strong affinity for each other, but we let it die before it ever really got started which, in retrospect, may have been the tragedy.

Don't Fence Me In

Even in this small valley, or maybe particularly in this small vale, two disparate worlds, ne'er to be reconciled, are joined at the hip, for better or worse. Which side of the fence is greener depends on which side one stands. Do they have all that security at "celebrity" parties to keep the riffraff out, or in?

The West, as we still believe it to be, reflects open spaces, blue skies, and "land, lots of land under starry skies above," in which to freely roam. At least according to Cole Porter's song, "Don't Fence Me In."

But there's a flaw in Porter's thinking: Fences are rarely about keeping livestock (or people) in but more about keeping critters out. Beginning in the 1800s, land barons built fences around thousands of acres of land they controlled, mainly to keep the cattle or sheep of free-ranging ranchers out of the water holes contained therein. Wire was cheaper than hired guns.

Early on, the biggest purchasers of newfangled barbed wire were the railroads, who used it to keep livestock off their rights-of-way. Governments today rely on fences to keep cattle, elk, deer and horses off public roads.

Range wars don't happen much anymore, but there's still an occasional flare-up over wandering cattle or horses. If you live near or alongside the national forest, you know that cattle begin wandering home in the autumn. You're probably also aware that cows are great opportunists who don't mind getting into what's left of your flower or vegetable gardens; they love scratching themselves against the posts holding up your porch, or evacuating their bladders and bowels all over your yard or driveway.

This is where the fences come in, for those of you who hadn't thought about it. If you fence them out of your property, they just keep moseying toward home, leaving your stuff alone. I know that may be antithetical as to whom some of you thought should be doing the fencing, but it's true, nonetheless.

In the early 1880s, the Colorado legislature passed the "Open Range," or what is more commonly referred to as the "fenced out" statute. This doesn't mean that ranchers can let their cattle vagabond all over the place without supervision; it means that for you to collect any damages incurred by roaming livestock, you first need to have a legal fence, in good repair, installed to prevent trespass by livestock. Gates need to be kept closed, and the property completely bounded.

From time to time, we hear the Pitkin County Board of County Commissioners discuss the applicability of agricultural zoning on certain parcels, and question the validity of those operations. It seems clear that a requisite of high priority would be the existence of legal and effective fences. That, among other things, spells serious agricultural use.

Some people obviously spend a lot of time designing a barrier around their property, but many of these are ineffective. If it doesn't completely surround your property, including a gate, it is impotent against an invasion from livestock. From the number of "No Trespassing" signs one sees anymore, it's clear many folks are a bit ownership proud, but don't forget, cows and horses can't read.

It can be frustrating driving cattle home from the forest when more than half of the properties along the trail don't have adequate fencing. Most ranchers try valiantly to be good neighbors, and will sometimes even help with major repairs, if you ask. But to totally ignore your fences to a "wing and a prayer" and help from God is irresponsible and unneighborly.

Fishin' With Granddad

It's a new season and thoughts turn to activities other than skiing. Unmined for years, memories of my grandfather and fishing are strong on my mind this spring. Growing up in a ranching family as I did, we never took the time (at least not officially) to pursue things like catching fish, so we always did it in the evening, after work. Saturdays were out because Grandpa (a widower) was in a hurry to get to town and hook up with his girlfriend, Jennie, and Sunday was a day of recovery and rest, although Sunday evenings sometimes had promise.

Out in Woody Creek, the gods seemed to be on our side as the creek was about a hundred yards from the house, which meant wetting a line could be done almost on the spur of the moment, and we never visited the rippling waters without some success. The first time he asked, I wasn't sure I wanted Granddad to initiate me into the sport, simply because he never did anything halfway and the thought of trying to keep up with him at something else besides riding horses wasn't exactly appealing. But, alongside the banks of the little stream, Gramps was about like me, just a kid having fun.

He'd drop me off at my house on the way by, to put my horse away and have a snack - he'd do the same at his place - and without spelling it out, we'd know where to meet in the cow pasture - the spot where the worms were the fattest. Whoever got there first gathered in a few (worms) and we'd be off, yakkng about where we ought to start, mostly based on the luck we'd had the last time out.

Catch and release wasn't a concept back in those days, and it didn't really matter 'cause we never wasted anything we caught. If we'd had good luck in a particular fishing hole more than once, we would avoid it for a long time, letting it recover. Fly fishing was big over on the Roaring Fork, but Woody Creek wasn't quite built for casting. Occasionally, some outsider would ask if he could try his luck, and unless mother cows were in the area, we always said OK.

A city-slicker from my mom's side of the family conned me into taking him down to Woody Creek for an afternoon one fine summer day, and it was a miserable experience for both of us. Now, this guy could tie technically correct flies with his eyes closed, could cast to within a quarter-inch of where he wanted his line and, even though he was from Denver, was a well-respected fisherman on the Fork. But he couldn't cast through willows so thick as what I led him to, he thought my choice of fishing holes to be deficient, and when he did manage to get his line in the water, it usually got snagged on something. I tried to give him some advice but he thought me and Gramps were barbarians when it came to fishing, so he ended up getting skunked. He never mentioned coming back for another try.

My grandfather died in March, the year I was eleven, an event which forever changed my life, in ways impossible to anticipate. On a warm summer's evening, one of the hired hands who had known Gramps came up to the house and asked if maybe I'd like to go fishing. "No thanks," I replied, "I just don't feel like it."

There have been excursions to Lake Powell and maybe a couple of trips to mountain brooks here and there, but I'm no fisherman and the last time I threw a line into Woody Creek, it was with Gramps.

Following the Homesteaders

No Man's Land, it's called. The Panhandle of Oklahoma is littered with abandoned ranch headquarters, dead to the world except in the imaginations of the living. It's good country for cattle and broom corn, but people find it a little rough.

Tiny towns dot the area, names placarded along the highway such as Hooker, Slapshot, Optima and Guymon. The most famous perhaps, is the ghost town of Beer City, the Sodom and Gomorrah of the Plains. Never an official town, it lured the best and the worst with more dance halls, saloons and whorehouses than most derelicts could ever imagine.

What does the song say: "Oklahoma, where the wind comes sweepin' down the plain, And the wavin' wheat can sure smell sweet When the wind comes right behind the rain . . ." If you like musicals, that's grand. I'm guessing more photos of the Dust Bowl years were taken in Oklahoma than anywhere else.

Drawn in by the promises of Manifest Destiny, suckered homesteaders wouldn't much care how hard the wind blew or the rattlesnakes bit once they got a taste of Oklahoma sunsets. The twilight sky comes alive, 360 degrees of a phantasmagoria of colors, breathtaking in essence.

Oklahoma can slurp you up and spit you out before you know it; it's not a place for the faint of heart or the ne'er do well. You'd better have your stuff together when you hit the border or you'll soon rue your naiveté. Highway signs usually don't tell you where you're going, but they'll tell you where you are, sometimes. When I inquired about a major two-lane asphalt road headed east, a grizzled black man told me it used to be marked but the wind blew the sign down, "a while back." Make a wrong turn and it'll cost you a hundred miles, easy. "No Vacancy" at the local inn might mean another 200 miles, or three hours, on the road.

When I thought I'd reached my destination, a town so small on the Arkansas border that a blink would have missed it, there was no sign informing me. A gas station and a non-descript run-down building were all that made up the traces of civilization. As I clumped into the gas parlor, an old man followed, asking if I knew where "the hell" we were.

A tall, slender forty-something bombshell with porn princess fingernails, blue on the ends and gold glitter down to the cuticles, an unnatural blonde with jeans tight enough to expose any imperfection on her well-preserved ass, called from behind the counter. "Can I help you, honey?" They're big on "honey" down this way, and it's always said with the kind of tone that makes you want to believe they mean it. "You got to go that way, honey. I'll ride down there with you, if you want, and show you." It goes with the "honey," I reckon, all that friendliness.

With my cargo now in tow, a shiny new, 25-foot tandem dually trailer, proof that I didn't come just for the scenery, I looked for a friendly Interstate to light my way home.

There's a certain aura of loneliness that encapsulates professional road riders, guys who live behind windshields and are at the mercy of whatever the road throws them. He was huge, mid-fifties with long, shoulder length hair. As I got behind him in the line, he put up a hand to protect his space without ever looking my direction. Like a dog waiting for a handout, he leaned his face into the glass and his washed out, gray eyes unshakably scanned the Subway "extras" in front of him. "More onions, gimme peppers, bacon, jack cheese. Oh, yeah, that's good. More chicken, huh?" A forgettable man who still rattles my memory.

I crawled back in my truck, relishing the familiarity and headed into the thick ink of a midnight sky. The haunting twang of Duane Eddy's "Rebel-Rouser" echoed throughout the cab as I pushed the pedal to the metal and ran the gears without thinking. Gonna be home, soon.

Another Season Gone

It's that time of year once again, when the readjustment of life begins. The ski lifts have closed and the days have a different glow now that skiing's not on the agenda. All, or least most, hopes and aspirations of winter have been realized, or dashed, depending on the case.

If you were aiming for 100 days on the hill and only made 85, well, that's the final count for this year. Perhaps you were gonna ski Highland Bowl at least once this winter, but woke up April 4, 2005 without getting it done. Odds are it's not going to happen very soon, but you could make a mental note to raise the altitude on your attention span next winter. Oh, sure, you could put on the skins and hoof it up, but do you really think you might? There's always tomorrow, but for now, the tomorrows have run out.

Except for those things you've put off all winter, those things you thought could wait until later. Later has arrived and some things need attention, the sooner the better. It might have been prudent if you'd skied fewer days, but that's just not the way it works in a ski town.

Good ski runs are a little like smoke - their essence only lasts for about as long as it takes to get back to the top for another one. You laugh and smile all the way up the chairlift or gondola, talking about this line or that face-shot, getting air here, or surviving a close call there, or who's going out with whom, and before you know it, the next run is done and it becomes the new focal point of discussion. You go home and put your feet up, trying to remember the best of the many layers of exhilaration, but mostly there's a blur of realization that it was a stellar day. And now, we can say it was a dynamite season.

Skiing's a funny game, when you get right down to it. We all have our group of "ski buddies" we beat it up and down the mountain with, friends that we see with unchallenged consistency, even if only for an occasional run or bowl of soup. That's in the winter, of course. If you're like me, most ski friends are winter friends, and summer, well, that's another story.

As the lifts close, the nostalgia creeps up on most of us, taking us a little by surprise. A last run down the Face of Bell, by yourself with no one within sight on the entire area, gives one pause to think of the good times that were had, and how short it all seemed to be. It wasn't that long ago that we were making the first ride of the season up the mountain, wondering how good the snow was gonna be and wondering how many friends we were going to see from last year. Those questions have all been answered, and already, at least for me, I'm wondering how it's going to be next year.

For some, the end of the season couldn't come soon enough. Maybe they're nursing the hangover from an ACL repair, or maybe had a rotator cuff overhauled and have been looking forward to "spring break" for a while now. No matter where; just a warm, long way off from Aspen. But you know they're thinking about next year, as well.

I've got a pasture full of horses to ride, some work to do around the place, and really should, at least, take a road trip up north somewhere. First, I have to throttle down, get used to a more laid back daytime pace, and give my mind, as well as my body, a little room to readjust its focus.

But wouldn't you know, just as I felt the slowdown coming, I looked out my window this morning and caught a glimpse of a snow-covered Mount Sopris staring me down. A lot of vertical, both up and down, and the energy won't quite subside.

Football Weekend

It wasn't that long ago a small group of us traveled to Boulder for a football homecoming weekend. Some were alumni, some football aficionados, and others just simple party animals. We stayed with a good Aspen friend, an engaging young law student who lived in a very stylish, 1930s redbrick two-story with his longtime girlfriend.

Space was tight and some of us planned to sleep on the floor, but before we could throw out our bedrolls, there was the Friday night kick-off party to get everyone in a football mood. Or a mood, at least.

About midnight, an obviously intelligent, but rather common looking, middle-aged woman from a few houses down took her place on the couch next to me and, after the usual pleasantries, began to get a little derogatory about my attire. "Why do you wear cowboy boots? Isn't that rather extravagant in today's world? I'm sure you realize animals had to die for the leather, and boots take a lot of leather?" What can a guy say, but "Hell lady, I wear 'em 'cause I don't like going barefoot, or in my socks, either."

It soon turned into a tug-of-war, and not a particularly friendly one, either. I reminded her that there are many things that come from sheep and cows, including such by-products as: leather, candles, cellophane, deodorant, detergent, perfume, paint, shaving cream, wallpaper, piano keys, mouthwash, some plastics, shoe polish and more.

To which she turned a deafened ear, saying "maybe so," but further, "we could learn to do without or improvise those things, because in an increasingly civilized and educated world, who would eat red meat, anyway?"

I really wasn't in the mood for a conversation of such seemingly one-sided momentum, and tried to deflect her continued negative comments about my footwear (which now included my belt) with grunts and disassociated "uh-uhs," while looking around the room for a polite escape.

"Well, my dear, perhaps you don't realize that cows contribute to medicines that we need on a daily basis in this country, including insulin for diabetes, blood plasma for hemophilia, bone marrow for blood disorders, intestines for surgical sutures; and they also provide hormone products, including vitamin B-12. And that's the short medicinal list. Furthermore, red meat protein plays a role in preventing osteoporosis; its nutrients provide memory enhancing zinc, and help to maintain the body's immune system. And if you need iron, meat's the place to get the best."

As we talked, she inched closer and closer to me on the couch, until at last our knees and arms touched, which began to put a new spin on our relationship. Her torturous demeanor relaxed a bit, and with a sexier and softer tone, mentioned that since the sleeping arrangements were a little crowded in the brick bungalow, maybe I should wander over to her place for the night. "But please," she said, whispering in my ear, "leave your cowboy hat here." Being astute to the nth degree, it finally became clear that I was the "second" in a hardened city girl's dance of emasculation and detente, all choreographed together in one potent formula, designed with unerring accuracy to entice unsuspecting, but willing partners into a night of mixed blessings.

I poured her another glass of red, and while gently setting the bottle down, casually mentioned that the condoms in my wallet were made of only the finest Wyoming sheep gut, for a more natural experience. Shortly thereafter, she excused herself, saying she'd be right back, but clearly, she never found the couch again. Maybe it was the wine?

From This Life into Another

I hear the clink of cubes against a crystal cold glass and know immediately she's across the crowded room. Her smile is tantalizing, inquisitive face fixed on mine, and with an almost imperceptible roll of her eyes, invites me to follow her. She ducks through the kitchen and just in time I see her velvet gown disappear down a narrow staircase, the sides lined with stone. Turning at the bottom with a flirtatious look, she sweeps into a small, windowless room, fast-rising water coming up the walls. In that instant, she turns to face me, the brunette of her long, luxurious mane suddenly becoming a short, pale blonde, tied together in pigtails on each side of her head, her face that of a twelve- or thirteen-year-old girl. Brilliant, ice-blue eyes penetrate my psyche and I feel as though I'm drowning and suffocating, all at once. "I don't like what you do to me," she says. So much for the dream.

"Momma, come quick," she pleaded from her upstairs bedroom. "I'm so sick, my eyes are blurred, can't swallow and it's hard to keep my thoughts together. I'm scared" "My God, you are racked with fever, my darling child. I'll send your father for the doctor right away," said the mother, trying to keep her voice from faltering. It was 1903, and going to get the doctor and bringing him to the house took about as long as it took for the young girl to die. As dawn approached, her parents laid her on wooden slats placed between two sawhorses and carefully and slowly bathed her body with cool ditch water, an emptiness consuming them that would never go away.

Here she comes, running toward me from across the hayfield, her long, blonde braids flapping up and down with each stride, a smile upon her face, as though she is happy to see me. Her dress is not velvet, but green gingham, the front covered with a dirty, white apron, and she wears black captoe shoes, laced up above the ankle, with inch-high heels and white stockings. "You understand, don't you? I can't work in the hayfields 'cause my allergies hurt me and then at night I can't breathe. Please tell my father." Yes, my dear, I do understand, but even so, I cannot interfere, for you have ceased to be, more than a hundred years ago.

Her quiet, unobtrusive grave rests in one of my horse pastures, a marble cross affixed to the homemade concrete covering. I pass her way four or five times a summer, moving irrigation water across the land, and I suppose, inadvertently flooding her final resting place. A creek tumbles and falls within ten feet of her tomb, and tall cottonwoods whisper their song, keeping her from the heat of day. No one seems to know much - age (12 or 13?), name (?), date (1903 or 1913?), or cause of death (?) - all apparent mysteries.

"Tell me then, what do you see," she asks, "for when I talk to you, I'm in this tiny cubicle, dark, with nothing to look at?" "Don't you remember," I wonder, "you lived and breathed here once?" Quietly, she says, "Yes, I remember - it was beautiful." "Oh, yes, sweetheart, it is still beautiful."

Maybe she has family that remembers some thread of her story, people that walk through the pasture when no one is looking, to pay their last respects. But I don't think so. It would not be impossible for her to be my maternal grandfather's sister, given historical scenarios, but highly improbable.

I know where she lies, and after I pass by, a wildflower can be found on the marble cross, just to let the world know that someone cares, still.

My Time in the Gulf

Brackish water in a backwater canal, translucent at best and typical of the Gulf of Mexico, lapped at my face and panic resided just under the surface of my being. The tips of my skis protruded in front of me and the rhythm of the water kept moving me in directions I didn't want to go. Suddenly, the tow rope slack disappeared and I was left with nothing but instinct for survival.

Me, a big-shot high school kid, learning to water ski, had let Padre Island become a feature in my life through one incredible experience. My host and girlfriend's father, Lawrence, and his buddy Paul, a Corpus Christi physician, had landed me there the year before in a Piper Cub, shortly after Hurricane Cindy and we taxied down streets once occupied by cars, dodging downed power lines and trees, hopping across washed-out roads, finally arriving at Paul's beach house to estimate the damage it had received.

"Waterskiing isn't that big a deal to a snow skier," someone had said, which was mostly true, although it failed to take into account my lack of practiced form and abiding fear of water. Paul's young son Ralph was there, tall, blonde, with piercing eyes and an excellent water skier, a kid much younger than I who could do tricks on skis, really knew how to swim, and who was soon testing my abilities by involving me in his prolific quiver of acrobatic sensations on skis.

Ralph also ran a trot line several miles offshore, getting there in a tiny boat that seemed incapable of surviving anything more than a piddling wave. I was very uneasy until, a couple of miles out, Ralph jumped overboard into water that might have been all of four feet deep. That kid knew his stuff.

Skiing on water began to grow on me, and when Paul said I could ski behind his cabin cruiser as he sliced across Corpus Christi Bay to the repairman, I jumped at the chance. We didn't go clear across the bay, obviously, but cut a wide swath over it, and taking Paul's advice, was glad I used two skis. The presence of sharks had been discussed, although being almost unable to see the shoreline was more unsettling, it seemed. Fear of the depths kept me upright in the choppy water, and when we finally reached the dock, I required assistance to get in the boat, so exhausted was I.

For a Woody Creek kid, not only water skiing but body surfing in the Gulf of Mexico and jumping over bushes along the beach that concealed rattlesnakes was fairly heady stuff. An adventure I'll never forget, but I've never been back. Oh, I visited Corpus several more times, but never saw Padre Island again.

The next Christmas, to finish the circle of friendship, Paul and his family stayed at our house, enjoying winter recreation. Ralph, the young son who taught me so much about water skiing, didn't say much, but went along with my dad several times to feed the cows, stationed on our southwestern mesa near the W/J.

The years went by and it all faded into history, the brief relationship between two families that hadn't known each other before that eventful year and who would never see each other again, almost.

The call came as I rode the gondola a couple of winters ago, a voice from the past, the youth who clearly dominated any water skis he rode, the waterman, was visiting Aspen and we set up a breakfast date.

Ralph, the kid, is still in Texas, a cattle rancher along the Nueces River near Cotulla. His life's work came to him that long ago Christmas as he and my dad slowly flaked rich, green hay off the horse-drawn sled and onto the winter feed ground for a herd of hungry Woody Creek Hereford's.

Springtime Gardens

Young kids are kind of like dogs, if you want my opinion. Although I had thousands of acres of unsupervised personal space to move around in, I usually stuck within whistle distance of the house, just so I wouldn't miss a scrap of what was going on. Every spring, I'd hear my dad coming up the road, clucking and talking to a team of magnificent horses pulling a plow.

Horses in harness create a unique sound and emanate tremendous energy, what with the leather and iron clacking, tapping and slapping together, all moving in cadence with the motion of the horses, and the vibration of the earth under their hooves, silently calling one's attention to an event of spectacular proportions.

We had tractors with lots of horsepower, used for farming, but tractors are not of the earth, and it would have been sacrilegious to plow up my mother's garden with anything other than a fine team of working draft horses. The aroma of rich, fertile black Woody Creek soil being turned, mixed with the powerful, unique smell of the glistening equines, and my dad's voice filled the panorama of the back stage, "Get up Queenie. Come on, Tom, pull dammit."

And before you could even get used to the scene, the horses and my dad disappeared back down the trail and my mother and grandmother began the truly hard work of busting up the dirt clods, getting the soil loose and fine, ready for planting. That's usually about the time I began losing interest, although I could be counted on to plant my share of seeds.

For my mother it might have been a spiritual experience of sorts, I don't know, but she and her mother always managed the ritual together, and my absence while the tough work was being accomplished didn't seem to bother her all that much. Sometimes she even encouraged me to go do something else.

Those gals raised a good garden, too, and a big one. We had a lot of ranch hands to feed, relatives to impress, and besides, it was something most industrious people did if they wanted fresh vegetables on the table. There were rows and rows of corn, potatoes, beans, peas, zucchini, raspberries, strawberries, radishes, lettuce, and on and on. Sweet peas, tulips, pansies, crocuses and other flowers filled the corners and other off places, and I loved going to the garden.

It was something my mother could call her very own, and she was proud of it. I'd hear her talking to my dad after dinner, saying how excited she felt inside that things had come up so well, that the garden looked really grand when you stood back and truly appreciated all its sweet nuances, and that it'd be a good winter because we'd have enough vegetables to last us through.

My grandmother, who never wore anything but a dress, and who stayed with us numerous times throughout the summer, would take me to the garden occasionally, and we'd get the pick of the day. Grandma would give me a pan to carry things in, but she'd carefully wrap her share in her apron, and carry it to the house that way. She was a genius at keeping the produce in her lap, holding it there with the dip in her dress between her legs, and shucking, shelling or peeling whatever it was directly into a bowl or box right beside her.

The garden died about the time we moved into a new house. The established patch was too far away to adequately manage, my mother's health was failing, and Grandma wasn't doing much better. It was just one of those changes that, taken by itself wasn't deafening, but in the collective, almost impossible to fathom.

Now, it's spring again, and I'd enjoy nothing more than to harness the team and plow up a garden plot for some lucky kid's mother.

Getting ID'd a Way of Life

I've been struggling with the Arizona border brouhaha, and honestly don't get it. I mean, if you cross the Mexican/U.S. border surreptitiously, most likely at night, there must be something wrong about it, or you wouldn't have to be so sneaky.

The term "racial profiling" gets batted around like a mosquito in malaria country, mostly by people who clearly live a long way from Arizona's chaos, people who have absolutely no realistic conception of the rising tide of brown skin headed north and its effect on the neighborhood. Call that racist if you want, but if I said it any other way, I'd be obfuscating the truth while glorifying political correctness. Maybe we should call it "nationality profiling." Is there something un-American about showing identification?

Early on, I was stopped by the cops for nothing more than being a kid from Woody Creek. OK, maybe an Italian kid from Woody Creek. John Loushin, the town marshal was happy to chat me up at the old post office, generally including something in there about "Be careful in town." He was one of my heroes.

Kris Kralicek, a later town marshal, used to flag me down for riding my bike too fast or for being in the "wrong" part of town. "What're you doing in town? Shouldn't you be out on the ranch helping your dad?" He taught me a lot about law and order - I'd see his car coming and I'd duck down the alley or through somebody's yard just to avoid the inquisition.

Those guys were nice, if you take the whole package into consideration. They weren't calling us Wops or Dagos. That generally got left up to those who didn't know better, like some of the local businessmen or newcomers. In case you don't know, Wop always applied to Italians, meaning "without papers," and was/is a totally derogatory term. We didn't particularly realize that at the time, or maybe we just didn't care. Later, I used to reply, without total malice, that "a Wop is a Wop. At least we know our heritage." Some wise-guy always wanted to know if Gramps had any homemade wine on hand; "Dago red," they called it.

Aspen got busier and the cops upped the ante. Showing ID became a regular ritual, if they were fast enough to catch us. They'd have never stopped us just for being kids, but we seemed to unintentionally draw attention to ourselves, if nothing else, just by acting suspiciously.

When a young man finally gets his driver's license, it's like opening day of hunting season for cops. I don't know if they did it maliciously, but I used to get stopped for all sorts of imaginary offenses, from "loose" license plates, dirty headlights, the trunk lid "looked ajar," even for having my girlfriend sitting "too close" to the driver. Every time I had to be polite and show my driver's license.

The last time I got a ticket, I was in my 40s, driving through Glenwood Springs when a well-known old man in a station wagon tried to take the front-end off my truck. The cop's look was derogatory, "You're from Aspen, huh?" Nobody wanted to hear my side of the story and though I tried, the cop played dumb and handed me a ticket for careless driving. When I protested, he rudely told me to tell it to the judge.

The judge was my last wife's divorce lawyer, and with a tin ear, he denied my objections. The old man, called as a witness over a $40.00 traffic violation, showed up with an attorney. They all were determined to see my upvalley ass fry. Nobody told me I could bring a lawyer. Nefariously out-gunned, I was guilty as charged, of course.

Anyway, whether you're brown, black, yellow, white or green, I don't understand the problem with showing your ID. Obviously, I've been profiled all my life and I'm uncomfortable with any group getting better treatment from the law than me. Maybe I could get the ACLU to help me sue somebody for past transgressions?

Gone to the Football Game

Hiking the Arbaney-Kittle trail on an early fall day, the activity and the warmth of the sun bring forth eye-stinging, vision-blurring sweat and long-banished memories well up, carrying me back to a warm day at Wagner Park.

A simple play; the quarterback fakes to his left, I hesitate and then charge into the line just off the right guard, taking the hand-off as I go by the quarterback. Lined up in position, listening to the count, looking at the defense, all eyes on me (they know we're gonna run it) and the sweat runs underneath the helmet, off my forehead and temples and into my eyes. Blurred vision and no time to wipe it away. The snap comes, I briefly delay, then charge ahead grasping the football, unable to see much, but know where I'm going on instinct and can feel the hole created for me without seeing it. I hit the line hard, snap a couple of tackles and emerge in the secondary, eyes still blurred with the bite of never-ending sweat. Most of the time, I get tackled before I can dance through the defense, but every once in a while, I kick free of the congestion and put on a show.

That was almost 40 years ago, back when I was a running back for the Aspen High School squad and can tell you there weren't all that many games the sweat poured off us. We played more than once with the temperature in the teens and a snowstorm wasn't unusual at all. We found the heat in other locales, such as Silt or New Castle, maybe Minturn or Basalt, Eagle, Oak Creek, Grand Valley, or of all places, Collbran. The names of the schools didn't always match up with the towns and there were names like Plateau Valley, Riverside, Roaring Fork and Battle Mountain. I'd like to think we put the fear of God into them when it was uttered that "Aspen is coming to town," but I suspect that was not usually the case.

We weren't the best team in the valley, but there was something in us that made that not be an issue. Many of us played both offense and defense in the same game and I'd get up on

Sunday mornings with trouble breathing 'cause my rib cage and lungs were acutely sore from the ravenous hunger I'd had for oxygen the day before. It meant I'd played hard and it brought a smile to my face.

There wasn't much going on in Aspen back in those autumnal days, and football was about the biggest thing in town. We played in downtown Aspen on Friday or Saturday afternoons around 1:00 P.M. and drew quite a crowd. The town merchants simply hung a note on the door, "Gone to the Game" and wandered over to the park, joining most everybody else in town.

We were a motley crew at best, with divergent interests. Some of us went on to become writers, artists and musicians; others made more money than they should have and some became satisfied in a chosen field. We've had at least one suicide, an alcoholic or two; maybe somebody got too fond of chemicals and a couple of us are still wondering what it was we started out to accomplish.

When we all finally lay the hammer down, it'll be as we played the game, each of us in his own way, but still part of a team from long ago. Our names won't be on the front pages of the newspapers or on the town marquee, but those who remain will feel the loss simply because we were part of something so seemingly big in our youth.

Sometimes today, when the sting of the sweat makes it hard to see, the thought comes that perhaps there is a tear or two for unforgettable days gone by mixed in, making the burn more poignant.

Good ol' Days in Basalt

The excitement is big down in West Basalt (is there really a coterminous line between the town's "east" and "west" portions or are the politicians just lazy?), now that a Whole Foods store has decided to buy into the frenzied and astounding growth in the mid-valley.

It could be said that Basalt owes me absolutely nothing, but historically, I may be somewhat indebted to her. It all started with my mother's paternal side of the family, who were early settlers in the Basalt area and until recently, still maintained a small claim on the town. My great-grandfather, John Sloss, owned the Emma Store and surrounding land for a time and then had an establishment on Basalt's 2nd Street, a building which still has the Sloss moniker across the front. He also ranched in the Sopris Creek area and his brother, Stirling, owned the Cap K Ranch up the Frying Pan for many years. My grandmother and grandfather Sloss (Nellie and Bates), along with other family, are buried in Fairview Cemetery. My mother, Kathleen, played basketball for and graduated from Basalt Union High School.

We used to run some of our cattle through Basalt on a two-day drive from Woody Creek to the Cap K, where we then turned them up the mountain toward the Red Canyon summer grazing grounds. The shopping center containing Clark's Market was, at that time, mostly a boggy swamp full of cattails, but a good shortcut through town for cows. Seemed like we always hit civilization too early to draw a good crowd, though.

Jimmy Gerbaz and I used to visit Basalt on school dance nights, get smuggled in by family friend, Arwinna Bogue, and have the time of our lives. Sometimes, she couldn't get us into the regular dance but would tell us where the after-party get-together was taking place and we'd be sure to show up. I fell in love a couple of times and remember my dad telling me about the call he'd gotten from a Basalt rancher, threatening my father to keep his son "up the valley" where he belonged.

In my 20s and 30s, a good night might involve a warm-up at Newt Klusmire's Frying Pan Inn, then a trip across the street to the Midland, where some live music could sometimes be found. It was a careful walk, however, as the Frying Pan "cowboys" seemed to stir up the mostly "long-haired" clientele of the Midland (or vice-versa), and fights were as common as Sunday morning hangovers. If you were smart, you wouldn't screw up badly enough to draw the attention of Buck Davis, the town marshal. Buck would give you every chance in the world if you were honest with him, but try to bullshit your way out of trouble and he'd have you in the backseat of the cop car quicker than a hobo on a ham sandwich.

Basalt really started getting upscale when they took out the wooden sidewalks, I reckon, but even then, she went kicking and screaming into the limelight much like a miscreant being dragged into church. But, alas, the cards had been dealt and there was slim hope of sustaining her originality and individualism, although she remains one of Colorado's last bastions of mountain hippies.

In the winter of 2001, a lady on a Highlands lift talked proudly of how her daughter and son-in-law had just moved here from California, eager to start his law practice and to raise their family in the mountains. The woman went on about how great Basalt was, and in her exuberance, asked if I thought Basalt would be able to maintain its small-town charm. Succinctly, the answer was, "No, not as long as yuppies from out of state keep moving here." Maybe I should have just kept my mouth shut.

Grab a Hold Before It's Too Late

A lady friend of mine from days gone by, who grew up in Aspen and now lives in another part of the country, and I keep in some sort of regular correspondence during the course of the year. In winter, the conversation at some point always turns to skiing, with her question being something along the lines of, "Doesn't skiing everyday begin to turn into a job or an obligation"? Or, "Don't you think you're pushing your physical impairments a little by skiing so much"?

If you're an inveterate skier, as I am, then you have no doubt heard similar comments from people you know and love. If you were going out the door to work every day, it would make so much more sense, but to be going up Aspen Mountain, or another area, every day to enjoy the passion of skiing, is hard for many people to understand.

The other day on the lift, a lady told me her daughter "snowboards" now because she became "bored" with skiing. I told her that if skiing bored her daughter, then she wasn't really skiing, not by any stretch of the imagination, and was in for a rather flat-line existence down the road. The look I got was memorable.

It's hard to explain to people the feeling, as my buddy Bob says, of "puttin' the zipper" on an almost perfect line through some big bumps and never looking back. Or how it feels to launch "big air" into Super 8 gully from the road, on any day, preferably a powder day for me.

Maybe you have one of those days, in mid-January, when the avalanche danger subsides and you finally get to your favorite backcountry mine dump and find it untracked? Exhilaration is a good word to identify how you may react when you first see the virgin snow, but there's really not a word good enough to describe how you feel when you serpentine your way down through the bottomless stuff in your own private stash.

If you're the type that might get bored by skiing, you probably check the weather before you go up. Nobody else checks because they're ready for whatever Mother Nature may throw at them. Oh, a look out the window is advantageous, but nothing technical is demanded. To some, skiing is about fashion and being seen, but that's more about just having lunch than skiing so I'm not sure how that stuff really works.

Inadvertently inhaling a mouthful of powder as a blinding curtain of Aspen fluff rolls over your face may not appeal to a lot of people, but ask the skiers you see at the bottom of a steep run on a powder day how they liked it (as though you'd actually stop to do so), and you won't really get an answer. Just a huge smile, or giggles, and a gush of enthusiasm, somewhat like a "Yesss!" at the end of an orgasm.

You know those moments. You've just totally ripped Summit, or hammered Walsh's, or maybe danced down Corkscrew Gully, and you look over at your partner, too depleted of oxygen to really say how great it was, but the smiles tell it all, anyway. An early morning stroll down Copper or Spar, "rippin' the 'roy,'" will leave your lungs happy and a smile just as big. Whether you ski the steeps and deeps, or prefer to cruise "groomers" all day, it doesn't matter 'cause it's all about lovin' the mountain.

Life offers a lot of things, but the things we go after and really enjoy are the ones that stir our passions. We can peruse actuarial tables and maps of our genetic code and figure out about how long we're theoretically going to live. On the other hand, we can't look into a crystal ball and see the errant car that might take us out early, or the unexpected, insidious disease that could deal us the lethal blow.

We should look deep inside ourselves and grab hold of our passions, nurturing them to their fullest for as many days as we have.

Graves of What Might Have Been

"That's where the babies are buried," said my dad from the window of his 1952 Chevrolet pickup truck. He'd just chewed my butt about something else and wasn't in the mood for my insistent grilling about the area in question. As he roared off, I spied a long tail of smoke billowing from his just-lit Lucky Strike and wanted to kick his ass for leaving those words hanging in the air, without any elaboration.

It was a small, untouched rectangle of land, sitting next to a corner of our cattle pens, parallel to the Woody Creek road. Every spring and fall, hundreds of cows filled the corrals and in the late fall guys like Don Stapleton and myself roped oversized calves, born in the summer, and drug them through a specially designed wooden chute for branding purposes. My granddad kept a herd of wild horses up on the apron of Vagneur Mountain, and every spring, we'd corral them and rope a colt or two for breaking. Through it all, the adjacent corner remained a quiet enigma.

As time went on, the undisturbed, pristine parcel of secured ground took up more and more of my curiosity, but about the most I could get out of my dad was to, "leave it alone." Granddad died and despite my best efforts, no one appeared to know the secret other than my father.

Still, I cannot understand Dad's reluctance to give his explanation, for simply enough, "the babies" were siblings of my grandfather, children who had died in infancy. They were born in different years and died likewise, and if we think back to Aspen's 1880s or 1890s, it becomes believable that no records exist of their deaths. In those times, the story usually went like this: "my child became sick one day, suffered through the night and died the following evening." It was of paramount importance to bury the corpse in a timely manner, for in a world without antibiotics and limited knowledge of germs, contagion was a life and death proposition, something to be feared. Any good rancher knew about the devastating effects of the spread of disease.

Out of necessity, it was a self-reliant world in those early years and my great-grandfather Jeremie, being a skilled carpenter, carefully constructed the tiny caskets out of whatever was on hand, probably working on the back porch for lack of a better place. Maybe his wife Estephanie helped him carry the coffins up the hill from the house, but most likely one or two of the older boys aided with the heavy lifting. The wooden crosses placed on the graves didn't last long, and the urgency for something more enduring faded with the passage of time.

Maybe that was the source of my father's angst - something left undone that he felt an obligation to complete. He honored the sacred burial ground - what more could he have done? We'll never know, and I doubt there is anything unusual about a couple of unmarked graves out on great-granddad's first homestead. With all probability, every major drainage along this valley contains the final resting places of young children, most of them unmarked and forgotten.

My great-grandmother Estephanie had eight children in all, five of them surviving into adulthood. One child died in Val d'Aosta, Italy, before they emigrated to this country, and two died in Woody Creek. It is said that until her own demise, great-grandmother surrounded her house and yard with many beautiful flower gardens.

One of the babies buried in Woody Creek was a girl, and I suspect that had that tiny creature, the only girl-child, lived, the music in great-grandmother's life would have played sweeter and the beauty of her flower gardens shown a deeper hue.

Great Shakes in Ouray

To be perfectly honest, I don't remember the drive from Silverton to Ouray, but I know we took it. We'd finished our last night as a traveling band for the Colorado 500, and were left to our own schedule to get home. We were hung-over, starving and mostly broke (check being sent via mail), with about five bucks between the three of us. Chris Winter (RIP), the English drummer, sometimes displayed a flash of parsimony on trips like this, saving our butts, but not this time.

We walked up the steps into the deserted bar, old mining-town typical with creaking hardwood floors and ordered tap beers. I mean, any establishment of serious drink that opens at 9:00 a.m. should be celebrated. How the hell that was going to get us breakfast, we didn't know, but it gave us a little time to think.

"Go get your accordion," said Buck, and before our beers were downed, I was laying out a polka of beer-barrel intensity to the empty room, breathing in the early-morning smell of stale hops and feeling like a damned fool. The bartender smiled, set us up with another round (on the house) and got on the phone. A local, gray-haired lady from next door stuck her head in long enough to see the music was live and said she'd be right back.

In the meantime, a few curious pedestrians had wandered in, standing like nervous, smiling stilts by the door; Chris had set up a snare and a cymbal, and we were starting to work the place, just a bit. Buck set an empty beer pitcher on a chair next to us and slung his guitar over his shoulder.

As if choreographed, a couple started doing a slow shuffle around the room, easing themselves down from the night before. About then, the lady with the pinned up gray hair, a tall woman of what appeared to be impeccable, fastidious taste, returned with a stand-up bass and began slapping the strings like she might a wayward boyfriend, spinning the thing around as if she knew the score. Her hair was already in half-cascade.

Friends of the bartender slowly sauntered in, the empty beer pitcher began filling up with green bills and I ducked my head and gave it up. We weren't going to eat, we were going to party and damn, everything was going to be all right. Buck was yodeling, the beers kept coming like ice melt off a Colorado summer glacier and for a short time we provided the vessel in which the spirit of life thrived in a splendid experience between strangers. For a fleeting spell, we were tinged with the soul of Ouray.

The night bartenders, one of them being the owner, had sequestered our tip jug behind the bar, "For safekeeping," he'd said, and when we finally asked for our money, reality crept back into the world with a chilling, unforeseen ugliness.

"You boys owe for the beer you drank," and by the time he got done recreating the flow of our jam session, using a scratchy, dull pencil and creative imagination, he'd fairly well drained our dreams of a healthy breakfast tomorrow. We'd brought in more business that day and evening than he'd seen in months and be damned if he was going to let a nickel slide by.

We should have gutted him right there and left him lay behind the bar, but that's not our style and besides, we were still coming down from a pretty amazing day.

That bar is open for business yet, last time I looked and there are people in Ouray, not as young as they used to be maybe, who still remember our visit as if it happened only last week. Ask my buddy, Marlin Vander Tuin, a stalwart Aspen icon who just happened to drift in during the midst of it all.

Growth Wins

Picture this - two guys riding into Aspen on their lily-white steeds, shiny-armored-up and at full gallop, just in time to save Pitkin County from the devastation of out-of-control growth (1972). That's a romantic notion of Joe Edwards and Dwight Shellman, if you believe in fairy tales, and there's a certain dogged population of unquestioning belief that adheres to the memory of that ideal, but the reality was full of contention and hard feelings that survive to this very day.

Swing by the Aspen Historical Society on W. Bleeker and check out its new summer exhibition, "Out of Your Mind, Body and Spirit - Voices of Aspen in 1975." It's an excellent look at the metamorphic convolutions Aspen was going through in the 1970s, one of which was growth.

In the late 1960s and early 70s, Pitkin County, Aspen in particular, had seen a tremendous increase in population. In an ironic twist of reasoning, those newcomers who themselves had been most of the growth decided they'd seen enough, and determined it was time to take over the politics of "their" town and put a halt to more kindred spirits moving in behind them.

The locals, those who had lived through the "quiet" years and had no conception of the Aspen-specific coined term "local," felt a little out of sorts at this turn of events, especially at the arrogance of those fledglings who thought they "knew better" than the long-time townspeople.

Edwards, a leading radical of the period who helped form Citizens for Community Action, a group designed to protect Aspen from the vagaries of growth, ran for mayor in 1969. The "old guard" was leery of Edwards and elected a woman instead, Eve Homeyer, a staunch conservative. Even CCA, Edwards own group, had endorsed Homeyer.

Then came Hunter Thompson's ill-conceived 1970 bid for Pitkin County sheriff and his loss, coupled with that of Edwards a year earlier gave the orthodox townspeople a sigh of relief. They figured, at least for a time, that the "new boys in town" couldn't win, not even by importing the "freak, head and dropout" vote from surrounding towns, anywhere from Basalt to Boulder.

Times change, and in 1972, Shellman and Edwards, both newly elected to the board of County commissioners and fueled by opinions picked up and reinforced during neighborhood caucus meetings (reminiscent of Chicago politics), went hell-bent on a mendacious mission of creating a down-zoning plan for Pitkin County that some thought would choke it to death. The problem was that a large majority of the people voicing their pleas for growth control owned very little, if any, local property.

The large landowners, found in Woody, Capitol, Sopris and Snowmass Creeks and other areas, amounted to little more than a handful of people and even though they owned tens-of-thousands of acres of agricultural land, they had almost no voice in a political land control scheme. The county commissioners ran roughshod over them, adding insult to injury.

One of the high-profile commissioners was heard to exclaim, naively, that the days of "fiefdoms" were over. It sounded like redistribution of wealth and a personal vendetta, even back then. Agriculture had recently been outranked by tourism as the number one economic indicator in

Pitkin County and ranchers were beginning to run scared. And now they were being told that Pitkin County would control their land, their lifeblood.

In the end, one can argue all day about the success of the growth control; there still isn't a compelling view. Ranchers survived the thuggery, but only in real estate values, for it knelled the end of agriculture in Pitkin County. Predictably, real estate prices are astronomical, about a third more than in "comparable" areas.

Aspen, for all its talk about controlling growth, looks more cobbled up today than it did even ten years ago. View planes are considered "passé" and today's Aspen Club, airport and hospital expansions are lighting up the grid. Don't you wonder where all the white horses have gone?

The Bully Deserved It

The hatred I felt at that moment was bitter on my tongue, but it was soon replaced with a ripple of excitement as the shadows in our dangerous relationship suddenly shifted.

He was standing several feet below me on a huge mound of excavated dirt, where soon the Yellow Brick Elementary School would emerge. On the sidewalk, side-by-side, he stood about six inches taller and at two years older, probably outweighed my skinny frame by at least fifty pounds, likely more.

The dark green airman's jacket he wore, the one with the big fur collar that was in vogue throughout Aspen high school that year, was a mite short for his long arms and his hands, even though he was only a freshman, already had the swollen, coarse fingers typical of someone much older who had worked hard all his life.

We talk about them a lot these days, bullies, social misfits who can make life hell for those they pick on. My first real encounter with such a person occurred in the third grade, although I can't recall the exact circumstances, other than he liked to slug and threaten me when no one was looking. It's a wider spread game today, I realize, with the advent of modern technology and it appears to be more psychological than physical, but the scars remain, either way.

The logistics of the old Red Brick School, which contained all twelve grades, didn't bode well for the younger students, especially when there was a bully in the neighborhood. One day, an older kid shoved my head into the drinking fountain apparatus, smacking my teeth and cutting through my upper lip. Although no one seemed to connect the dots at the time, it eventually cost me a front tooth. We learned to warn each other of his lurking presence.

That same kid later developed a penchant for viciously slugging a couple of my buddies and me whenever he caught one of us alone, and among the three of us, we decided something needed to be done. We were in the 7th grade, he was a sophomore and every day without fail, just after math class, he'd swagger into the men's room for an afternoon bladder drain.

On the appointed day, two of us hid in one of the stalls while the other hollered at him to come to the rear of the restroom. As he went by our stall, we jumped out behind him, effectively cornering the bad ass. We whipped him up pretty good, no visible marks, and although we didn't exactly leave him standing in a puddle of his own tears, he left us alone after that.

Anyway, there we were, just the two of us, standing lopsided on a lonely, hard-packed pile of fertile black earth, one a belligerent personality in a green fly boy coat, and me. He looked smaller, standing downhill as he was, and something told me I might never get a chance like that again.

He looked away for a moment and I shouldered him square in the gut with all the strength my body contained, and down the mountain of barren soil we rolled, a feeling of satisfaction rising from deep within my being.

Killing this kid who had, during one dismal night, terrorized me and a friend with a knife and his father's police revolver in a game of Russian roulette, did cross my mind and it wouldn't have hurt my feelings. The bully got up, dusted himself off and said, "I can't believe you did that." And then, he tried to beat the hell out of me, but couldn't, not really. I was laughing and swinging and cussing so hard, he finally walked away. And that was, forever, the end of it.

If there's any justice in the world, and maybe there is, I reckon it could be said that I outlived all three of those threatening brow beaters, but that's about it. I'll never forget them.

Heart

He just turned two the end of July, so you could say he's still a pup. Naturally, he doesn't know that, and basically thinks the world turns around him, unless he gets around other dogs. A shy boy that Topper, until we get on the trail, then all his instincts kick in and he becomes what God intended, an incredible vision of athleticism and grace.

Just as in pro sports, or even high school athletics, where a player can become well-known for one spectacular play, or one truly boneheaded flub, dogs and horses take their place in local folklore based on the same demonstrations of excellence or mediocrity.

You might think a two-year-old border collie too young to make history, and I agree, but for now, he's riding a swell of admiration and respect that is almost impossible to elicit from a jaded, curmudgeonly cowboy of many a dog/cow skirmish.

We'd already spent a couple of long days moving cows up the mountain, arriving home a little after dark each day, with only the briefest of respites for lunch. Early the third morning, Topper moved slowly, like a wise old dog, keeping a close eye on me and appearing to hope that maybe we'd go a different direction that day.

It was a bit tedious, cutting a neighbor's cows from ours in an expanse of many acres and no corrals, but at last we got on the trail. To us, the word "trail" connotes an established way to travel, whereas cows generally view trails as impediments to their direction of locomotion. And so it was on this particular day.

My horse, Billy, and I were off the path, doing our best to chase cattle through an area of immense, fallen aspen trees and it was a close contest, keeping the cows gathered. My riding buddy, Niki Day (with dogs Chief and Rex), was off on the right, dealing with problems of her own, and I had kind of forgotten about my dog, trying to navigate Billy through a dangerous logjam.

Then, just as I happened to look around, Topper ripped into view, in mid-flight, traveling at what seemed to be a hundred miles an hour. We were on a steep hillside, and this first sighting was of a dog at my eye level, crossing directly in front of me and briefly touching the top tree on a twisted, tortured wind-blown pile of downed aspens for the briefest of a millisecond. When he first launched, it would have been impossible for him to know what was on the other side of the tangled mess, but that was a consideration he obviously decided to make in mid-air.

Without leaving a bit of his stride behind, Topper was already on his way to negotiating the next fallen tree, a drop of considerable distance, eyes narrowed to the target looming large ahead. He sucked up that next tree like a good skier breathes in a mogul field, and hit the ground in mid-turn, his move so quick that his butt swung wide from the centrifugal force. An obstreperous, black cow who erroneously thought she might have a chance of outmaneuvering a horse in devastating terrain, had no time to see the black-and-white streak of a dog headed her way. The application of sharp, shiny white teeth to a relatively huge back fetlock of the wayward cow led her to believe her line of travel was in error, and with a bellow, she immediately made a course correction.

And there was no time to say, "Good dog," 'cause before you could even blink, Topper was quickly moving across the terrain, looking to see where he was needed next.

Sometimes I hug the dog and tell him I love him, and it makes him uncomfortable. He's a professional and doesn't have time for such anthropomorphic pap. But still.

Hidden Cave

For more than a hundred years, my family has called it the "Cave Ridge," a long skinny finger going up the side of mountainous terrain, eventually so steep a horse's front feet seem to slap near his nose just to get enough purchase to keep from falling backward.

It's a lonely ridge; cattle don't wander in that direction, nor is it close to any trail, recognized or imagined. But given its reclusive location and for reasons unknown, the existence of a small cave close to its spine has really never been that big a secret. I've talked to townspeople, "old-timers" who have read or heard of its existence, but couldn't come within 3 or 4 country miles of actually locating the cave itself.

The Utes may have used it for one reason or another, but it doesn't seem likely even though there are remnants of their once-potent presence still visible in the area. If one were caught in a huge rain or hail storm, the cave would provide excellent cover, but just getting to it from any nearby path would provide a challenge greater than the storm itself.

The rather large entrance is hidden under a plethora of serviceberry bushes, and without knowing how to access the opening, a hiker could walk within three feet of the cave and not find it. Going in, the entrance is steep, and minds inquiring as to animal tracks quickly realize that footprints are almost impossible to discern in the sliding dirt.

Then the corridor jogs sharply to the side, cutting off all earthly light and in the same instant, one is suddenly on a very narrow, flat ledge, high above a modest but deep room. It's dark, but not like on a moonless, pitch black night, when one can see very little. No, this is the sweet blackness of a world absolutely without sparkle, an environment in which only God and the Devil could safely move around with any assurance.

A quiet man most everyone knew found solace there in the 1940s, a tale almost too gruesome to tell. He'd take a couple jugs of rot-gut whiskey and crawl into the cave with his lantern, down a homemade ladder leaned against the ledge; then he'd traverse a small room, cross under a rock overhang and emerge into a large, colorless cavern, desperately crying out to ease the pain of a twisted and hideous home life that caressed every fold of his mind.

Sophocles, on his best day, couldn't better describe the Oedipal behavior between the man's wife and their son, and eventually, when the cave and the whiskey could no longer drown the torment, the man lay down under a chokecherry bush near a stream of soul-soothing rhythm, placed a stick of dynamite in his mouth and lit the fuse.

If you go there today, the cave is almost as empty as it has been for millennia, unfriendly to animals and man alike. There are no underground rivulets of water seeping through the walls, no echoing drip-drip of life-sustaining liquid. The rickety ladder has given itself up to dry rot, sixty years or more in the process, and deep within, a lonely candle from long ago lies on its side, validating the haunting presence of a man racked with anguish.

The quiet stream still flows, incessant in its soft caress of the colorful rock that lines its bed. Under the branches of the wild chokecherry tree is visible a small depression, now gentle in its grass-covered curves, a silent reminder of the violent end to a psyche that must, at one time, have been full of dreams and vitality.

Ghost Town, My Ass

Coming off the singles line at the gondola, I was suddenly thrust into the midst of a cabin lecture about Aspen's history, conducted by one of those people who seem to know everything. As she explained how Walter Paepcke "saved" the teetering ghost town of Aspen, I was tempted to speak up, but to do so would have contorted the idyllic looks on the faces of her adoring cohorts. It's a twisted trail we took to get where we are today, but being a ghost town wasn't part of it.

To look deeper than the woman in the gondola, it is well-documented that Walter Paepcke, a businessman from Chicago who, through the urging of his wife, began to look upon Aspen as a good place to "get away from it all," a location that could be molded into a vision reminiscent of the thinker Plato, a planned community, if you will, a spot where busy corporate executives could rejuvenate "mind, body and spirit" in a relaxing atmosphere. It would be foolish to argue against such an appealing inkling unless one is concerned about social class distinctions, for in any shade you wish to color it, that was an elitist idea. Oh, I know you can argue that if given the synergy produced by a conclave of the brightest and best minds of the day, great ideas could/might have lasting impact on the world.

To implement Paepcke's concept, a certain amount of genius had to be employed, for if word of his strategy was leaked prematurely, the price of real estate would skyrocket and his plan would become unaffordable. Through the assistance of local judge, William R. Shaw, Paepcke quietly put together a sizeable string of Aspen properties, enough to begin execution of his plan. The Paepcke's carefully selected those whom they invited to share in their new-found Nirvana, and the horses were off, so to speak.

There were a couple of snags along the way, things that couldn't be ignored. For one, there was an existing population of hard case survivors already in town, folks who weren't thrilled with Paepcke's big-city tactics, and who fought him on several fronts.

Music, art and grand ideas were okay, but most of the locals had been on the short end of the monetary stick for a long while and were starting to like the tourist income that fishing, swimming, hiking, horseback riding and skiing was beginning to attract. It was unlikely that any of them were going to hobnob with great minds or play first violin in the orchestra. And, don't forget, tourist Elizabeth Paepcke first visited here in 1939.

The Aspen Ski Club had been in existence since 1936 (originally the Roaring Fork Winter Sports Club) and had already established a certain modicum of expertise in that realm. And besides, Austrian immigrant and 10th Mountain Division veteran, Friedl Pfeifer, had convinced the town fathers to put him in charge of the boat tow and related activities. In anticipation of grand things to come, Pfeifer had founded the Aspen Ski Corporation, but didn't have access to the kind of money needed to make his dream come true. And a brilliant idea he had: Put in a chairlift rather than the common European tram, at a fraction of the cost.

Re-enter Walter Paepcke, a visionary but also a pragmatic businessman, and as revolting as the idea of ski bums residing in his cultural haven might have been, winter revenue would be welcome. Paepcke took over the fledgling ski company, allowing Pfeifer to retain control of the ski school, and began selling shares to investors. Early on, it became clear that some arrangement needed to be worked out to attain access over the many mining claims on the proposed ski area. Aspen stalwarts, D.R.C. Brown and his brother Fletcher owned many of them anyway and soon were on board with the Ski Corp., as it was always affectionately known.

A lot happened in the 1940s, but "saving the ghost town" of Aspen was not one of them.

Honest Business

It's happened to most of us at one time or another - a longtime friend or business associate slam dunks us on a deal and ends the conversation by saying, "It's nothing personal, it's just business" - which sort of means that you've just been bent over the nearest fence and abused.

What is there about much of today's business world that has become so disgusting, so aberrant, so obvious to most of us, but seemingly ignored with complacency? People with a yearn for bigger bank accounts put Ivy League graduates and MBAs somewhere on the same level with doctors and other high-dollar professionals, thinking that there's a well-kept secret to be learned with higher education and fancy degrees. It appears that, for many businessmen, the only secret is developing a propensity to continually check the bottom line with a skilled right hand that can manipulate a calculator faster than any three office assistants put together, and make adjustments above it whenever and wherever necessary in the blink of an eye, based solely on that day's profitability.

If you live in the country, check your phone bill, and you will no doubt find a city tax on it. It's only about twenty-three cents on mine, but just think: If the phone company erroneously charges one million rural customers $.23 per month that comes out to about $230,000 each month. Do you really think it, or any other company, is going to voluntarily surrender that amount of money to the appropriate city when it's not required to do so? And its reps will argue with you over the $.23, somehow thinking the company is deserving of its ill-gotten gains. Over the course of a year, that's $2,760,000, not chump change. Phones aside, the internet has created a wealth of bogus "tax" revenues for companies brazen enough to do the "collecting," including a nationally well-known provider of business software.

Oil companies have made higher profits the last two years than even when J. D. Rockefeller was at the helm of an almost monopoly. The word "gouge" is gaining traction, and we've all certainly felt its stab. European nations pay $5.00 or so for a gallon of premium gasoline, but they also get health care for almost nothing and their Euro is kicking ass with our dollar.

I learned a few things about pricing after I graduated from the University of Colorado business school and came home to Aspen. I learned that for some businesses, it is necessary to double the wholesale price to make a decent retail profit. If the wholesale price is $50.00, common sense would tell you that raising the price to $100.00 (fifty plus fifty) is doubling the price. Ah, but not so fast. It's necessary to double it one more time ($100.00 to $200.00) to truly "double" the wholesale price.

That way, you've doubled it twice, right? Which is double, actually. You see, it's not really about math, after all. It's more about greed.

An associate of mine in the trash business, a terrible businessman, used to say that if you couldn't post your prices on a roadside billboard and defend them, they were too high. Probably the only honest thing he ever said, but in his defense, he obviously hadn't been to the 21st century school of commerce. We used to try to make an annual 35% return on investment for our stockholders, but found that many times we were making 60 -70% profit every month, which translated in some cases to over 400% return on investment (sometimes much more). When I suggested we give some of that money back to the customers, I was suddenly made aware of how fragile my existence really was.

So, as some of the highly skilled and educated businessmen hunker over their calculators, looking at you out of the corners of their eyes, remember that ethics and morals are not necessarily a part of the pricing structure. As my neighbor Hugh said one time, "It's no fun getting screwed without sex."

Honor the Past, Live in the Now

Some months ago, in a distant city, a delicious-looking younger woman and I strolled into a dining establishment of impeccable Eastern tradition. She was seated very near, within inches - precisely where I like her. The background hum and clink of the bustling restaurant coaxed us even closer together, giving an intimacy to our space that otherwise couldn't exist.

"Do you think you live more in the past, rather than the now," she asked? "To tell the truth, sweetheart, you just zipped me out of the now and into the realm of nebulous philosophical thought, which could be anywhere. Of course, I live in the present."

"Oh, I'm not so sure. Most of your columns are about things that happened a long time ago. Don't you ever want to write about recent happenings? Even the stories you tell me are mostly about the past."

"I appreciate your observation, my dear, but think about this - I write and tell them all in the present." was my response. "And besides, I'm enjoying every minute of being with you. We're on to something good here and if we continue the mood after we leave, living in the now with you tonight may become an unforgettable night of special memories, perhaps to be told in some future column a long time down the road. It can't be any other way, not if I don't want to embarrass you, or me."

On another day, my friend Detweiler and I were talking about heading north to Montana or the Dakotas, buying humongous-sized cattle ranches and living out our days as focused, crazy ol' cattle barons. "I've thought about it a lot," he said, "but we'd never fit in. They'd never accept us because we don't have the stories."

He's right. We have a lot of good stories between us, but if people don't feel part of the tale, it's mostly meaningless. Up north, by the time we built up some good, repeatable yarns about ourselves, we'd be dead, and after the funeral, nobody'd give a damn, anyway. Exceptin' maybe a few coyotes. No history, no stories, no credibility.

Just as an aside, let me say that horses might be close to living in the now, compared to dogs or humans. When you catch your horse, he doesn't know whether you're going for a 20-mile ride or you're gonna give him some oats. Either way, he'll live with it without objection and, probably, with enthusiasm. And he won't talk about it when he gets back to the pasture. That's truly living in the now and I don't think I could put up with a schedule like that.

The thing about stories, in my estimation, is that a good narrative isn't much, no matter what it depicts, without the details. To collect the details, you have to pay attention to events as they happen, which definitely requires that you live in the now. That's the easy part - it's more difficult to have a capable memory, one you can draw upon at will. At least that's what I hear.

We're the sum of our experiences, I reckon. Truth has little meaning without lies. Tears can only make joy ring stronger in our hearts. Say what you want, but we can't escape the past, not by twisting a crystal ball, nor by a long shot. That's not to say we should pack our past around with us like a debilitating showboat deformity reminiscent of the hunchback of Notre Dame, but we should be aware of where we came from and what we've learned.

My philosophy has always been that life is a journey, not a destination. Savor what comes your way. If you're reading these words right now, you're close to living in the now, but because I wrote them last Tuesday, they're history to me. Still, they say the same thing. Whatever that is.

PHOTOS: The following photos from the Tony Vagneur Collection unless otherwise noted.

Four generations: my dad Cliff, my great-granddad Jeremie, me,
and my granddad Ben Vagneur

Me as a budding irrigator in front of the Elkhorn Ranch
main house, 1950

At Woody Creek, circa 1905, my grandfather Ben on left, with his brothers (left to right): Jim, Sullivan, Louis, and Dellore

My father Cliff and his best friend, Mick Bogue, both about 15 years old, 1935

Wild horse race at W/J – Johnny Chiodo and Keith Patterson with yours truly holding the saddle, 1971

My father Cliff and his dad Ben, on the Elkhorn Ranch, Woody
Creek, 1934

In the 1950s, my grandfather Ben with some of his prized Herefords on the Elkhorn Ranch, Woody Creek

My mother's Stapleton family on the feed sled, about where the Sardy Field runway now exists - the boy is William C. Stapleton.

Circa 1920 at the Stapleton Ranch (Sardy Field today): my grandfather
Bates Sloss and grandmother Nellie Stapleton Sloss with McLain Flats
and Red Mountain in the background

1919 - My grandparents Vagneur, Ben and Grace

Circa 1930 – Stapleton Airport Ranch, great-aunt-Julia Stapleton
on right, McLain Flats and Vagneur Mountain in background

1937, skiing at Highland Bavaria up Castle Creek;
1980s bump skier upper right

Top of Independence Pass March 1 1935. My aunt Eileen Vagneur
Goodhard standing on left next to my grandfather, Ben. My
father, Cliff, standing on the far right. They drove up in the car.

Waiting for WWI soldiers to return home, 1918, at the Midland RR
Station - photo taken by my fraternal grandmother,
Grace Prindle Vagneur

Then and Now - my dad and granddad plus my grandson Cash and
me sitting on the porch of the house built by my great-
grandfather and grandfather.

My lovely daughter, Lauren, an excellent horseman and rancher, in 2006- Overlooking the Fryingpan Valley

Tony Vagneur doing what he does best - telling stories; Aspen Hall of Fame Banquet, 2012 – Photo credit Burnie Arndt

Horse Sense

The first thing every morning, I open my bedroom curtains to check out Mount Sopris. An early morning weather report, so to speak. Then, I turn up the shade at the foot of my bed and every time I do, the horses standing in the corral take notice. Their reaction isn't a big thing, but a slight modification of their body language tells me they know I'm up, which translates into a Pavlovian reaction of sorts on their part. After they've been fed, I saunter into my office and throw up the window blinds, without provoking a stir from the corral. Or so it seems.

Stationary horses can see almost 360 degrees around themselves and the corral sits about twenty yards from the house, so it isn't a mystery as to whether the horses actually see the movement, or simply "feel" my presence. A lot has been written about the relationship between man and horse and the intuitive ability of the equine species to understand man. Pure anthropomorphic pap, I believe, but it makes good reading, nonetheless. However, as blunt as that statement is, it still leaves room ideologically to give credence to certain abilities the horse has to communicate with others in his domain.

I've had a lot of conversations with horses, and have come to believe that one of the endearing qualities of the horse is its refusal to speak any form of human language. That has enabled me to impart most of my philosophy of life to more than one horse, or repetitively to one horse, without getting a word of argument in return. Say what you want to a horse, but he won't start pressuring you to take sides or further explain yourself and he just seems to understand.

I left my horse, Kiowa, alone at Tommy Moore's ranch most of one summer, and along about August, found myself with a depressed Equus caballus on my hands. He needed someone to play with in his pasture, and late one evening, after our irrigation rounds, he let me in on his problem. He started at me from about fifty yards away, coming toward me in a full-on gallop, and as he passed by, he let fly with his hind legs in a playful sort of way. Not one to be intimidated, I waited for him to stop in the corner then took the initiative in his direction, full bore (in a pair of hip waders, no less) and as I ran toward him, he started back with an eye for me again. As we passed in perambulating flight, flying kicks were exchanged and we both grunted. It was hard to run, breathe and laugh so hard all at the same time, but we kept it up for a good seven or eight minutes. As weird as it seems, I think that was one of "our" favorite memories.

It may be possible to imagine the horse as more of an intuitive thinker than man, but only if we use our "scientific" and "inductive" minds to delineate the difference between a sixth sense and reason. Which, if we do, clearly leaves horses as the winners in the intuition department. They live connected to the earth, while we live thinking we're somehow detached from the earth. Only when we forego our "intelligence" and let ourselves react naturally do we begin to communicate unaffectedly with the horse. In the dark of night, we give ourselves up to our dreams; so must we also give up ourselves to the natural world if we are to have meaningful communication.

So, I head for the corral in the late afternoon, halter in hand, and my blue roan Drifter fixes a big, black eye on me and I can instantaneously sense that he's imperceptibly flexed his muscles up a bit, getting ready for flight if he feels the need and, almost unperceivably, I adjust my steps and mental attitude accordingly. We communicate on a regular basis, he and I, and I find myself listening more often than not, anymore.

Talking Horses with Bert Wells

Years ago, I bought a pair of big-boned, blue roan Quarter horses from a man in Grand Junction by the name of Bert Wells. Meticulously well matched and beautiful to look at, they had the gentle dispositions of large draft animals and were, without a doubt, one of the flashiest horse teams ever to be seen around Aspen. I sold them a few months later.

There's an old saying that "Good horses are where you find them," meaning that pedigree often takes a back seat to heart and natural ability. It's the same for people, although most of us seldom think in terms of pedigree as it relates to humans, other than we hope we know who will "horse trade" fairly with us or who should be looking over his shoulder for our retribution.

Bert and I became friends long before he sold me the horses, simply because he was about the only sled and wagon maker on the Western Slope and we had something of a synergy between us. Stopping at his house to pick up specially hand-crafted parts for one of my sleighs, or to get ideas about how to improve this or that wagon would generally allow the hands of time to turn a bright afternoon into the dark of night before it was over. We converged on a few projects, such as providing top quality carriages for Jimmy Buffett's Redstone wedding and hauling an unidentified casket to a private, obscure mountain burial site. He had at least as many stories as the best of them (and just as good, too), and had been introduced to me through our mutual friend, L. E. Wheeler, who without argument, was one of the best.

Many times, Bert's quiet wife cooked us dinner over a coal stove that had warmed more than one generation of family, the aroma of her concoctions filling the large kitchen, and as we all sat around talking and waiting for dinner, there was the buzz of much to be learned from each other. My first wife, Caroline, went with me many times and more than once, my accomplice Buck Deane filled their living room with boot-stomping yodels and cowboy songs from the past. Bert's daughter, Nettie, a fine piano player, would trade off with me on the upright and through her playing, unintentionally taught me to be a much better pianist. The house would rock with the rhythm of the music and the joy it brought, especially to Bert and his wife, clearly thinking back about many good times and trials in their long life together.

Times change and people's lives suddenly don't coincide anymore, and I didn't see Bert for many years. Oh, a couple of times, I'd gone looking for him, but missed the turn, or got on the wrong road, and gave it up too soon. Almost unconsciously one day, I found myself in front of the bridge leading to his house, and pulled in with a bit of trepidation. The once busy yard, cluttered with wagons and buggies of various design, was empty and unkempt, covered with wind-blown weeds. I knew the story then, but couldn't let it go just yet. A peek in the window revealed nothing but bare floors and empty walls, the once breathing, living house now only a shell. I left my card in the window and drove off, feeling somehow like I'd let Bert down by not having a final visit with him, although it had probably all been said, anyway.

Within minutes, my cell phone rang, a call from another of Bert's daughters. Telling me of the events that had ended it for her parents, she finished it all by saying that Nettie had died shortly thereafter.

I spent the next week in a crazy search for a couple of old, blue roan Quarter horses, a search I knew was futile, but one I had to make anyway.

Horse Sense (Eastern Thoroughbred Farm)

There was an autumn, once upon a time, when I put my Aspen life in a box and indulged in life-threatening activities on a racehorse farm in the fair state of Maryland. My first wife, Caroline, and I anticipated going into the horse racing business with Buck Deane, and headed back East to get some first-hand education about it all. Caroline, a native of the Eastern Shore of Maryland and a true horseman with the proper connections, found us a great place to work.

It's a vastly different world from that of a Woody Creek cowboy and my education started almost immediately. I had cleaned one stall (the horses stay in), a learning experience in itself, when the manager caught up with me and told me to be careful mucking out the next cubicle, home to a Thoroughbred mare named Rimark. She'd kicked the daylights out of the last inexperienced farm hand and killed him. "OK." What else could you say, first day on the job?

By the time I'd cleaned three or four stalls, Charlie, the manager was back, telling me they needed someone to ride a recently gelded three-year-old who had been caged for the past few days, healing up, and was ready to jump his skin, he was so riled up from lack of exercise. The manager allowed they'd saddled the horse with the largest English saddle they could find (a courtesy to the Colorado cowboy), and as he explained about the horse, gave me a look similar to the kind your uncle might give you as you board a ship bound for war. "OK."

For a warm-up, I climbed aboard in a small, round pen used for breaking colts and was relieved to find the horse halfway calm, although the steam blasting from his nostrils could just as easily have been the fiery breath of a precocious dragon. As this well-bred, sorrel dynamo danced the perimeter a few times, I noticed that people from all over the farm were setting themselves up on the white fence surrounding a five-acre paddock, the site chosen for my maiden voyage on an Eastern race horse. Someone had brought a cooler and it was starting to look like the typical Saturday at a down-home western rodeo.

Once in the paddock, what might have been a nightmare turned out to be a good show. The horse tried his best to unload me, and although it wasn't pretty, I managed to stay on and give him his exercise. Apparently, a little skill, some luck and a bit of class got me a promotion and I was allowed, starting the next day, to exercise the hunting horses kept on another part of the farm. "Whew!" although I still had to clean stalls.

First thing every morning, we took the breeding stallions from their stalls and out to their personal paddocks, a death-defying walk if there ever was one. Handling a stallion is much like trying to tame a wild lion inside a cage. For a hundred yards or so, the lifeblood, the foundation, the reputation of the farm was on the end of the lead opposite me, often reared up, teeth occasionally bared, and had I ever weakened and lost control, a myriad of things may have happened to a runaway horse, none of them good. I felt fear on occasion, but had I ever shown it, a stud horse, full of astounding energy and quick to spot opportunity could have pounded my skull with hooves quick enough to cause mortal injury. The challenge was soon irresistible and I volunteered to bring them in at night, as well.

It wasn't all danger, and we laughed and learned a lot, much of it after hours over stout drinks poured by the owner. But the longer I worked there, the more obvious it became that farm hands such as myself were totally expendable, and the horses, king. Just as it should be, I guess.

Horse Wreck

Events, taken by themselves, are rarely earth shattering, but sometimes the culmination of small, seemingly unrelated matters can conspire for resulting ugliness. Such was the case the other day.

I had an afternoon piano gig, so I attempted to get an early start on my livestock salt packing expedition. I'd intended to use the new horse in the pasture, my daughter's mare Babe, as the pack horse and was going to ride my big roan, Drifter. Except, I couldn't catch Babe, seasonally "in season" and predictably difficult to catch, nor could I catch Drifter, who although a gelding, had taken on the personality of an over-protective stallion and ran after Babe's every escape maneuver. Two hours later (embarrassing), I finally had Babe in one hand and strictly by default, my newest horse Billy, in the other.

Now I was running late, riding Billy instead of Drifter and the paradigm shifted without notice. With steady diligence, I loaded Babe with the salt blocks that would be spread out hither and yon along the cattle grazing area. It was Billy's initial ride of the year, and he was a little skittish, his first time leading a pack horse part of the cause, I reckon.

The shortcut trail took an unexpected, precipitous dive down the mountainside; Billy tucked his haunches under himself, sliding and walking at the same time, his tail swishing around in a display of unhappiness over having Babe right on his butt in the steepness.

Suddenly, all hell broke loose. Billy dove to the left, Babe ducked to the right, and in the quickness of the impending wreck, I had a split second of fear before the adrenalin kicked in, telling me I'd better think fast. With the speed of light, the horses suddenly faced each other and then lunged forward, rock-hard blocks of salt aimed directly at my left leg. I narrowly managed to avoid that possibility when Billy, having thrown caution to the wind, decided the only way out was to go into a bucking horse demonstration.

By now, I'd figured out that the lead rope had gotten under Billy's tail and he wasn't taking to it in a good way. Usually, in such rare situations, I just let my horse have a buck or two, and the ensuing disagreement between the horses, one pulling forward and the other back, results in the rope being jerked out from under the tail, and everything returns to normal. Except that wasn't happening, and "why the hell not?" I began to wonder.

Billy got in four or five good bucks (thank God he's a smooth bronc, kind of fun actually) before I got him shut down, and then he decided to put it in reverse, trying to dislodge the agitation under his tail. Normally, we'd have been long free of the packhorse by now, but we weren't, and I was pulling with reins, jabbing with spurs, and softly cussing, my left leg now totally imprisoned against Billy by the force of the lead rope that wouldn't turn loose. I was fully cognizant of the cliff about 10 feet behind us, but Billy's whirlwind state of mind hadn't accounted for that, yet.

I managed to yank Billy around to the right and give him a view of the 30-foot drop-off, which slowed him down a bit, and then Babe decided to quit pulling back. Things were at a momentary standstill, and I bailed off Billy to see what was keeping that damned rope, the possible instigator of our death knell, under his tail.

In a heartbeat, it was obvious. With Billy swishing his tail around and Babe right on his butt going down that steep trail, the slack lead rope had inexplicably and irrevocably tied itself in a clove hitch around Billy's tail. Without the opportunity to get off and untie it, we might be there still, ducking and diving, twisting and turning, eventually testing the landing at the bottom of the cliff.

Horsing Around in Amish Country

We were standing in the middle of a quiet Iowa farmyard, overcast sky and sandy soil damp from recent rain, waiting for Joe Borntrager, the sole proprietor, to turn loose of the draft horses I'd just bought. He clearly liked those big boys and wasn't eager to see them shipped to Colorado, but he had his reasons, I reckon.

I'd bought an almost identically-matched pair of blonde Belgian geldings, Pete and Pat, who weighed about a ton apiece, and Ted, an enthusiastic, dark brown Clydesdale, weighing in at a little more. It's tough fitting three horses that size into a trailer designed for four regular-sized animals. Leading them out of the barn, Joe said, "These horses haven't been in a trailer before. Hope we don't have trouble." But Borntrager knew his charges well and leading with a pitchfork full of hay the size of a VW Bug over his shoulder, he coaxed the team directly into the trailer. I eased the door shut, capturing them before they could back out.

My wife, Caroline, fired up the truck, my buddy, L.E. Wheeler (a mentor), pulled out a generic, "fill in the blanks" bill of sale, and I hurriedly wrote a check. We were conscious of getting on the road before the horses got anxious and started acting up, causing problems.

In a heartbeat, we were out of there, twisting and turning down a labyrinth of back roads, lined on both sides by the quiet, well-tended Amish farms we'd been visiting for the past week in our quest for draft horses. Aspen, here we come!

We were traveling on the edge, as usual, but if everything was perfect it wouldn't be much of a trip. Our conversation was flushed with success, the accomplishment of a mission we'd thought impossible a week earlier. It was about canceled horse sales, a friendly librarian who'd put us on to the Amish, a fellow named Andy Mast, crippled harness maker in the center of the Amish community who both helped and sabotaged our efforts. And Joe Borntrager, who finally decided we were worthy of owning his horses.

About 20 miles into our journey home, I had to hitchhike into town to buy a jack big enough to lift the trailer and horses so we could change a flat. It being Sunday, there was no way to get the horses certified by a veterinarian and to travel without such papers was foolhardy and the jack was a bad omen. But, L.E. had a brother near Hutchinson, Kansas and we figured we'd get there sometime Sunday night and weigh our options then.

The horses were well-behaved, almost motionless, and the trip droned on. Among the three of us in front, we had enough equine stories to last a long time, but not long enough. My wife, unfamiliar with the trailer and its cumbersome load, didn't want to drive and L.E., who'd somehow found a quart of I.W. Harper whiskey during my hitchhike to town, was nipping at it every ten miles or so.

It was about 600 miles from our starting point to Hutchinson, the speed limit was 55, and about sixteen hours after leaving the Borntrager farm, we turned into a pitch-black rural abyss off the Interstate, totally trusting L.E., who with thick tongue and selective memory was relatively certain we'd found the correct road. Don't get me wrong, I loved L.E. like a father (he was about 75 at the time), but our banter was no longer friendly.

And before we knew it, we were lost. It was pushing midnight with not a sign of civilization anywhere. The roads were endless and we turned here and there, hoping L.E. would see something familiar. Wait, is that a light over there? Ten miles away on the prairie or more, but we zigged and zagged and finally pulled up in the driveway, desperate for directions. L.E. says flatly, "This is my brother's place."

"Oh, bullshit," I cried, even as L.E. and his brother were shaking hands in the yard. We unloaded the horses and called it a day.

How Death Became Him

If you turn toward State Bridge off of Interstate 70 and head north, it's a fine drive, especially in early summer. Every slow-turning bend reveals a new perspective on the land, creates enthusiasm for adventure between two people falling in love, and makes conversation easy.

We spied the notebook-sized piece of paper stuck to the windshield, just like he said it'd be, with the address numbers wildly scrawled in pencil. There was a moment of hesitation, perhaps a touch of ambivalence, before we climbed the stairs to what could be best described as a hurriedly-built, 1950s log-sided cabin, and made our presence known.

He'd advertised treasures for sale, of the kind seldom found anymore, and my future paramour had asked me to tag along on this journey, part of the mating dance we all do, never sure of the future.

You don't find people like him around these parts much, although they used to be common. Beat up bad by hard work and forced to live on Social Security and odd jobs, his gnarled and stiff fingers from a lifetime of using tools such as hammers, axes and shovels kept going to his front shirt pocket, pulling out the fixin's for a smoke. ZZ Top papers and a white canvas bag of Bull Durham tobacco, with the drawstring top. He was good, too, rolled 'em tight and full.

The worn-out woman came and went, at first appearing to be his wife, but the disinterest she had in our presence soon had her pegged as an interloper. The whiskey bottle quietly came out for a brief appearance and then she left on foot. A big grin creased his unshaven, wrinkled mug as he said, "Man, I'm so lucky I hooked up with her."

Sitting next to the sink, a large pot roast thawed, its blood puddling around thick freezer paper, the whole package collecting concentrated rays of sun that bore through the window. "You wanna leave that out," I asked, drawing his attention to the situation? "Oh yeah, that's our dinner for tonight," he responded, and I could smell a fresh blast of whiskey on his breath.

"Any luck, we sell a bunch of this stuff to you guys and we're moving to Las Vegas in the morning. Kinda like a honeymoon, only we ain't getting married. No way! Less a course, she insists." And he quit trying to hide the booze bottle, just left it on a nearby bookshelf.

Quietly, the woman came through again, leaving a big bowl of something in the refrigerator, presumably to go with that night's celebratory meal. Wobbly, she'd been nursing her own brand of rotgut down the street some place, and was a little agitated to find us still there. She left again.

The flies had found the roast in the kitchen and made a loud buzz every time I shooed them away with my hand. "Yep, soon as you leave," he said with a wink in my direction, "I'm gonna have a heart-to-heart with that woman. You know what I mean?" Unable now to easily find his shirt pocket opening under the protective flap, he tossed the papers and the sack of tobacco onto the kitchen table.

We drove away with a pickup truck load of stuff, some of which I still have, and there was the satisfaction, I guess, of lacing his jeans with a few hundred bucks. My partner and I had some good times for the next year-and-a-half.

Like many stories, we never know the ending, but it's seldom pretty. Did he die of a broken heart and an enlarged liver, back in his small cabin on the hill, wondering where it all went south; or unable to return, did some security guard in front of a fancy Vegas casino roll his dying body off the sidewalk with a kick to the gut before he called the medics?

How Hyrup's got Its Name

He was a rough talkin' SOB, who wasn't afraid to get in your face with an idea, although he never really cussed out anyone in particular - except politicians. Johnny was the kind of a guy who could get a lot of people stirred up over something, just through the energy he expended talking about it. If you took the long view and left the filigree and frills off the edges of the argument, you had to admit that he was usually right.

He used to clean the Salvation Ditch for my family every spring, using a behemoth, yellow D7 Caterpillar bulldozer, and it didn't take me long to figure out he was a soft touch for a ride. And we took a lot of rides together.

He built the existing road up the face of Larkspur Mountain, above Lenado, and all the logging roads on top, as well. Occasionally, he'd stop by the ranch on his way to work and pick me up. We'd ride in silence, 'cause who wants to talk much at 5:00 A.M.? A ten-year-old kid, I'd sit in the dozer seat with him all day long, figuring that cat skinning was my destiny.

I'd learned enough by watching, I thought, to run that monstrous machine, and one day when he'd parked the big D7 across the road from our Woody Creek house (and everyone was gone), I got to tinkering with the thing, and before long, had the diesel engine purring like the big Cat she was. Johnny happened down the road about then, giving me his blessing. Being ranch-raised, the operation of machinery came naturally, and before my folks got home, I'd filled in the pond across from the house and widened half the road up the draw behind our house. About then, the cable that lifted the blade broke, and I was forced to give it up. At eleven years old then, I figured the punishment would be severe, but all Johnny did when he came back was to laugh and have me help him fix the damned thing.

When I was in junior high, blue suede shoes were the "in" thing, stemming from Carl Perkins' song of the same name, and I'll never forget the day, in front of Matthew Drug (Carl's Pharmacy now), when I spotted Johnny coming down the walk. "Hey, look at my new shoes, man." They didn't impress Johnny all that much, and he held me tight with a big arm while he totally scuffed up my shoes with his dirty work boots. "Does your dad know you're wearing crap like that around town?" It was the only time he really pissed me off, teaching me that heroes are only human, no matter what we think.

He worked fourteen winters for the Ski Corp., running the snow cat crew and then after dark, hauling water up the Midnight Mine road for the Sundeck. One inauspicious day, while plowing the Midnight Mine road, disaster struck, burying Johnny in an avalanche. When the spray settled, he was totally buried but for one hand and through very fortunate circumstances, managed to dig himself out. There weren't enough employees in those days to provide a spotter for him on the back side, but then, Johnny was usually a one-man show anyway, too damned tough to be taken out by an avalanche.

Another winter, he was asked to pick up the ski patrol at the bottom of Walsh's, after they'd bombed it. The scratchy radio in his snow cat blared, "All clear," and he rolled down Loushin's Road just in time to see the then unnamed Hyrup's slide in front of his cat, nearly rolling him over the side. There's no doubt he singled out the culprit.

So, the next time you ski Hyrup's on Aspen Mountain, you'll know a little bit of the history, for it was named after the tough cat driver with a soft spot for kids, Johnny Hyrup. Johnny ended up a cattle rancher around Parachute until his death in 2006.

How to Be a True Ski Bum

Back in the 1960s, when I graduated from high school, a couple of buddies and I wanted to buy a Victorian house in the West end. It wasn't much compared to today's overdone extravaganzas, but it would have suited us well without much repair. We thought it was a little expensive at $12,000, but when the owner told us he'd talk price when we came up with some serious money, our hopes were lifted.

It was a career move that, in the end, we failed to make, mostly because twelve grand might as well have been twelve million back then, but I've always wondered where it might have taken us. Our goals were lofty - a few parties here and there, chase some women around the pot-belly stove and pursue the lives we'd dreamed about (and witnessed) from our perspective as Aspen high school students. Like ski every day and hang out at the Aspen Institute. I kid you not.

My dad was one of the most level-headed guys to ever have kids, much to my chagrin, and once he'd convinced me a house in town wasn't in my best interest, I started hammering him about ranches in Australia or Canada, and in the absence of any enthusiasm from him on those subjects, how about if his eldest son joined the Peace Corps or lived in Europe for a couple of years? In the end, I promised him I'd get an undergraduate degree and then, as he gently put it, "You can do whatever the hell you want."

It was a gamble I'm sure he thought he'd win, but before the ink was dry on that college diploma, I was back in Aspen, skiing almost every day (December graduation). My dad was true to his word and didn't complain, but he didn't support my decision, either. But, thanks to my aunt and uncle (Vic & Eileen), I had a ski pass, a job and a place to live. It's hard to get over being a first-class ski bum like that.

The party was on for the next seven or eight years and, given the latitude we enjoyed in those days, especially my cousin Don Stapleton and me, we're lucky we didn't self-destruct from the responsibility of maintaining our niche. Luckily, we weren't into drugs - how odd, as it was the days of Drug City, USA. Of course, there wasn't a drink in town that didn't have our names on it and some of the wildest adventures and craziest ideas were attracted to us with regularity.

It was also a time for sporadic, but serious introspection and I spent a lot of time in Wyoming and Montana looking for something serious to do, finally accepting that I was just looking for another Aspen, or maybe just a way out of the one I had created.

Realizing there wasn't much life elsewhere, not for me anyway, I committed my future to that of Aspen. I went into business, carved out a career in town, and did OK for a kid who never took life too seriously. But a lifetime of work, unless in the arts or literature is, for most of us, as vaporous as being a skiing fool.

Oh, there are some guys you can think of, such as Ralph Jackson or Red Campbell, who couldn't help themselves when it came to skiing, even if they tried, but they represent only the tiniest fraction of the crazed skier population. To be a true ski bum, it helps to have a lot of money (and free time), but one of the cardinal rules is that, to be authentic, you must never pay for your lift ticket, at least not in cash.

Go ahead, dream of buying a cheap house in town, get on the ski instructor call list, party hearty, but remember, no matter how you do it, you'll only be as good as your last run.

How to Dismantle a Ranch

Gray light came slowly down the valley to reveal a foot, maybe half again that much, of fresh, spring-wet snow. Overnight, the temperature had plummeted almost as fast as the precipitation had come down, and the beginning of a nightmare was unfolding.

Blasts of condensation emanated from the nostrils of my dapple gray mare, forming the top of a giant "A" which spread out toward her feet and almost touched the ground. Ironically, it was the first day of spring, and the mood of the crew was as somber as the quiet, bone-chilling air.

In preparation for a dispersal sale, things were turned upside down at the ranch, and confusion wrangled against common sense in my mind. The old man had sent me down to the creek bottom to see how many new calves had been born overnight, and through the rising mist of the water, I witnessed a travesty of things gone wrong. The long shed we normally used for birthing calves (near the house with a roof over it) had clearly been appropriated for something else, and the poor mother cows, those giving birth and already distressed at a change in the decades-old procedure, had been forced to calve out in a partially frozen Woody Creek swamp.

I fashioned a sled of sorts out of old sheets of roofing tin tied together, caught the struggling and freezing calves in the snow, hogtied and loaded them up and headed for the dry of the tack room, the only unused place out of the weather. There were twelve newborns that I found, and I could only haul one or two at a time, an arduous task. My young horse soon felt my frustration and occasionally reared, bucked and otherwise did anything to create problems. My language and its volume degenerated with the continued deterioration of the day, drawing curious onlookers and my dad finally sent some help my way.

How do you dismantle a ranch? You might think it difficult; thousands of acres of land surrounding you, hundreds of cattle to sell, hay still in the stack, saddles and bridles lining the tack room walls, pastures full of horses, houses and barns full of memories.

Do you have a big sale like the Elkhorn Ranch was having that day, a family-owned operation trading beef, horses and machinery for dollars?

No, you just kill the dream. It doesn't happen overnight, but when the wind no longer blows through your hair at a gallop, when the cattle bring frustration instead of smiles, when nuances too subtle to notice, change, it's gone. Whatever it was, my dad's new vision of freedom was "get out," and the soul of the place cried.

Whether we got all the calves in, I don't remember, and then I watched my dad run some yearlings through part of the corrals for prospective buyers. He was angry at me for not bringing in the calves alone, quietly, and I didn't much care for him that day, either.

There were sandwiches for sale on the back porch, but I went into the kitchen to make my own and was told by some self-officious woman that it was off-limits. Too tired to argue, I stumbled through the back hall leading to the living room, and found it full of bee-hived strangers, running adding machines and collecting money.

The reality of it glanced off me as bile rose in my throat. I spent the rest of the afternoon in my upstairs room, face down on the bed, trying to comprehend what the hell we'd done to ourselves.

Spring came begrudgingly, late. The old man had to use our stock truck to deliver all the horses we'd sold since none of 'em had ever seen the inside of a horse trailer.

By early summer, my parents had left, but I stayed, belligerently sleeping on a mattress on the floor of an empty house, heating tea water with a blowtorch. Until I started college. For the next twenty-odd years, I wandered elusively, a party boy and general mess, a cowboy without a dream.

Cooking Joe's Goose

In the days when McCulloch Oil owned much of the Hunter Creek valley, memories of Lamech sheep bands wandering the valley floor and Jenny Adair's entreprenurial sawmill weren't so distant as to be indistinguishable from the "olden" days. Van Horn Park was summer home to cattle herds from Woody Creek, Brush Creek, Starwood (Trentaz) and points in between.

A group of us, hooked to McCulloch Oil in one form or another, scored the key to the locked gate and gained permission to spend the weekend in the old cabin not far up the valley. It wasn't any spur of the moment camping trip, for we were going first-class, at least for the times. A couple of the boys brought along a cooler full of crappie and bass, we rounded up some steaks, potatoes, corn-on-the-cob and, naturally, brought along enough beer and whiskey to float a solar energy company loan. Someone had the brilliant idea we should cook a goose, literally, and Joe "No Problem" Candreia's name came up as the obvious source of such a fowl.

Joe lived at Buttermilk (before Bumps Restaurant) in an upstairs apartment over the ski shop with a blue-haired woman who no doubt was a lot of fun, but who had a tongue sharper than a barber's straight-razor, at least when she was talking to Joe, which seemed to be most of the time. His reply was the toothless and usual, "No problem," softened by a plug of tobacco in one cheek or the other and a tongue habitually numbed by alcoholic libations. In addition to being a Ski Corp. mechanic, Joe was considered to be the night watchman and as such, entitled to live about any way he pleased, which meant raising chickens, ducks and geese on the roof above the ski shop. Joe wasn't sure he wanted to see the goose leave home, but for $5.00 and a bottle of hootch, the deal was struck.

We left work early on a Friday afternoon, loaded our gear into a brand-new Dodge pickup truck, including the gawking goose, and followed it all in an open-topped Jeep, about a 1952 vintage, stocked with fishing gear and other accoutrement that likely could have been left at home.

Deep-fried fish, the first I'd ever had, was great on top of about a case of beer and we finally got around to dressing out the goose. I guess the idea was to cook it and let it sit overnight, ready for a lunch time feast the next day. More savvy cooks than I lowered it into the deep fryer and the last I remember hearing was, "Somebody wake me at midnight to check on the bird." To coin a phrase, "No problem."

About 3:00 am, I heard a commotion and one of the cooks running outside, yelling, "The goose, the goose!" Upon inspection, it wasn't a total loss, but what the difference was, I couldn't say. It was a tragedy, there's no doubt, and we felt bad about it all weekend. Still do, as a matter of fact.

That was in the early 1970s. The man many of you knew as "No Problem Joe," the man for whom "No Problem Bridge" (Neale Street) is named, had something else to say to the rest of us (every time we saw him) after we explained what we'd done to the goose. Like a little kid, his eyes would tear up and he'd let his face contort into a sad expression, and he'd say, in that inimitable way he had, "Go away, you ruined my goose."

I thought he might never get over it and would hold a grudge forever, but sometime in the early 90s, not too long before he died, he invited my uncle and me into his house to share in an after-breakfast snort. He took a big swig off a table-top bottle, passed it to my uncle and then elbowed me in the ribs with a teasing smile, "You're the sumbitch who cooked my goose. No problem."

Avalanche at Hunter's Pass

Lined up single file, nose-to-tail, the horses stood exhausted in the narrow trench, thankful for the respite, while the men accompanying them spread out among some large boulders close beside the avalanche path. The snow along the sides of the constricted passage towered over the horses heads, and yet there was two or three feet of the soft stuff under their legs, creating a nightmare of hurried escape in the mountains nine miles east of Aspen.

Billed as one of the worst in Colorado history, the 1899 storm had raged intermittently for weeks at the Hunter's Pass gold mine and at the now-ghost town of Independence, putting a stop to all mining operations and preventing supplies from reaching the intrepid miners. Little did the inhabitants know, but this latest January storm of nine days was wreaking almost perfect havoc on their little mining town.

In spite of the heavy snows and incessant, howling winds, the tiny town of Independence had not seen a snow slide all winter, not until the afternoon of January 30, 1899. A quiet, unobtrusive release, opposite the town, slid harmlessly to the edge of civilization, without causing much consternation. Then, about nine o'clock that night, a blast of snow came down a draw opposite the conglomeration of log structures, the sheer size of it obliterating a large barn that housed George Frost's freight teams. Buried under heavy snow, beams, freight wagons and other accoutrement of the trade, the horses were eventually extricated, largely unscathed.

A small cabin next to the stable was buried under about ten feet of snow. Quick attention to the matter by other citizens allowed the occupants to be successfully dug out from the still-standing structure, although it was said they were a little "scairt." Most of the residents did not hear the slide coming and were caught off-guard, although no one was injured or killed. One cabin was totally demolished, but its tenant was visiting down the street.

With unstable snow all around, at a depth never before seen, with 300 cords of wood essential for heat buried under tons of snow from a third avalanche and supplies running out, it was decided the best course of action would be to move the horses (their feed buried under the debris, as well) down the pass to Aspen. Before gasoline power, horses and mules were major transportation links between civilization and the frontier, and to save the horses, so rudely put out of a home, was a noble gesture.

At least that was the excuse used, as a force of nearly 100 men volunteered to dig a trench down the mountain to extricate the horses, a reasonable way to escape the impending doom at Independence. Many men were on homemade skis. Fearing a return of the storm and instead of waiting for the snow on the bottom of the trench to freeze overnight, the caravan plunged forward early on February 2, the soft snow underneath causing the horses to struggle and flounder, the men assisting as best they could.

About midnight, the miners were exhausted and hungry, the horses possibly worse off, and just at the edge of what they considered to be the last avalanche path, the men took a "lunch" break, letting the horses regenerate as well, before a last-ditch effort to reach a safe overnight stop.

The sixteen horses quietly waited, trusting their fate while the men rested behind in the shelter of some rocks when a loud, "Boom," rocked the clear night air. Scrambling for safety, the men managed to dodge the brunt of the avalanche, although some were buried in peripheral loose snow. The horses, about 20 feet in front of the men, were trapped forcefully in the fast-moving flurry, crushed by its weight. Several horses were later found on top of the debris, crushed to death by the force of the rumbling snow. Only two horses survived, and one of those had to be put down due to serious injuries. The buried men were quickly dug out and the entourage limped safely toward Aspen.

If there were any old-timers left, they'd still be talking about it.

Insanity in Aspen

Maybe it was a hangover from the big bicycle races last week, stress getting the better of folks, or maybe it points out an old Aspen problem that has found new heights for expressing its madness.

While driving east on Durant, I spotted my ski buddy Bob getting out of his car, which was parked on the north side of Durant. I stopped to holler at him, just to say "Hi," a rather common custom around here since the Utes began the tradition thousands of years ago by saying "Mique" as they passed each other on the trail.

A quick glance in my rearview mirror revealed a woman coming up on me at a fast clip, and rather than go around (there was plenty of room), she pulled up on my butt with mere fractions of an inch to spare. It was clearly an expression of displeasure and, as you might have guessed, she had a cell phone stuck to her ear. "She'll get over it," I thought. A quick greeting to Bob and I'd be on my way, but wait!

Headed west with a couple of toy-like kayaks on top, an SUV (painted Druid black, apparently to dispel the murkiness of the driver's gender) pulled up and stopped, asking if I had "broken down?" If not, "why'd you stop in the middle of the street?" came the clipped voice from behind the wheel. He then pulled forward (still blocking the opposite lane) and began a loud conversation with the occupant of the car behind me, something about how I clearly must be from out of town to be so oblivious and obtuse.

Evidently they were unaware that their rudeness was overshadowing mine. I'd stopped on a mostly deserted street to say hello to a friend, and in their eagerness to point out the inaccuracy of my ways, two people had now committed egregious errors of driving etiquette themselves, one with her nose up the ass of my vehicle, the other blocking traffic in the opposite lane while bitching about my actions.

If you've been around a while, the above scene is probably not a news flash – there are more self-appointed "behavior police" per square inch in this town than likely anywhere else on the planet, and many of them are the same folks who fatuously complain about "lack of messy vitality."

Anyway, thinking I could make a longer story short, I pulled off to the side, allowing room for the unhappy woman behind me to get on with it. And that she did by stopping directly alongside my vehicle and giving me a fake-smiled lecture about driving laws, about how "it's illegal to stop in the middle of the street to talk to a friend." Apparently, though, it is quite legal to stop in the middle of the street to lecture a complete stranger about how pissed off you are.

To top it off, that same emasculating lady delivered said scolding over the lap of her passenger, a young girl not more than twelve. A rare case of a "skirt hiding behind a skirt," I reckon, except it involved a child. It did serve to keep my profanity at an acceptable level, although I'm still wondering what was more important to this woman – the need to express her ire or setting a good example for the kid?

After I thanked her for the information, she said, "You're a real piece of work." I hoped it to be a compliment, but the nastiness in her voice implied I may as well have stomped a puppy to death, so deep was her frustration over my banal error of driving judgment. I realize some people's sensitivities overwhelm even them, but this was ludicrous.

After she was all said and done and had driven off, sanity returned. A smile slowly crossed my face as I realized the circus had come to town and I got to be a part of it.

Interruption of Memory

You could tell she was a tall woman, just from the way she sat her wheelchair, back straight with knees jutting out a little past what might appear to be comfortable. I was very pleased to see her at a family soiree last fall, but as I reservedly offered my hand rather than a hug, she eyed my name-tag with suspicion and wondered aloud why she didn't know me. My surname and her maiden name were the same, she said, and asked if perhaps I was related to her father, Ben Vagneur (my granddad), or at least knew him, and the question caught me off guard.

We can't know for certain when people leave us, and I've never been that close to it, but somewhere along our intricate paths, the thread of a lifetime breaks and we can no longer communicate with a loved one. It's easy to categorize the problem as "Alzheimer's" or "too old to remember," or whatever else we might come up with, but throwing words at such a complex problem fails us when we need to understand the most.

My dad's sister, Bernice, was born in the Aspen Citizen's Hospital in 1927 and grew up on the family ranch in Woody Creek. My first horse, Stardust, was the same steed she rode to the Woody Creek schoolhouse every day when she was a kid, but as Bernice succinctly pointed out in "Aspen, The Quiet Years," we never really "owned" our riding horses. They were ranch property, assigned to us.

Maybe it was the horses, but more likely it was that we both were outspoken, had a sometimes unusual view of the world and generally seemed to be able to find common ground on divergent issues that made us close in a special way.

Perhaps that's why she called me one day, saying she couldn't remember where she'd parked her car. I didn't think too much about it, but she was genuinely scared so I walked her slowly through the available options until she finally said, "Oh yes, I remember, now!"

She was a big woman with a big heart, and a laugh to match. She could see behind the stage, look past wrinkle-causing events, and many times, sitting through a serious discussion, her hand would all at once go to her mouth with an exclamation of, "Oh, my God," and then a roar of laughter (or rush of tears) as she explained the epiphany that had just passed through her vision. Not everyone took this in a humorous fashion, but then, not everyone got it, either.

A long time ago, she took me into her confidence, showing me an old, abandoned, hand-hewn log cabin she wanted to restore. "I'll buy it, move it to your place and we'll fix it up," she'd said. Of course, the ol' boy that owned the cabin wouldn't cooperate, so our plan didn't pan out. But can't you imagine that if Aunt Bernice had, through the blending of reality and a great metaphor, through a stretch of the imagination almost too great to comprehend - and while those with the easy answers sat dumbfounded - gotten hold of that rickety cabin, perhaps she'd have fixed the lengthening synapses in her brain just as surely as she repaired the cabin.

And so it was that later, as I sat down beside her and as she once again questioned me, I told her that I knew her father well. Her eyes lit up with a burning curiosity and for a brief time, we had a most pleasant conversation. It was our last.

The Price of a Good Ranch

While catching a break at Bonnie's restaurant the other day, the unambiguous epitome of laid-back cool, Jim Spann, pointed out an ad listing one of my family's old ranches for sale at 88 million dollars. That's not a joke, either. Well, it isn't meant to be humorous, but it does bring a cynical smile to anyone who's due to make a mortgage payment or meet the rent.

Let's knock off the bullshit early on - for that kind of money, it's not a ranch, say what you will. No self-respecting rancher of even the most rudimentary ability would pay that much for a ranch. It's kind of like horses - why pay fifty thousand dollars for a horse when you can get a good one for say, $2500.00, or less? We could call it a large piece of land instead, even though its expanse is not nearly its original size. It's been piecemealed off, here and there by previous owners who needed a quick buck for the here and now. People have a penchant for talking about the high price of land around here and the billionaires it takes to buy it, but it seems like most of them can't really afford it, as don't you know, the new outfit will eventually be going through the land use process, trying to advantageously develop the "highest and best use" of the land. That's real-estate (and government)-speak for "development."

88 mil - that's a big wad to carry around in the front pocket of your jeans. Once the deal is struck, buyer or seller can celebrate by having a party or two - "at the ranch" - and mouthing off about it around their circle of peers (the choir), but if you have to brag, you're already a loser. As a friend of mine, a youth beyond his years, says, "A good cowboy doesn't have to show off - his personal worth becomes apparent through his actions."

Lamentably, our delirious trend toward conspicuous consumerism has turned us into a valley out of control, putting most everything we own up for sale to the highest bidder. Some of that is OK, 'cause we're all entitled to make a living, but at what point will we look up and notice that our souls are buried somewhere deep in the deed of trust we've just signed away.

As my good buddy, Bruce Carlson, asks, "Whatever happened to the days when someone bought a house because they needed somewhere to live?" Many people have to work two and three jobs just to keep pace around here and we've priced all but the most affluent local kids out of this valley. Flip this - flop that - kill the golden goose. It's going to be tougher and tougher to find anyone willing to take the reins of community responsibility. Money doesn't come with or create that kind of accountability in people. Folks who've lived here briefly and think they know what's best for the town all lack one important attribute - a sense of history.

Not that many years ago, we used to describe to anyone who'd listen how great we thought Aspen was. Then, as things became more complicated, we became quieter. Walking around town the past couple of days, though, with all the wondrous snow, has brought back incredible, magical feelings I used to have as a kid, walking the same streets. And, it has nothing to do with money.

Through the fairest favor that destiny can deliver, Aspen is deep in my soul. One can only hope there are kids growing up here today who, when they're my age, will be able to say they've been here all along, that they have phantasmagorical memories, and that they didn't get pushed out by the misdirected, but very real, power of money. Eighty-eight million is nothing compared to that.

Whispers

It's there sometimes just before I drift off to sleep, this place with emerald grass beside the tiny mountain brook. Sunlight filters through the tall, swaying stand of quivering, silvery aspens, creating soft contrast between light and shadow. Sounds, if they can be heard at all, come in whispers and the air is always still.

A tiny path, found completely by accident last summer in the middle of 20,000 acres, leads to this sanctuary, and once there, one must retrace his steps to get safely out again. Any other way is almost impossible to navigate due to huge trees blown down over the past few years, and it is a nightmare for a horse to navigate, worse for a person. Once discovered, this spectral cathedral of solitude became a focus of my attention every time I ventured near, tending to our grazing cattle.

Long winters make for a change in thought patterns, and by the time spring rolled around again, my secret spot in the mountains existed only in memory, the hidden path totally forgotten, a fact that became self-evident when I eventually tried to revisit the place in reality. On some level, I felt betrayed and began to wonder if perhaps my memory was of a dream or a blur of several dreams and I was merely kidding myself into believing I had actually visited this place.

Over the course of several weeks, I'd try this direction, that way, over this hillock, through that small draw, and each time, I'd end up facing forests of aspen, spruce and pine, finding no trail through the maze and eventually wondering if I'd ever find my way out again. It was rugged, frustrating, and sometimes cold, and in an odd way, exhilarating each time my horse, Drifter, and I would finally battle our way out of the trees and onto some small cow trail that we recognized, disappointed we hadn't found our coveted hideout in the woods. Drifter was happy just to be headed home, and I guess to be totally frank, I was getting tired of looking.

Unwilling to spend any more time looking, I finally gave it up, pleased to at least have the memory of such a place and realizing there was never any guarantee that I'd touch that sacred ground again.

It was late October, and the cows had been gathered weeks before, but I took a ride just to make sure we hadn't missed some, and traversed the high country that looks out toward the majesty of the Elk Mountain Range, peaks such as Capitol, Daly and Snowmass visible in the distance.

The wind was raw, blowing snow that was little less than hail with a force that made my horse dance, trying to turn away from it, and I had little sympathy, urging him onward because of the cold in my feet and fingers.

Neither of us was happy and in a sudden display of bravado, I ducked into an aspen forest, thinking the trees would lessen the effect of the wind, making travel less difficult for the both of us. We crashed over deadfall, worked our way around impassable gaps in the trees, and about the time I reckoned my thought processes had doomed us to a truly miserable day, we came out in the very glade I've been discussing.

To be honest, in the flat light of a snowstorm it didn't radiate itself quite like it does on a sunlit summer's day, but still, my smile was wide and my heart warm as we stopped briefly to admire what we had found. Our journey out on the small, snow-covered path was a blessing to our travels and I'll not soon forget, again, where it all exists.

And the realization came to me that we all have special places we carry in our hearts, whether we learn of them through photographs, hikes in the wilderness, travels in the forest, stories in books, or dreams we've had in the night. We just need to remember that if we are patient and caring, the special places will find us, for that is the way it works.

Jammin' and Slammin' at the Old Sleepy Cat Ranch

As usual, we were running late but we'd been doing that for so long, it seemed normal. We threw a public address system, several amplifiers, microphones, speakers, guitars, a drum set and an electric piano in the back of my 4-door Dodge pickup and headed to Meeker, for a wedding reception. At the old Sleepy Cat Ranch. It seemed like a big deal and it was, but if we didn't pull a miracle out of our hats to get there on time, they were gonna be throwin' rocks at us instead of smiles.

As with all good ideas that come just in the nick of time, we decided to take the Buford Road out of New Castle, believing it to be a shortcut. We didn't realize it usually takes about an hour longer to get to Meeker using the Buford route compared to Highway 13 out of Rifle, so we intently flew along, making the fastest time we could. Buck Deane navigated, I drove, and the English drummer, Chris Winter, sat in the back seat, wondering if anyone would ever find the wreckage.

If you've never driven the Buford Road, it is a dirt byway full of switchbacks, potholes and gnarly turns, and it parallels the Flattops Wilderness Area. In spite of this, we made it to the Sleepy Cat in just under an hour, still late, but not terribly so. The lead guitar player was waiting for us, more than a little nervous, but that's what he gets for riding with his girlfriend.

The gig went remarkably well, the bride being a good friend of Buck's, and we kept the crowd going until the bitter end. Almost the bitter end. Buck, in his inimitable way, got me to telling a couple of jokes, and then the guy down the bar told one, and before long, I was scribbling them down on a pad of paper, they were so good. Around 4:30 A.M., the bartender said he couldn't take anymore and about 25 of us wandered out into a cold fall morning.

Johnny Zurfluh had gotten us accommodations at a cabin down the road, and by the time we arrived, the gray of early dawn was but a breath away. It was colder than a witch's nose in a north wind and there was some trouble getting the propane furnace to light. Having had a water heater blow up in my face once, I took on the role of expert and before long, was unencumbered of my bushy eyebrows and some of the hair on my head. But the cabin warmed up rapidly after that.

We slept for three or four hours and headed to Buford, looking for breakfast on the recommendation of a friend. It had been a long night; silence ruled in the truck and as we sped along, I looked out the passenger window to see a one-humped camel wandering along a forsaken ridge in the distance. I don't know, but it just didn't seem right to bring it up at the time. Maybe I saw it and maybe I didn't, but by the time I'd thought about it, the camel was gone from sight. A guy doesn't need something like that hanging over his head, at least not the morning after one of those nights.

With impeccable timing, we were back at the Sleepy Cat around lunchtime, jammin' in the lounge and slammin' back a little bit of the hair of the dog. I was gonna take some guy outside for saying I didn't look like much until I started playing the piano. That's what you call turning a compliment into an accident, but like I said, it had been a rough night.

In the end, we stuck around for two or three more boisterous nights, playing the music like crazy, chasing some local gals around, and buying drinks for those that looked at us sideways.

Safely out of town, we wondered what it'd take for a return trip. A couple of weeks later, the Meeker Cattlemen's Ball beckoned, deja vu if there ever was any.

A Man You Should Know

Gondola Plaza is a thriving gob of adrenalin-laced people midmorning, reminiscent of a country marketplace. Folks scurry by statues of icons past, looking for tickets, ski partners, or just looking straight ahead at whatever they hope the day will bring.

A quick look at the ski rack reveals that your skis are nowhere to be found. There's a rising sense of urgency overtaking your demeanor and just before the panic mode sets in, a tall, graying gentleman with a smooth, southern accent offers his help. He listens to your story as he walks you to the nearest rental shop, tells the man in charge to give you whatever you want, and says as he walks off, "Don't worry about your skis. I'll have 'em right here when you get done today."

The only thing missing is the silver bullet as you wonder, "Who was that uniformed man?" We all know the Skico big-shots; Carolyn in guest services, Frankie the equalizer, King the manager, Burkley in operations; Mike-something-or-other, the head duck, and then there's the Colonel. "The who?" you say.

If there's one person who operates under the radar, who takes responsibility for keeping Aspen Mountain running smoothly, it is the Colonel, John Holsonback. It's not so much that anything is particularly his province, but if he sees a problem, he owns it until there is a resolution.

It doesn't matter who you are, he'll help you, and this writer has personally witnessed, time and time again the Colonel displaying pure genius when it comes to finding misplaced, lost or stolen ski equipment. Or lost partners, kids, even overstimulated minds on the verge.

Many Skiing Company name tags contain the hometown of the person wearing them, and the number for Holsonback might be long, listing either his homes in Germany as a military brat, or Charleston, South Carolina, where a big chunk of his soul resides, or any number of other places the Colonel knew growing up. He met his bride, Hilde, in Germany and learned to ski all over Europe, a past that uniquely qualifies him to work on Aspen Mountain as an internationally sophisticated skier, fluent in foreign languages.

The Citadel in South Carolina is one of America's top military schools, up there with West Point and the Air Force Academy, but is the only one that still embraces the "fourth class system." You don't necessarily need to know what that means, but if those other schools are designed to turn boys into men, you can trust that the Citadel turns boys into tough men, the kind you want on our side. The Citadel is John's alma mater and precursor to a successful military career which earned him the rank of "Colonel," only one field rank below "General."

I mean, let's face it, if you're used to commanding infantry brigades (3000-5,000 soldiers each) in Vietnam, Turkey or anywhere else, finding someone's lost skis or helping out a friend in need is not something to flinch about. And I suspect that most everyone who has come into contact with John now counts him as a friend.

We could talk about John's good attributes all day long, but that's not why we're here. Some people want to know how many scalps he took, how many bronze or silver stars he earned, and other bloody basic stuff. I'm not gonna say. And it's just a hunch anyway, but I think he'd like to be a cowboy.

But, I will tell you that John cares deeply for Aspen, for the character of the town, not the characters in town. He'll emphasize that distinction. According to John, the good character of Aspen is built upon the personal independence of its citizens, those pioneer miners, ranchers and skiers who are the foundation of today's Aspen. And that group includes John Holsonback.

Josie and Me

A few day ago, there was mention in the national news about a 9-year-old girl caught driving her mother's car, with the mother in the car. It made me wonder how badly I would have been chastised by the politically correct of the world for letting my 5-year-old daughter drive my truck while I fed the horses. With the pickup in its lowest 4-wheel drive gear, she'd stand on the seat and steer whichever direction I pointed. By the time she was 10, she could put a five-speed manual transmission through its paces, up or down, with flawless precision. She could also take a 16-hand horse over a 3-foot jump without blinking.

So it was no big deal the other day when, just before we began the monstrous job of separating 750 bovine animals into pre-arranged groups, the big boss looked at me with a bit of a grin and said, "Do you think you and Josie can keep the cutting alleyway in the corrals loaded with cattle?" Without being demonstrative, I said something like, "Hell yes," realizing too late that my reply might have been a little salty for a 7-year-old girl.

It was our job, Josie and me, to separate 30 or 40 cows and calves off of the main bunch (in a huge enclosure) and push them through an ever-narrowing corral passage and hold them there until men on the other end had properly sorted them into various pens. This is the kind of job you do over and over again until finally, the entire herd gets through the corrals and separated.

Josie rides a small, well-proportioned dark-brown horse named Glenn, the two of them ideally suited to each other. Glenn responds with the quickness and alertness of a pony who is enthusiastic about his job and is, in the words of some sun-creased, leather-faced old timers, a seasoned cow horse.

Taking turns, one of us would hold our cows in the corral without help while the other rode back into the main herd and cut out 30 or 40 more. With that teamwork, we kept a smooth and continuous flow of cattle going through the corrals, keeping everyone busy, without a wait for more cattle.

You might think it impossible or immaterial to know individual cows in the midst of a bunch that size, but that's not how it works. In particular, I was concerned about a big, cross-bred Angus-Brahma cow with low, wide-flung ears, a dedicated momma with red tag number M-209 stuck in her ear. She has been known to charge horses, sometimes without warning, so I advised Josie to keep a careful eye on her.

Now Josie is, like many girls her age, shy and soft-spoken, so about the most I had gotten out of her was the name of her horse. But after the second warning on M-209, she pushed her wide-brimmed, black hat back and said something through the swirling dust I couldn't quite understand, except for, "off our horses."

M-209, 1400-1500 pounds of vibrant beef on the hoof who has no fear of a twelve-to-fourteen hundred pound horse, can be kowtowed by a two-legged person on foot, something Josie was trying to tell me.

Almost done, I left Josie to watch the corral cows while I went back to gather up M-209 and the few cows remaining with her. I hopped off my horse, had a short stare-down with the old broad and whistled the big beasts into action.

Here came Josie at a lope, back out of the corral, unwilling to leave me on my own. She went to the opposite side, dismounted and quickly tied Glenn to a rail. She was on foot next to me, arms stretched wide, feet moving quickly to prevent any cows from turning back. Just as if we'd been working together for years, we covered each other's backs and before long, M-209 and the others were corralled.

We gave each other a big smile, not wanting to spoil the moment with words, or even a high-five. We mounted up and rode off together towards the chuck wagon.

Just Gramps and Me for Christmas

My big black horse, Spades, put his head down and pulled us up the steep incline, blasts of condensation coming from his nostrils in regular rhythm, just like the chuffing of a steam locomotive leaving the station. It was a good five below zero, with about 1 ½ feet of new, dry snow on the ground and no wind. Gramps led the way, riding his bay horse, Slim, and between the cold and the new snow, it was about as close to perfect as it ever gets.

We crossed a low ridge and ducked down a draw into Collins Creek, with gobs of snow occasionally spiraling up from the horses' hooves and landing in our laps, or hitting us on the arm or chest. The steepness of the descent made the horses dance in a way reminiscent of first tracks down a slow-moving powder run and the silence made it all surreal.

The beauty, the richness of the ride was soon interrupted by the deep and compelling voice of Granddad, calling me to address the purpose of our journey. "Whaddya think of that one?" or, "That one looks pretty good, huh," he said as we traveled up the creek bottom. The Christmas tree closest to home was as good as any, and with a whack of his hatchet and a toss of his lariat, we headed for home, Gramps dragging the tree behind his horse.

We were a two-man team, and once Grandpa got the tree situated in a living room corner, we climbed the narrow stairs to the third floor and dragged down the decorations. The yearly trees, as I've come to realize from looking at old photographs, were less than stellar, and to say they were ragged and non-symmetrical might even be kind. But, by God, we thought they were good, and as Gramps sat in his rocker, puffing on his pipe, hollering out suggestions here and there about what ornaments to put where, we thought it entirely possible that we might be on the verge of creating a masterpiece.

My grandfather lived alone in a very large, five bedroom house and Christmas Day was the one time of the year when all of the family got together. For Gramps and me, once we got the tree up, that was pretty much the end of Christmas between us, mostly I guess 'cause he and I operated alone all the time and having family around threw us off our game. Although, when I was eight, he gave me one of those great Schwinn bikes, a used one because no one knew how I was going to react.

One year I had a great urge to do something special for him, and why I did it, I'll never know, but with the help of my dad, made him a candle holder out of an old piece of wood I'd found along the way. I gave it to him early, hoping he'd put it on the library mantle with other Christmas stuff, and sure enough, there it was when the family showed up, complete with red candles, ready to be lit.

I figured we'd witness that unique tallow bearer every year after that, sort of a tradition like some of the other decorations, but Granddad died before he saw another Christmas. Several years later, we moved into his "big" house, and my mother surprised me by setting out my childish rendition of a candelabrum, which had been languishing in a ranch shed since Granddad's demise.

In the end, it's safe to say the candle holder became a tradition after all, as I've kept an eye on it since. Just today, I gathered in Gramps candle holder, rubbed the dust off and set it up on a living room table. It doesn't say nearly as much about Christmas as it incongruously does about Gramps and me, two lonesome ol' cowboys who loved livin', and whose destinies and memories will hopefully live on after my daughter inherits the damned thing.

Drifter's Sixth Sense

It's not really wind, but more like a steady breeze or a stiff drink, right in your face. Three days of unending snowfall and it might total eight inches, up here near timberline so desolate that the odds of seeing another person are nonexistent.

My business, as a Forest Service volunteer, is sparse; actually, there isn't any work at all of the kind I was expecting. The three-degree weather must have scared everyone off, and there's no need to be in such a location, but it's the aloneness, the quiet, which draws me higher, further away from the usual trails.

Billy, the black and white paint pack horse, is staying right with us, and in conditions like these, he's about the best friend I have, carrying enough to get me through an emergency stay in the wilderness - tent, sleeping bag, survival kit, axe and fuel. Little food, but how long would it take to be found, or to die hurt?

There's a responsibility riding on this, one that the horses are seemingly oblivious to, but being the joker that dragged them up here for such an adventure, it's up to me to get them safely out. It leans on me for a couple of miles, but then, there are other things to wonder about; where is that shortcut we found last fall, what's the temperature, when should we turn back to reach camp before dark?

Mounting up the next morning for another look around, my big horse Drifter has a surprise for me. As soon as my butt hits the saddle, he shifts into another gear, one relegated to his past, I thought, and his ears go straight out to the side, helicopter ears, Willie Fender always called them. Recognizing this, it's like sitting on a box of lit dynamite for in a second, maybe two, Drifter is going to go totally berserk. I can feel him gathering his muscles under him, a totally awesome sensation, and that's my clue to push my feet out, hunker down, and be ready for the explosion.

There's no disappointment on this day. One huge leap into the air and he tries to duck his head on the way down, but I'm ready for that, so he rears up, dancing backwards on his rear legs, until he slips into a deep rut and almost goes over backwards. "You SOB, don't mess with me like that," I'm thinking, but then he whips around to the right, still tensed tighter than a just-wound gyroscope, and I spy a shallow depression in the earth along the trail, pointing his head in that direction. Bucking down into the hole, he has a real fit, spinning both directions, and I stay right with him, for in the cold, the snow, and being all alone, I can't afford to get bucked off.

Suddenly he stops, 1400 pounds of quivering outlaw under me, and I quietly soothe him down. But for the first five or 6 miles, he's a total handful. Sure, you readers may have a lot of theories about this or that - a cold-backed horse that was jumped too soon, etc. Keep 'em, for I know how useless they would have been in this case.

Drifter's never come unglued except in that particular area, and it's not related to the weather. Sometimes, when I lie in my camp bunk at night, the almost inaudible hum of a vibration, way off in the forest or in an underground hideaway, keeps me half-awake. Maybe Drifter's inner self is somehow shaken by that unknown tremor.

Or, the ghost of a long-deceased Ute Indian chief's pony, shot dead by a rival for one of the chief's wives, gallops across the undulating landscape, visible only through the eyes of a horse. A soft breeze drifts through the spruce branches, carrying the nicker of a pony who'll never get home for the bad medicine that's trapped him, and Drifter takes up the cause.

You can't say otherwise unless you're a horse.

Keyboards and Clowns, a Time to Remember

The guy was a powerhouse on the piano, you could tell, big hands deftly pounding out original blues and boogie beats, but hanging back, not wanting to steal the show, not just yet, waiting for later, when he could really lay it down without offending anyone.

It was the 70s, a time period in Aspen's history that every party boy who was here claims not to remember, but they're mostly full of crap. I mean, if they're still alive. A lot of good things were happening in those days, especially on the music scene, and we got to be a part of it. Including a connection with the Rolling Stones.

Chris Winter, renowned European drummer, regular with the internationally-famous Hazy Osterwald Jet Set, decided to stick around after Osterwald's last whirlwind, worldwide tour, which auspiciously ended at the Red Onion. Burned-out and tired of traveling, Chris wanted nothing more than to be a western cowboy, to become a horseman, and he moved onto Buck Deane's thoroughbred farm in Carbondale to do just exactly that.

Being a neophyte piano player, I was more than thrilled to have Chris around, just for the pointers he could offer, and in addition to gigs with Buck (it was after the Buckin' Strings), we often struck out on our own, playing for beer and tips anywhere we could find a piano and an audience.

After a couple of years of living on the ranch, Chris fell in love and decided to get married. His chapter in the Roaring Fork Valley was nearing its end, but not before a huge wedding bash at the T Lazy 7, which was, if nothing else, a great jam session, composed of most of Aspen's prodigiously talented musicians.

Having established good rapport and being friends of the first order, Chris asked if I would play the piano at his wedding. That was a huge honor, as he had his choice of musicians and I took my job seriously. In addition to Wagner's "Wedding March," he requested, quite specifically, "Send in the Clowns," a song not only indicative of how Chris felt, but of our whole philosophy during those mind-warping years. "Isn't it queer, losing my timing this late in my career? And where are the clowns? There ought to be clowns. Don't bother, they're here."

If you know much about the Rolling Stones, you know that Ian Stewart has always been considered the "sixth Stone," a moniker richly deserved, for had it not been for Stu's big chin and clean-cut appearance, he would've died a full-on Stone. Or the Stones might have died without Stu's quiet, behind-the-scenes prodding to stay focused. Although not a live stage presence, most piano riffs on Stone's albums prior to 1985 were provided by Ian Stewart, and Stewart was a popular pianist in his own right, having toured Europe with various boogie and blues groups in the 70s and 80s.

Stewart and other notables had flown over from England for Chris' wedding and provided the cutting edge for a party that lasted a very long time. For me, it was a privilege to play with so many valley musicians, but sharing the stage with Ian Stewart that day has remained one of the highlights of my life. We traded off on Lou Deane's magnificent grand piano in the old lodge before fire claimed it all, with Stewart, ever the nice guy, asking me my method for learning this or that, and asking my advice from time to time. "Come on, Stu, you're the piano player."

We were working on a trip to visit Stu when word came that he'd suffered a fatal heart attack. We held our own wake, listening to him play the original "Rocket 88" on vinyl and in the end, we drunkenly serenaded his memory with "Where Are the Clowns?"

Killing a Parade

You might have noticed there was no Winterskol Parade again this past weekend. Some claim to know why, but the reasons they've thrown have been half-hearted bombs. Dumping a 58-year tradition should be treated with more than cavalier shrugs.

The first death blow might have been delivered years ago when public notice was made by the City of Aspen that all parades would henceforth require a permit. That's kind of like a dare, isn't it, and before the week ended, I'd loaded up a team of Belgians and headed to town. A buddy followed with the hay wagon and we reconnoitered by the Forest Service offices with some local musicians.

Headed east on Main, I glanced up just in time to see the mare's headstall come apart, the bit dangling to the side, clearly not in her mouth. Quick action was required to prevent a runaway, and I hollered "Whoa!" before the mare even realized the change in tack. A leather strap corrected the situation, and we headed down Main with renewed vigor, totally aware that dodging such a disaster made us impervious to the usual rules of human endeavor.

We popped some beers, dug the guitars out of their cases and began to pick up a crowd near the Hotel Jerome, lazy afternoon folks looking for something to do. A couple of bikini-clad ladies jumped up and put the moves on every street we covered. Another gal asked if we could meet her over by No Problem Bridge and took off on the run. By the time we circled around, she was coming up the hill with 3 or 4 goats.

Word was out and people began looking for us, waving and whistling as we clip-clopped by. The goats seemed to like the commotion better than anyone and soon were jumping on and off the hay wagon with gay abandon, bleating out a certain degree of excitement, tinged with confusion. My cavalier attitude toward the goats made their owner a little nervous and she wasn't sure if she'd done the right thing, but she stuck with us.

My cousin, Clyde Vagneur, known to be flamboyant, spotted our little shindig and jumped aboard in front of the Elks Club. He grabbed the lines, gave a big whistle to the team, and we thundered down the mall at a gallopolus gait. The cops soon arrived, but just to oversee the excitement, and it all stayed friendly.

With our entourage still in tow and the hay wagon loaded to capacity we headed west and home. Well-known town character, Baltimore Jim, was leading the procession, laying down a line of BS on the public address system connected to his Toyota Land Cruiser.

Baltimore Jim and I, who were occasionally used to meeting up either as the late-afternoon sun burnished the hallowed halls of the Hickory House or just inside the old Red Onion bar, usually had the same conversation. We were going to buy an elephant, mostly to ride to Snowmass Lake. We thought the trail users were getting too numerous and aggressive and needed to give up some right-of-way.

It's worthy to note that Baltimore and I both quit drinking, which has no doubt benefited the town because sober, that plan and others we concocted never seemed to materialize.

Baltimore was walking outside of his Toyota, yakking away on the end of a microphone cord probably twenty-five feet long, once-in-a-while steering the vehicle back on course when it began to wander to either side. I was a little put out that he was upstaging my Belgians with such nonsense, and with propitious timing, sidled up the passenger side of his still-moving Toyota and locked Baltimore out of his vehicle.

It started drifting toward Main Street Bakery, and the look on his face when he realized he'd been locked out was worth the whole prank. The thing with a guy like Baltimore though, is that he's prepared for any contingency, and the spare key he'd hidden probably saved us all a lot of explaining.

We made it home without anyone getting arrested or hurt.

Knocked Down But Hardly Out

It's that kind of place where people walk in under their own power without recognizing that they'll never leave via the same doors. Within minutes, I'm stripping down to my skin, physically and psychologically, pulling on some ankle-high, no-slip booties over my feet.

When I was five or six, I had my tonsils out in the old, three-story Pitkin County Hospital, and putting on a hospital gown for the first time since is a bit disquieting. How do things come our way, these things that supposedly only happen to other people?

It's certain, I'm a fast skier who's known for ripping up the bumps, an Aspen Mountain snob, and I'm also a dyed-in-the-wool cowboy who keeps a couple of high-spirited horses around for moving cattle through the high country. At 63, I'm not exactly a kid anymore, but neither am I convinced there's anything kids can do that I can't.

Which is to say, I've always gone at it hard, not afraid to lead with my head, and never fearful of the landing. My knees and hips are solid, skinny legs stronger than iron, and my mind disdainful of people who think "aging gracefully" has conceptual meaning.

If you've been following the story, you know I crashed on Silver Queen seven weeks ago, laid there in a paralyzed heap for several minutes and likely would have suffocated had it not been for the actions of my buddy Bob. Later that day, I left the emergency room with the knowledge that I had a couple of prolapsed cervical discs pressing into my spinal cord, not only as the direct result of that ski mountain fall, but probably others, as well, all exacerbated by non-symptomatic spinal degenerative arthritis and a narrowing of the spinal column. The degeneration is not uncommon in folks as they grow older and, no matter how tough you are, you can't limp your way out of stuff like that.

"You may not be afraid of much, big boy," but some things are beyond one's control and as such, inescapable. Had I not tried to self-destruct riding a pair of sticks, it might have just as easily come as a slip in the driveway washing my car, or stepping off the curb wrong, or falling backward on the slick talus of a favorite hiking trail. Any of these has the potential to cause catastrophic injury to those susceptible, particularly those of us in the over-50 crowd.

At last, I'm needled, gowned and "bootied" up, those elastic white anti-clot hose hugging my calves like thick second skin. I'm more curious than apprehensive for I've already given my trust over to this team, one of excellent reputation and there's nothing I can do about it anyway as surgery is my only option. Lizzie, my surgical "aide de camp," throws a couple of blankets fresh out of the dryer over me, and announces to no one in particular that "we're ready."

My daughter gives me a good-luck hug and off I go, a wild-driving nurse steering me down the loneliest hallway in the world, halting in front of "Operating Room 1." It's a good sign; we're getting the numbers right, anyway.

We enter the surgical theater and it's as if we landed in a different reality or something. There's dark blue cloth everywhere, the operating table glaringly apparent under a serious-looking, modernistic light. Everyone's face is covered and I quit looking at people, concentrating instead on what they say. "We're gonna give you something to relax you," says a voice to the left and I know it won't be long. Briefly, I recognize the friendly eyes behind the opaque face on my right and whatever's blasting through my face mask isn't oxygen, and I wonder . . .

In recovery, smiling doctors tell me my spinal cord was almost totally crushed, but the surgery has been successful. Lizzie squeezes my hand and asks how I feel, and my reply is a simple, "ecstatic."

If You Live Here You Might Know More . . .

Now that the election is over and the wounds have begun to heal, it's time to get back to the stuff of importance. What's important? Only you know for sure, but while we all twist and turn in suspense over various changes facing the town, we need to keep one thing in mind - the history of Aspen is what it's all built upon.

It's mostly common knowledge, the fact that each of us thinks Aspen was at its best about the time we each arrived, give or take a little. Aspen includes a staggering majority of people who came to town from somewhere else and who all seem to have an idea of what Aspen should be like indexed away somewhere with that first day or two they spent here. We all have a different baseline upon what we can compare "acceptable" change to, whether it is 1950, 1975, or 2005.

I'm always amused by those who say they've lived here 20 or 30 years, with the concomitant implication that their take on the town has more significance than someone who has lived here only five or 10 seasons. Having lived here over fifty years (whoa!), I wouldn't pretend to know too much about how things work. People occasionally say something to me, such as, "So far in your lifetime, you must have seen a lot of changes around here?" and I always reply with, "The skyline is still the same," or "The mountain skis about the same way it always has."

As the community changes, so does our philosophy of the town and the land surrounding us. "Let's re-zone agricultural land, let's build employee housing," or "let's 'revitalize' the downtown core." No matter when we arrive, and based upon our experience from the past, we have an inkling of how things should be run around here. Unfortunately, most of us have our feet mired in an urban past and can't get beyond how it was where we came from. That is the "totem" from which most of us get our references as to what is good or bad for this area, and without realizing it, our ego sometimes lets us forget that although the town is "new" to us, - we are actually the new ones.

I'm on a history kick because I see and hear so much misinformation from people who live here, people who are well-meaning, but who have little sense of history. When I studied international marketing, we came to learn that it takes two or three generations for those not used to machinery to learn how to operate it in a reasonable fashion. You can't take an adult from Uganda, or Brazil (or Aspen, for that matter), who has never seen a tractor, place him on it, and expect him to be a good operator of said tractor. This is true simply because there's a learning curve mandated by machinery that requires more than one natural life cycle. A man may begin to get proficient with the tractor, but he won't be nearly as good as his son, provided the son is exposed to the machinery during his growing years.

It's the same way with living around here. If you came from a city, no matter when, many of your ideas aren't really appropriate to Aspen or this area. That's not to say you don't have some good ideas - it's more to say that your children will have a better sense of the way the town operates than you do.

Some of the names of our prominent old-timers are mispronounced with regularity, street names are misspelled, on purpose it would seem, and very few, at least those in the public's eye, seem to care about any of it. And yet, we blindly pursue our dreams for the future of Aspen, taking stock in what baggage we bring with us from other places, and combine it with what we casually learn about Aspen over the time we live here. We're an odd bunch, if you ask me, but consistent

Going Solo Can Be Deadly

If you talk to my friend Margaret, she will tell you the thoughtful words from her father as she headed out on a hike through the high country alone. "The mountains have no favorites," he'd say.

The tragic death of lone cyclist Linda Sellers a couple of weeks ago in Cattle Creek has turned up the volume on whether one should ride, hike, soar, or whatever alone. It's doubtful her death will change anyone's behavior, but there has always been a cautioning chorus of those against doing outside activities alone.

My neighbor Jane confides that after the Sellers accident, a group of friends, knowing her penchant for biking alone, coerced her into a group ride, but she wasn't convinced. "It's nice to see my friends, but that's a social event, not a bicycle ride."

From the time I was about twelve, the old man would throw me, a couple of horses, a tent and enough groceries for a week into the Diamond T stock truck and deliver us somewhere into the mountains above Lenado. I'd pack salt for the cattle, fix fence, sleep a lot, learn to cook, and dream about girls, without ever seeing another person. One time, I got disgusted with the whole thing and was trailing out when I met my dad coming up to check on me. I expected an ass-chewing, but he seemed glad to see me.

During the summer, I keep my eye on about 200 head of cattle in the mountains above the Roaring Fork Valley. "You don't go up there alone, do you?" people will ask. "Well, hell yes, alone. If I waited for everyone that said they'd like to help, I'd still be back in 2008."

Truthfully, I've grown up operating alone, and haven't given much thought to whether it's healthy. The forest service started requesting I carry an official radio, for personal safety and potential emergencies. It gives me honest weather reports; I hear a lot of chatter from the sheriff's office and know when the summer and fall work crews head home each day. About the only thing I can't do with it is call out with any reliability. I've given in to a cell phone in deference to those who profess to worry about me.

Winter before last, I took a hard fall on Aspen Mountain, landed with my face buried in the packed snow, and found myself to be totally, but (thank God!) only temporarily, paralyzed. The one thing I could move was my chin, and I furiously cranked it around in a circle, trying to get airspace. Had I been alone, I might have suffocated, but my ski buddy, Bob Snyder, came to the rescue, creating a hole in the snow around my face. Do I still ski by myself most days? Of course.

The other day, my horses (Billy and Chief) and I were zigzagging down a steep, jack-oak covered hillside without the benefit of trail, keeping a sharp eye out for hidden drop-offs that could spell trouble. We'd had a long day, packing salt to distant ridges, and the horses were eager to get home; I was totally relaxed and encouraging them along. "This is how it happens," I briefly thought. In a heartbeat, disaster lays its nasty breath upon you and your world is forever changed. No one would have purposefully looked for me in that location, at least not for a while.

Pursuing activities alone in the mountains isn't necessarily macho or brave, dangerous or dumb. One weighs the risks, makes a decision and it becomes a personal preference. For that no one should be made to feel reckless, uncaring, or unreasoning.

In the end, and in the words of Dylan Thomas, those of us who travel alone will "not go gentle into that good night."

Leaving the Party Early

To tell the truth, I miss the drinking and the running around. When you're dialed into that kind of lifestyle, there isn't much thinking about what to do on weekends, or week nights, either. One thing's for sure, though, I never met a hangover I liked, and I'd rather crawl for miles down a wind-scoured ridge in 20-below-zero weather than face another hangover, but who wouldn't?

I grew up bumming a sip of beer from anyone who'd cooperate, which allowed me to cultivate a taste for hops and barley. About junior high school, I discovered my great-uncle Tom's stash of chokecherry wine in a bathroom closet, and learned to chug that "Dago Red" straight from the bottle, just like any number of "chug-a-holics" I'd seen in the movies.

In high school, and I'm not bragging but, as a sophomore, I set the-then Aspen High school high-jump record at a meet in Delta with a hangover, something I'm not really proud of, and then went on to place 2nd or 3rd at the state championships, abstemiously. The "sobering" thought to my young mind (if one can use such a word in an essay about drinking), was that it appeared possible to do anything, in any condition.

Going out drinking is similar to writing a column. Once you get started, you can't be totally certain of where you'll end up. A vow to have only a couple at the Tavern after work could likely find you at Maroon Lake in the moon glow at 3:00 A.M., skinny-dipping naked and shivering in the water as you clutch a woman whose name you'll never remember, if you ever knew it. Romantic? Give me a break.

There were signs along the way that I was losing the grip on my party-boy reputation. The unopened 12-packs of Budweiser I'd bring back from a weekend retreat at my cabin was one of the most troubling signs, but there were others. A broken heart used to be good reason to salve my pain with smooth sipping whiskey, but the last time I felt that kind of anguish, I screwed the lid down tight on the jug and haven't looked back, although I know precisely where it is.

I didn't exactly quit drinking. I just sort of walked away from it. Fortunately, too, I reckon. There was no hitting bottom, no epiphany of any significance, no dark depressions or stupid acts of potentially life-ending proportions. There were all of those things, to be sure, but they weren't the motivation behind my drinking cessation. At least not that I can remember.

I quit smoking about ten years ago, and as much as I loved sucking up nicotine, I knew full-well if I ever found myself in a smoke-filled bar with too much whiskey in my belly, the demon-driven quest for oral gratification would overtake my mind and I'd be back to square one. As much as I liked to drink, I hated smoking even more, so I enthusiastically gave up the mind-altering alcohol.

Really, now that I've thought about it, I don't miss the drinking a damned bit, although it certainly can be beneficial in helping to lubricate the sometimes awkward and bashful wheels of a fledgling romance. But then, too much lube can spoil the intricacies of almost any assignation; and besides, any woman who would curl up with me is likely more articulate than I could ever hope to manage, so why would I want to muck up a good conversation with the ramblings of a slurred and besotted brain?

A Grandfather's Influence

There comes a time in every man's life when he must break the bond with his mother and amend with his father the days he let his mother hide him behind her skirts. The son must do this to be able to tell his father he loves him. But how does the transition take place between a boy and his grandfather? It is more subtle, I surmise, but perhaps more powerful.

The gruff voice was persistent as it called out my name, and I was wishing it would go away and let me sleep, when suddenly I realized it was my grandfather calling. Fully awake at this reckoning, I figured it must mean trouble, as he usually only hollered at me when he suspected I had messed something up.

Peering out of my bedroom window into a bright, warm morning in early June, I saw the big bear of a man, sitting astride his horse, motioning me to come on outside. It's a picture forever etched in my mind: He sat there under a wide-brimmed, off-white straw cowboy hat, brim laid out flat, covering gray hair, bushy eyebrows, and shadowing a ruggedly handsome face. He wore a gray work shirt, buttoned up through the very top button, with the sleeves rolled down and buttoned. His left hand held the reins, right hand pushed against the swells, and both hands were covered in leather gloves. He had on an almost new pair of Levi's and his old standbys, a pair of lace-up leather work boots. There he was, sitting patiently in the middle of the Woody Creek road, scaring the hell out of me.

We went on the first of countless rides that day in the summer of my sixth year, up Collins Creek or through Kobey Park, moving cows or chasing wild horses high on Vagneur Mountain. It became a way of life for me and carried him through the rest of his. I felt threatened and not too pleased about it all in the beginning, but by trying to emulate him, mostly in silence, I quickly learned how to hold my own with Ben Vagneur, the "big boss" in our neighborhood and began to look forward to our daily convolutions through the mountains above our ranch.

It wasn't all the best of times with us, and I can honestly say I learned some creative ways to string cuss words together, some of them directed at me or my sometimes clumsy attempts to close gates, rope cows, tie knots or ride unruly horses. But when his temper had reached a high point and I thought he might club me with the nearest prop, only once did I fail to see his face soften, the eyes look away, followed by the always surprisingly gentle nudge to "let's try it again."

He taught me how to saddle a horse and get on by myself, even though I could barely lift the saddle. As the years went by, his house became our headquarters and we'd pack a lunch together before hitting the trail. Rarely, we'd split a beer, or for more excitement, we'd fire up his green and white Oldsmobile and head for town where we'd have lemonade with the ladies or play pool at the Elks Club.

Some years, we would ride our horses up Collins Creek in fresh snow to find a Christmas tree for the annual family gathering at his place, the only day each year the house didn't seem so lonely. He and I would put the ornaments on, if you can believe old pictures, some of the scraggliest trees ever used for such a purpose.

In his 67th year (my eleventh), we took our last ride together in the cool, golden breezes of September. He never rode again and by late winter, death's merciless claw, aided by an insidious and incurable disease, stilled his strong heart. For me, it was a blow as deep as a human can feel, and it took a majority of my journey through this life to finally accept the loss of my first real mentor, good ol' Gramps.

Life's Pageant

The horses snuffled between themselves as we topped the steep rise, streaks of sweat glistening along massive shoulders and their ever-diligent ears snapped forward, alerting my partner to the ramshackle group of buildings in the distance.

My grandfather bought this place back in the days when ranching could still make a buck, and one of my earliest memories goes back to a picnic out the back door, a gathering hosted by the hired hand and his family who took up residence there before we abandoned the buildings.

My partner rolled up to the decrepit, barely discernible corrals at a gallop, flopping the reins over an imaginary rail as her horse slid to a stop, and without missing a beat, she quickly tiptoed up the outside stairs leading to the loft of the old farmstead, now visible through a large hole in the roof. A dresser with drawers intact and an opened suitcase, its contents strewn about, had caught her attention.

I stayed on my horse, which put me at about eye level with her as she maneuvered around the cramped space on her hands and knees, looking through the remnants of someone else's life. It wasn't our first ride together, and as she crawled over to talk about her findings, there was something about the way she let the top of her loosely buttoned shirt fall open that indicated we might be on a mission of long-awaited physical consummation. A tiny curl of delicate hair clung to the dampness of her neck, and I was transfixed.

As we lay in the afterglow, tall grass around us, her head easy upon my chest, the reckoning settled in. For a man who's trifled away the better part of his life, it's safe to say that women have come and gone, and the biggest risks lie in the relaxed conversation after sex.

"We could buy this place," she says. "It'd take a lot of work, but we could fix it up, look out the windows and watch the horses and cows graze. It'd be so great, wouldn't it?"

"Well, hell yes it would," I attempt, trying to sound enthusiastic but imagining myself in a relationship like that with this much younger woman. Geezus, if I was more her age, maybe, but I've tried that, too, and I don't think my heart, or my head, could take it, not again.

In a way, it's humorous when you begin to pick up after an interlude like that, the way it all returns to the beginning in a different fashion than how it all came apart. Horses that seemed content to munch on succulent grass and who barely received a thought suddenly become objects of intense worry. "Where are the horses? We shoulda tied 'em up."

Tight jeans that got turned inside out on the way off are now difficult to straighten it seems, and tall cowboy boots, notoriously difficult to remove but somehow miraculously slipped off in the heat of passion, now require strength and determination to get back on.

We hug, we giggle, but the mood has changed and my mind inescapably wanders to horses of yesteryear, standing in the now-almost-invisible barn, waiting to be harnessed for their role in life's pageant, pulling two abreast. Almost inseparable, do they feel secure strapped to a load they cannot see, courageously laying their hearts out for the world to witness, giving it their all? Is that what grounds them in an existence they'd never choose, gives solace to their very vitality?

Sometimes, when you know the answer it's foolish to ask the question, but I stumble ahead anyway. "Wanna go riding tomorrow? Today was good."

"Are you crazy," she asks? "I gotta work."

Listen For Life's Real Sounds

Clouds knock the muffled, rolling thunder around, similar to the clacking of a soft break on an after-midnight pool table, or the slow motion rattle of bowling pins as they bounce without energy after a gentle roll of the ball. The ground is already wet and the sky grim, but the deliberate thunder gives me feelings of great comfort.

Sometimes, along a narrow, hidden trail, you can tell the rain is coming solely from the sound as it approaches. The drops hammer the ground, creating a hum of natural activity, sending mud and water back toward the sky, creating the wonderment of how many droplets they must explode into as they kamikaze themselves against the needles of a pine forest. The intensity never seems to sustain itself for long, and soon the delicate roar softens to a slow drip.

Thoughts come and go, and suddenly I'm back in a little mountain cabin, nestled in warm covers with the woman of my dreams in the middle of a dark day, listening to the thunder rock around the black sky and feeling cozy and supercharged by our energy. Soon, rain will pound the tin roof, again, and we'll close the minuscule gap between us, one more time.

Her breathing intensifies, eventually caught up in the deeper, more powerful and guttural but absolutely feminine expression of an uncontrollable release, deep within the physical. Such extremely pleasurable and delightful sounds cannot be mimicked in any other fashion than that which brings them forth and hasten me to my own expressions of ultimate pleasure, sounds of the same indication.

On a clear day, the wild birds sing; I don't mean the ones around our houses, the black-billed magpies, swallows and such. I'm writing of the vesper sparrows, hawks and others that are truly wild and grace the forest with the cry of their songs, the birds I try to share the sky with when my heart is broken, the ones who can brazenly wake you in the morning with their enthusiasm for the coming day, but who, at the end of the same day, slowly sign off one by one, species by species, until at last there is silence. Your eyes drop and your pulse slows, until the roosting birds feel your presence in their nocturnal rest.

If you ride horses, or hike with friends, there is a certain, strangely human catharsis in knowing that you heard the elk bugle before your horse or the other hikers. Or maybe you just heard the surprised snort as some unseen wild creature zeroed in on your footfall first and paused for that wondrous microsecond to assess the danger before crashing through the underbrush.

An experienced golfer knows by the sound whether it's a good ball long before his eye can track the trajectory and I'm sure I'd miss the almost-silent glissading hiss my skis make, edge against bottomless powder, each time we snake through a good stash.

Remember the days of closeness, sharing and your last true romance? Your lady friend left you alongside the road of life and you wonder why. Something bothers you, but what is it? Had you listened, you would have noticed that somewhere along the way, the spontaneous laughter you used to share so precisely on beat, had become, from her side, a second too late to matter.

What I'm distinctly saying is, put the iPod or MP3 (or motorized toys) back on the upper shelf once-in-a-while and listen to the honest and non-reproducible sounds of the world around you. You may learn a little more about the universe, yourself, or perhaps someone else.

Long Ups, Epic Downs

First there was the boat tow, and then around 1947 the Aspen Ski Corp. (the "p" on Corp. was always pronounced if you were a "local") began operation of the "Tuna Trolley," the combination of lift numbers 1 & 2, that started near the top of Aspen Street and ended at the summit of Aspen Mountain, near the Sundeck. Those two single lifts carried everything to the top - not just people - including restaurant supplies, lift parts, booze and an occasional dog. It was quite a production that, at the very least, was highly effective.

Of course, there was the T-Bar on Little Nell and then along came Lift #3 (Ajax Express) which changed the way everyone skied the mountain. Without the existence of today's modern contrivances, there was nothing to miss, nothing to bemoan, 'cause it didn't exist. We took what we had and made the most of it.

Ruthie's Road got a lot more use in those days (no #6, euphemistically called FIS, now) and we planned our descent with excruciating care, knowing it was a long ride back up the mountain. We skied each run as an adventure to last - had to or we'd have spent our lives riding single chairs, going back up for one more run. Some days we skied nothing but the Ruthie's side, from Midway (top of 6) down.

Elevator Shaft in Silver Queen was (is) a perennial favorite, not just for the speed, but for the close calls it involved. We'd line up at the top, and watch each other shoot the Shaft, learning from those in front of us just how ugly and bumpy the transition was that day. Wrecks weren't very common, but when they occurred, a certain enhanced meaning of "yard sale" became evident.

Next, it was easy to cut around the corner to the FIS Slalom Hill and line up on the eastern edge of Lazy 8 Gully, watching each other catch air off the western side of Lazy 8 as we came screaming up and out of the gully. Foibles in individual style were more readily exposed at this spot and sometimes Lower Magnifico could look like a landfill in transition from the scattered equipment. Launching a hundred feet in the air wasn't uncommon and the mogul field in the landing area was tough to tread. I bruised a kidney there one year in a spectacular fall, and that and the attendant broken ribs kept me off the hill for about a month while I got my innards back together.

We skied bumps differently in those days, using them as a field of challenges rather than as something to "artistically" manipulate. Watching Melvin Hoagland, legs gyrating as pistons might in a red-lined engine, taught me how to tuck Snow Bowl with huge moguls in place. Grooming report, you say? Yeah, once mid-winter, with shovels, maybe. You had to be really loose, keep a wide stance, and know in your heart that you damned-well could do it.

One year, my dad worked for the Ski Corp. at the bottom of old Lift #2, and the advantages to a kid my size were immense. I was in the 6th or 7th grade and two or three days a week, I'd go up the mountain with him to Midway and then rip it down Ruthie's, just in time for school to start. Red Rowland eventually caught on to our game and I was unceremoniously forbidden to have so much fun. Something about safety, he said. Other days, though, I'd wait for my dad to get off work and ski down with him after most everyone else had gone home.

Anyway, the next time you get in the gondola, think about the old, relaxed way to the top and remember that back in those days, we called a single chair on the Tuna Trolley a "bucket," just as we call a gondola cabin today a "bucket."

Magic in the West End

My friend Margaret recently bought a house in the West End. That's not terribly remarkable if you consider how many houses reside there, but there is something remarkable about the West End.

Growing up at my grandmother's house in that vicinity (at least when my parents let me off the ranch) has left indelible memories, the kind of childhood stuff we all cherish. But there is more to the West End than that, although if it wasn't so special, the memories wouldn't be, either.

I've written columns about that area, maybe more than I can remember, but there are still things left unsaid, things that came mostly after childhood.

My "aunt" Geri Vagneur, during her life of building, remodeling and living in West End homes, rented the Marquand Studio on the banks of Hallam Lake for a couple of years. A more peaceful setting could not be found, then or today, and I was lucky enough to be invited to her special wine tastings. Geri loved wine, loved people more and by propitious circumstance, had a grand piano in her living room, its keys about my size.

Robert Langenkamp (RIP) attended all of those parties and became a friend. Robert's brother, Arthur, was the gregarious founder of Arthur's Restaurant, who at one point took to bragging that business improved noticeably when he took down his sign out front. Freddie Fisher publicly castigated him for such outlandish thinking, claiming it was the ad Arthur ran in the Aspen Illustrated News that prompted such a fattening of the purse.

Robert was cut of a different cloth, quiet and reserved, and on slow afternoons I'd make a pass through the West End, knowing I might see Robert (never "Bob") out for a walk. I'd park and stroll with him a while, the two of us engaged in deep philosophical discussions, including the story of the periphery of Robert's life and how grand it was to live in Aspen. He'd shyly pull a candy from his pocket, asking if I'd "like a Werther's," as if there was no greater gift.

For a couple years, my high school friend Bronco Tunnard (that was his real name), lived in the house my friend just bought. Bronco came to town around our sophomore or junior year, played football, and about the time he finally made friends and got settled in, his family left, taking Bronco away.

A few years later, Bronco came back as the proprietor of the Pomegranate Stables, west of town. He rented horses out, wrote songs and played a mean guitar. We talked a couple of times, but his short return to town ended before we ever really got caught up again.

The West End quiet is a bit stifling, unless you go by the park where two or three people might be having a lunchtime conversation. Walking these streets again after a long respite, I see my faded tread everywhere I look; going to piano lessons, playing cowboys and Indians, walking girls home from school, running from cops, playing Mah Jongg in a third-floor enclave above a knight in shining armor, hoofing it to the music tent or the Aspen Institute, and pounding on that grand piano in Geri's various living rooms.

Like everywhere else, it's a neighborhood, but one that perchance hearkens back to Aspen's roots more than any other. Neighbors leave welcoming gifts and notes on your porch and come around to see who you are. They live passionate lives and peacefully die in homes they've loved for years.

To paraphrase my friend Lee Duncan, it's impossible to describe the enchantment of living in Aspen to those who have not experienced it. To me, the West End is the icing on the magic.

Magical Affairs, Enduring Marriages

It was one of those parties that come around very seldom. A lifetime (and I mean a long lifetime) of friends invited for a birthday party, and as it always is, prolific lives create large circles of friends that don't always know each other. But, for the most part (and like a group of valley bandits), we'd all heard about each other so conversations were easy to start, or finish.

Anyway, I opted for the secluded back deck to enjoy my dinner, and soon found myself joined by a most articulate and entertaining woman, one who knew a lot about cowboys and who could easily have been a university professor had she not chosen the Roaring Fork Valley for her home.

With a modicum of history and rapport established, she offered that, "My husband and one of your cousins had the most wonderful love affair imaginable. It was almost magical." As I waited silently for the rest of the story, she abruptly finished with a long exhalation, "Of course, they never consummated it." She was certain about that.

Her words resonated, as I recalled a similar situation in my own past. In the 60s, my college days, a graduate music student from a neighboring pod of academia had been granted the task of getting the University of Colorado symphonic orchestra into shape for a spring concert. A friend of mine was a soloist in the musical society, so I stopped in from time to time to get an inside view of the entire process. Thus it was that this particular guest conductor, having been introduced to me earlier (and supposing I had no tangible assets with which to further his career), requested that I take his bored spouse out of the constrained conservatory and show her around campus.

The wife, a recently graduated college cheerleader, had a rather delectable look about her and it was with some enthusiasm that I began my job as a diversionary device. She was undeniably in love with her talented husband, but felt a terrible neglect due to his tedious schedule, and could expound for hours on her feelings and desires, hopes and dreams. Almost immediately, we fell into an easy alliance that moved slowly, albeit effortlessly, from meeting in the nearby coffee shop, to lying in the campus grass, to the eventual day we nervously opened the door to my basement apartment.

When it was all said and done, we knew each other in the most intimate of ways, both physically and mentally, but in the words of another, never "consummated" the relationship, at least not in the strict Biblical sense. For reasons that seemed indisputable, she wished to retain some allegiance to her matrimonial commitment, and that was her way of accomplishing it. The ultimate physical act between us would have created trauma in her marriage, but our otherwise sensuous wanderings, both delicate and furious, apparently did not.

I suppose you could call it an affair, and although it definitely bordered on "magic," it wasn't exactly "wonderful." Still young, we learned much from each other that we might not have in any other kind of affaire d'amour.

In the end, my recent dinner companion's marriage remained intact, as it deservedly should have. The effects of my own dalliance (tragic or otherwise) would have been impossible to calculate, since I never saw the girl again, had it not been for the continued friendship of the symphony soloist. The husband, that whiz kid with virtuoso genius flowing through his veins, eventually became relatively well-known on the dinner theater circuit, and a 1990s photo shows his still-striking wife, my illicit lover of a spring semester, smiling at his side.

The Meeker Incident

A clear and bright, warm fall day, it was not the type of weather that spells tragedy, but the galloping hoof beats of two different groups, miles apart, were bringing down the last curtain on a centuries-old way of life in Colorado. Clearly, something of that magnitude doesn't happen in one day, but it's usually the blowup of long-festering incompatibility on the last day that tells the story.

North of the Milk River, near Craig, a contingent of 150 U.S. Cavalry, led by Civil War veteran Major Tipton Thornburgh thundered casually toward the White River Indian Reserve, trying not to get too far ahead of its supply train. Thornburgh had been summoned by a distraught Nathan Meeker, who feared for his safety after an intense argument with Ute leaders about the plowing of their horse pasture.

Coming up from the south, with a well-concealed desperation in their chests, rode 4 or 5 Ute Indians led by Nicaagat ("one with earring"), wondering what business the troops had in coming toward their land. Thornburgh promised Nicaagt that he would enter the reservation with only 4 or 5 of his officers, leaving the soldiers behind. After all, the latest treaty with the government promised that no cavalry troops could enter Ute lands.

Two disparate views of the world, hurtling toward disaster, were attempting to communicate without any understanding of the other's life philosophy. In the middle sat seemingly manic-depressive White River agent Nathan Meeker. The Utes had lived with absolute independence for centuries and could not comprehend a religion-based agrarian society or its hierarchy of intervention. Utes feared that giving up their hunting culture would mean a loss of their natural identity. Typical of the western settler's view of the time was the slogan, "The only good Ute is a dead Ute."

Indian agent Nathan C. Meeker, naively trying to enforce his own convoluted philosophy of socialism, religion and pastoralism upon the Utes found his influence to be sorely lacking. Meeker resorted to lies and the withholding of provisions in an attempt to coerce the Utes into compliance and finally concluded his only chance of gaining their conformance was to destroy their allegiance to their horses. He made bizarre threats, claiming that if the Utes didn't start farming, the government would take away their land or would put them in chains and send them to Oklahoma. "Not according to the treaty," the Utes replied, knowing in their hearts that Meeker lied.

Nicaagat knew well the stories of the 1864 Sand Creek Massacre during which Colonel John Chivington and 700 men, without provocation, attacked an already-surrendered village of Southern Cheyenne and Arapahos, killing around 200 defenseless women and children. Was Thornburgh's march signaling a repeat? On the way home, Nicaagt stopped at the trading post in Craig and bought 10,000 rounds of ammunition.

The next day, September 29, 1879, Thornburgh and his entire troop erringly lumbered across the Milk River into Ute lands, still unsure of what they might accomplish. Nicaagt and other Utes were out in force, unsure themselves what to expect and the two sides came to a standoff, with the Utes on a rim above the soldiers, exposed on the valley floor.

In the usual way, and no one can say who, someone fired a shot and the battle was on. Given their poor position, Thornburgh's troops were immediately pinned down, and remained so for the length of a week. Thornburgh was killed at the outset as were about 15 of his men. Ute casualties remain unknown.

Meanwhile, at the agency, a few other Utes decided it was time Meeker pay for his lies and particularly his egregious error of plowing up the Ute's race track and horse pasture. To this end, he was shot, along with ten of his employees, the finale being a stake driven through his mouth, pinning his head to the ground. This symbolic act was to guarantee Meeker could not tell lies in the next world.

There's more, lots more, but in the end, enough resentment toward the Utes surfaced that their land was taken from them and they were shuffled off to an already crowded reservation in eastern

Utah. Sadly, our understanding of each other's philosophy is about as unintelligible today as it was in 1879.

Missing an Aspen Icon

Harvey T. Carter died last week. If you didn't know him, you missed a true Aspen icon. This isn't the definitive obituary of Harvey, likely no one has that capability, but for those of us who knew him, the memory is strong.

He was a legendary climber, founded Climbing Magazine in 1970 and had a string of first-ascents that is impossible for many to fathom today. I never climbed a step with him, although he invited me on a trip or two around the neighborhood. We were skiers, Harvey and me, ski patrolmen on the world's finest mountain and there was a time I hung close, hoping a bit of the legend would rub my way, a foolish thought of youth.

Few could tell you what the "T" stood for in his middle name because most assumed that portion of his moniker to be "Balls." On Aspen Mountain, there wasn't much Harvey would go around and if the term had been invented, he might have been called an "extreme skier." There's the celebrated big cliff jump to the skier's left of Kristi, the tight landing now grown in and dangerously congested compared to the days when Harvey negotiated its charms. If that's too much for you, launch off of "Harvey's Rock," to the skier's right of Blazing Star (what kind of a name is that?). A homemade sign is still stuck up in a nearby tree, announcing the original designation. Most skiers are afraid of Harvey's Rock; it takes off sooner than it should and its landing is very close to the trees. When Harvey hucked it, there were trees on both sides of the run out. Few dared call him "Balls," and in the sheaves of ski patrol documentation that accompanies reality, he's generally listed as "HTC."

Like a good stuntman, Harvey weighed the risks, calculated his chances and then pulled out all the stops. If you visit the Mikey Houser shrine at the top of the Short Snort cliffs, take a peek down towards Spar on a good powder day and pick your line. That's how Harvey did it, but if you miss the landing, your hip joints will be up in your armpits by the time you remember where you are.

The tough rescues seemed to draw Harvey and me together and we pulled off more than a few. The ugly wrecks seem to happen in the most mundane of places, many times on the flats, but once-in-a-while you find one in an unsuspected place. Maybe best remembered is the dislocated shoulder victim we found near the top of Elevator Shaft, with a ski stuck between his legs to keep him from sliding down the pitch, his buddy hanging on to his waist for additional support. Harvey truly liked to muscle a one-man sled, but usually wanted me to help on the steeps. We made a good team on the Face of Bell, Hanging Tree, the Ridge of Bell. And Elevator Shaft.

Harvey was fueled by a fifty-year-old dream of developing a ski area on the west side of Pikes Peak, a life's work that consumed him in every way imaginable. During the Aspen Mountain ski patrol strike in the early 70s, Harvey spent an entire winter on his Pikes Peak property, a total hermit, a perimeter man if there ever was one. In 2008, he finally found a sponsor willing to back him, just before the economy went south. Perhaps, just the fact that he found an enthusiastic investor made the dream happen, at least in his mind.

Near the end, Harvey divided his life up into four segments, in his own words: "I got a college degree, which I figured I had to do: I got a job on the best ski patrol in the world, that was lucky: I got the most first ascents in the world, that was stupid: and if I get this done (ski area developed), it's the last thing I'm doing."

Unfortunately, Harvey died before he got it all done, but not because he didn't give it all he had. The man, and his life, lives on in the hearts of those still here.

Rescue in the Mountains

"This is 9-1-1. What is your emergency?" And thus, the Pandora's Box of an unknown journey is opened. "I'm in Hay Park, and my buddy is down with a definite shoulder injury and a possible closed-head injury." Trying to be helpful, I gave up our names when asked and further tried to define our position, it being obvious the dispatcher had no idea where Hay Park was. When she said such a location was not on her map, inferring I might be incorrect, I gave her a calm, "I hate to tell you, but it's near the base of Mount Sopris. I could climb the son-of-a-bitch from here." With that, she rang me through to a sheriff's deputy. Now, by God, we'll get something done.

As an EMT, I used to work with Mountain Rescue Aspen and have participated in more than a few deliverances from the brink. It was always easy to take the call requesting my services, and the answer was most always in the affirmative. There's a certain excitement in figuring out the logistics of getting something done, especially when time is of the essence and the rewards for helping someone in need are great, just in personal satisfaction alone. For me, the thought process paralleled the Golden Rule - provide the assistance as though you were the one in need. But now the tables were turned and I was given a new perspective.

It's the little things that can screw up an operation of the most meticulous kind, things you might never think of, such as having a charged-up cell phone in your possession. Cell phone service is sporadic in the mountains, and I had to travel all over hell to finally get a signal. Then, and I'm sure there are good reasons for this, the sheriff's office kept a leash on me. The deputy said, "Check back in twenty minutes," to which I replied, "No, I'm not gonna do that. My friend is seriously hurt and I'm going back to check on him." We got all that worked out, but it takes an inordinate amount of time on the phone, provided you have one, so keep your battery charged. If you're like me and don't use a map, carry one anyway, just to avoid arguments with the dispatcher.

For the last time, I checked in with my injured friend, which mostly involved saying I had to leave once again to intersect with the expected arrival of the first responder team, about a mile distant. There's no more bullshit now - the rain must fall as it will, bringing hail if it wishes, and we can't worry about it for I'm stuck in one place waiting for rescuers and my buddy in another, barely able to move, left to his own devices to protect himself.

The rescuers are expected to appear from the west, but briefly I hear faint engine noises from the north. "Might be a plane," I think, wondering who would be flying in such low visibility. But wait, there's an old jeep road in that direction; oh yeah, that's a rescue team who took a shortcut to get here. My horse starts acting up at the vision of an all-terrain vehicle and I don't care, for my smile's a wide one. The boots on the ground have arrived. Damned right, these folks know what they're doing. Jody Anthes and David Brown from Western Eagle County Search and Rescue are first on the scene, followed shortly by the Mountain Rescue medical team. I tell 'em where we need to go and they nod with the knowledge of years of experience, and we're off.

I've been seriously traveling the mountains around Aspen/Basalt for at least fifty-five years, and I've never called for help before. It's a sweet feeling to know there are Mountain Rescue/WESAR personnel who will quickly and competently come to your aid, with a smile on their faces. We should all be wise enough to send them a generous donation.

Corral Full of Renegades

If you have to think about it much, you might not be one, but even so, those who have the affliction recognize it with a certain sense of pride. "Goddamn right I'm a cowboy, 'til I die." At least that's what an old boy in the historic Fryingpan Inn told me a few years back. He was right.

If you live in this country, being a cowboy also means being a farmer and unlike some of the flatland boys, we never took umbrage at doing a few farm chores, like plowing, sowing oats (wild ones, too), harrowing fields or spreading fertilizer. It all goes with ranching territory and around this valley there never was what one would call a specialist, a guy who was only a "cowboy." But, the cowboying is what keeps most of us in the game.

When we were kids, riding rough stock was the draw, the meaner the better, although most of 'em weren't too bad. Riding out the string in early spring was a good warm-up for summer, throwing saddles on broncs that didn't much cotton to the idea of going back to work after a long winter off.

There's something about the smell of a horse that is relaxing, but mystifying. If you look long enough into a horse's eye, you can see eternity, and if you take the time to hug a horse's neck and inhale his smell, you can be one with him, at least for a little while. Tough old cowhands facing rambunctious colts use this as a survival tool – a brute thinking about unloading you has a different aroma.

It's one of those things I maybe never got over, riding the rough bunch, and I might never have been that good at it, but I learned that I seldom mind an honest SOB who flat out likes to raise hell, but a dishonest horse, one that'll fall over on you, or rear over backwards and try to hurt you has no future in my herd. Another thing I learned is that it's much easier to communicate with a horse than argue with one. An ounce of anticipation usually prevents a pound of craziness. Such personal predilections have brought some unusual horses my way, some damned good horses actually, those that respectable horsemen just couldn't trust but wanted to give one more chance to before they shot 'em or sent them to the killers.

My buddy Bob, who spent a summer or two breaking colts, calls my corral "dysfunction junction," saying there isn't a horse in there who "hasn't killed or maimed other people." No one in the know wants any part of my equine collection. At one of last spring's brandings, I offered my paint, Billy, to a damned good horsewoman as a rope horse, 'cause hers had turned up lame. "Now, why would I want to do that," she said with a smile, just before Billy decided to buck his way through the branding fires and show his stuff. He caught me shooting the bull instead of paying attention. So, yeah, Billy's a little excitable, but there isn't a bovine alive that can out-maneuver him when he's on his game.

Horses have a sixth sense that we humans don't always grasp. They know when we're vulnerable, know when we don't "get it," and in the interest of fairness, they almost always give us a clue as to what they're thinking. They're pretty honest, really, but I've known a couple that seemed to get genuine pleasure out of making life downright miserable for their riders. I sold one of them to a rodeo string and the last I heard, no one had been able to get a qualified ride on him. Kind of makes me like him a little better.

It's hard to talk about cowboys without getting lost in the world of horses, and if you're still with me, that's apparently what happened here. Besides, I know a lot more about horses than I do cowboys.

Travels with Topper and Drifter

It was daylight, but before the sun had risen, and we bobbed along, my horse Drifter and me, following Topper up the trail. The climb was steep, the air a delicious September cold, and somewhere deep inside, a smile was keeping me warm.

Topper reached the top of the pitch before we did, jumping high in the air to clear a sagebrush bush, just in time to catch the brilliant flash of the sun topping the ridge. Until then, he appeared to be just another dog, slogging up a seldom used cow path, but in that instant, he was transformed into a dial of beauty, sun glistening off his wet chest, droplets of dew reflected in the halo of sunlight surrounding him, his red tongue out to one side, eyes focused with intent.

Drifter picked his head up for a moment as if to say, "Yeah," and that one instance cemented the three of us together like we hadn't been earlier.

It's an undeniable thing about good working dogs or horses; they'll give you all they have, with total honesty, and if you ask for more, you'll get it. It comes naturally, from their hearts, an irrefutable thread of instinct that lets us humans in just long enough to offer a bit of coaching here and there.

Topper and I talk to each other most of the day without verbalizing very much of it. He watches me closer than a virgin's chaperone after midnight and knows, from experience and almost before I do, what his next move is going to be. It's a curious thing but Drifter, who doesn't let me in for much unless we're in the heat of battle with the cows, keeps a sharp eye on Topper.

Animals have a way of communicating that those of us with linguistic capabilities have mostly forgotten but could sorely use. Only in our world of words can we see the husband, frozen in angst as he watches his marriage self-destruct, waiting for the door to slam on everything in the world he loves, including his only child. A thousand thoughts race through his head as he struggles desperately to open his heart, but he can't think of the words. Stoically, he seals his fate.

Clearly, I remember the names; Stardust, Spades, Snicker, Thunderbird, Wishy, Kiowa, Willie, Donald, Billy and Drifter, and a slew more; horses who have carried me all over these mountains with little complaint, galloping after cows across hillsides so steep a fall might mean serious injury or death, giving it their all without miscue.

Growling, ankle-biting monsters to a herd of cattle, good dogs make life much more enjoyable for cowboys trailing a herd through the mountains and save a horse and cowboy a lot of work. Names like Wolf, Tag, Freckles, Blue, Calvin, Tipper and Topper roll off my tongue, all border collies or Aussie heelers, dogs all gone but Topper, dogs to always be remembered for their contributions to the cause.

In the early-morning chill before a big spring cattle drive or fall roundup, the horses snort and stomp with anticipation, the dogs run back-and-forth sniffing and wagging while the riders, fingering their reins, laugh too easily and anxiously await the cue to move out.

The boss "clucks" his mount out the gate and suddenly it's all business. The horses walk easy and with purpose; the dogs line out behind their human partners, knowing which horse and which rider they need to listen to, and from any perspective, it's an interrelated group who enjoys what they do, a page taken straight out of history books worn thin by centuries of loving use.

There are those who say that dogs and horses don't have souls, that they're just animals, and if that's really true, then I'd like to volunteer mine to those creatures I have experienced life with, for God knows, they truly deserve it.

261

W/J Rodeo

The arena has been gone for years and there's not a smidgen of rotten bleacher left nor any stray strands of horsetail stuck on a bent nail to remind us of the raucous days of the W/J Rodeo.

Two or three thousand people used to show up every year for the annual event and folks forever went on about how, "The whole town shows up," and they were at least half right. The Aspen Lions Club sponsored the two-day extravaganza, putting on a big community barbeque, as well. Incredible hands-on backup for the actual production was provided by the Aspen Roping Club and more than once the participating cowboys and cowgirls voted the W/J, "Best Rodeo in Colorado."

The first year was an inauspicious beginning, a shot in the dark it seemed, but the seed (or should I say germ) had been planted. From our ranch in Woody Creek, my buddy Jim Bixler and I would ride our horses over there 2 or 3 evenings a week, bucking out Wink Jaffee's prized steers and bulls until dark. Soon, Jaffee admired the enthusiasm of our shenanigans and posed the question, "If I held a rodeo here, would you guys ride in it?" We thought it was about us, so large were our egos.

Every year, the grandstands were expanded, the parking became tighter, and the crowd got more frenzied with every squeak of the bucking chute gates. Cowboys came from miles around to test their skills on the broncs and bulls, well-known team ropers seemed to appear from everywhere, and sharp cowgirls laid the iron to amazingly fast barrel horses, flying to whoops and hollers from the creaking bleachers. Alcohol flowed and undoubtedly chemicals too, and if you weren't smiling about something, you were definitely in the wrong place.

Some animals stood out and we felt like we knew them, such as the home-grown bull, Snuffy, and a later one by the same name; both nasty, with wide, hooking horns who'd rather hurt a cowboy than holler at a heifer in heat. Maybe you remember Chipmunk, the stout, black bull who broke his back fighting the bucking chute.

Towed out of the arena with a tractor, we all got a reminder of the inherent dangers as a rifle shot echoed from somewhere behind the parked cars.

I made my first rodeo money there, on a reliable bareback horse named Wishy, the perfect horse for a beginner. "How come you named him Wishy," I asked. "You know, wish he'd buck harder so a guy could win instead of place."

One of the rodeo contractors was 7-11 Rodeo Company, and for reasons you will soon see, I took up with the owner, Pat Mantle of Sombrero Ranch fame in Northern Colorado. Pat worked his butt off, making sure it all ran as smoothly as possible. He was the main pickup man for the bucking events, ran the bulls out of the arena after they'd performed, helped cowboys get their rigs on recalcitrant horses, and did whatever else was needed to keep it moving. Pat wasn't afraid to take a drink after a day of eating dust and barking out orders, and that's where our friendship began. "Come on," I said, "I know every waterin' hole in town," and off we headed.

We started at Pinocchio's with a pitcher of cold beer where a good-looking gal in a blue, pleated skirt started coming on to Pat. She was a too-young romantic, in over her head, and about the time she'd let the skirt climb to half-thigh, showing off some creamy white panties, Pat flashed her a lascivious grin, saying, "Honey, I'm gonna have some fun snortin' in those flanks." She left, but it was early.

Irreverence, dust, tight jeans, good-looking cowgirls and cowboys, snot-slingin' bucking stock, sex, booze and bullshit, great rodeo, whispered tantalizations, fine performance horses, incredible apres-rodeo, and God knows what else, it all came together with the W/J Rodeo. 1964 - 1985.

My Very First Muse

She's almost always been there, taking a position in my peripheral vision, arms folded across her chest, one ankle across the other, a slight smile upon her face and a shine deep within her eyes. The antithesis of any imagined matriarch, she was out-of-place sexy in a khaki skirt with a blue silk scarf around her neck, just enough older to maintain an intellectual integrity that enticed and allowed my young mind to blossom.

She arrived at the old red brick Aspen high school late, a couple weeks into the fall semester, bringing with her an air of excitement, although I doubted she'd ever earn my allegiance. Her charge, and I doubt anyone fully explained it to her, was to keep vigil over a small group of misfits, six of us in the beginning, somehow labeled as "gifted," although an attempt to put any two of us into the same category would have been a misappropriation of the original intent. Advanced English? I could fake it an hour a day.

If we can believe poets, life is about roads less traveled or fates twisted tortuously between light and dark, passion and indifference. Once a star pupil, a seriously considered candidate for "skipping" a grade, certain events in junior high had started me down an academic path of intolerable consequences, a downward slide that could not have ended well.

If I wasn't entertaining cheerleaders in the back of my '58 Ford coupe or carrying the pigskin on the gridiron, I was locked in my second-floor room, feet propped on my desk, reading maudlin poetry, short stories and encyclopedias from the 1940s and 50s. Each year, every textbook I owned sat on an easy chair, as unopened and untouched as the day I received them. Until that fall of my senior year.

Meg Heath wanted us to write, to express ourselves, to dig down into the depths and express what we held inside. She didn't tolerate insincerity. If it was teen-age "saccharin-sweet" crap, she let us know, in front of the class. It had to be real and it had to be well-written. And I thrived on that, almost impervious to the flow of red ink that accompanied my neophyte attempts as they were handed back to me.

But we didn't just write; we read, probably the most liberal reading list of any public high school in America. Henry Miller's "Tropic of Cancer" was on the list, and we did "Tropic of Capricorn" for extra credit; "On the Road," of course; "The Lord of The Flies," Herman Hesse's "Siddhartha" and then we moved to Shakespeare, wrote sonnets, delved into "Canterbury Tales," including the Old English prologue, and Dante's "Inferno." Poets Donne, Milton, Byron, Dickinson, Bronte, and T.S. Eliot entered our thinking. And she went to my football games.

My first college advisor (and football coach) was not happy when I insisted that my major be English literature. "You're making a big mistake," he said, as I walked away with a sense of academic liberation, silently thanking the woman who had made it possible.

Had I followed my passion for written creativity instead of that for powder snow and whiskey and crafted a life out of the artistry of writing, she and I might have stayed in touch and I may well have spread my dreams under her feet, entreating her, as W.B. Yeats wrote in "The Cloths of Heaven," to ". . . tread softly because you tread on my dreams." For years, she was my unattainable Maud Gonne, something known only to me.

Through the short months we shared, she became my Muse, a force of inward strength, who still looks over my shoulder when the verbs and nouns don't add up, nudging me deeper when I think I'm done. I have kept her close in my thoughts because I cannot do otherwise.

Myths and Reality

Myths, superstitions, suppositions and otherwise superficially irrelevant trivia have the potential to become the stuff of legend, particularly in Aspen town.

First and foremost, we should be aware of the "Ute Curse," cast over the land by the retreating Utes (attributed to various Ute chieftains depending in which part of Colorado you live), which says something like " though the white man may take this land, it and everything on it will never make him happy and his endeavors will forever fail . . ." Some say the curse goes on to describe that those who visit this area will never leave, or are destined to return if they do. Tough stuff, except the never leaving part. Ask any ski bum.

While we're on the Utes, lets' clear up another misconception. The Ute Indians did not start forest fires in an attempt to drive off settlers in the Aspen area. It's a convenient story concocted by whites to defer responsibility for the woodland infernos that did occur. If you think about it, there were miners scrambling all over these mountains, looking for riches of silver and gold, building campfires, smoking tobacco and otherwise taking chances. Also, to shore up the many mines that were producing ore and to provide lumber for spontaneous civilian development, there were logging camps and sundry sawmills (utilizing steam boilers) located everywhere in the high mountain forests surrounding Aspen. Tragically, at least in hindsight, there weren't any Utes living in the Roaring Fork Valley after 1879.

How many times have you heard it said that a honeycomb of silver mine tunnels exists under the town of Aspen, ready to cave in when condition are just right? How many people have you talked to that claim to have walked and belly-crawled through that labyrinth of human labor and genius? Old maps of mining activity in the area clearly indicate that a couple of tunnels may have been excavated under parts of the East End. End of story.

This, of course, brings up the fable of the Glory Hole, which used to be located under Glory Hole Park, and probably still is. Some say it swallowed up several steam engines as it sunk, along with the attendant rail cars. Balderdash! It really wasn't that deep of a dent, and when we were kids it was known as the "Snake Pit," as it seemed to have a steady population of garter snakes. The sides were partially lined with trash, but the town fathers had put an end to that rather quickly. In years past, there have been sinkholes of similar size on various agricultural properties in the valley, none of which have gained the same notoriety. Perhaps that's due to a definite lack of exposure?

My friend Romeo brings up the notion that Aspen's original survey does not line up exactly with the points of north and south. If you stand in Gondola Plaza, such discrepancy is clearly demonstrated by the placement of a large arrow in the concrete, delineating true North. The streets are definitely off-kilter from the established rules of laying out a township.

With the urgency and devious nature of the land grab engineered by B. Clark Wheeler and Charles A. Hallam in their takeover of Ute City (to create Aspen in 1880), magnetic north could well have been used rather than true north, a surveying no-no. In addition, charting equipment in those days was not of the highest technological standards, from which evolved today's surveying edict which states that if the original land measure is off somewhat, that's the way it shall forever stay. A common sense and simple way to deal with errors.

When it comes to myths and reality, it's kind of like kicking tires and digging up bones. Not everything coincides with what we've been told, and we would do well to remember David Bentley's insightful take on the matter: "Any lawyer will tell that if two people tell the exact same story, they are both lying." This writer likes to characterize the perpetuation of such stories as the propagation of inert minutiae.

New Year's Eve (At the Woody Creek Tavern)

In the aftermath of a New Year's Eve celebration, memories of the event itself are sometimes blurred, unwelcome, and unavoidable. If you want unpleasant stories, folks, I could tell you a few, but picking one above the others is a difficult task.

It started out peaceful enough, a celebration at the Woody Creek Tavern. My buddies, Andy Arasz and Dan Goldyn, owners at the time, had sponsored a successful Oktoberfest the previous fall, so hopes were high for New Year's Eve. The same biker gang returned to play free verse rock n' roll and yours truly strained the bellows on his squeeze box for a while. A valley-wide contingent of cowboys, hippies, bikers, city slickers and rabble rousers packed the house and the booze flowed like mountain run-off in the spring.

The trouble started about 1:30 AM, when in the middle of an argument, a flirtatious and decently put-together woman informed her boyfriend that she had been sharing bunk time with one of the few black men in town. The boyfriend went berserk, spewing out a string of racial and murderous epithets that, taken on their own might have drifted off into the night, but given the mix of the crowd, served only to dredge up mostly unrelated, but bad, feelings on all sides. The tension that had that simmered under a patina of politeness rose like bile in your throat and the war was on.

The bartender saw it coming and wisely booted most everyone out, locking the door and drawing the shades behind them. A few of us remained, friends of the owners, wondering how long the brouhaha outside was going to last.

Several minutes into the brawl, a woman appeared at the door, desperate to get in. She had gone out to her car much earlier to take a nap and hadn't realized how far the party had deteriorated in her absence. As we quickly pulled her inside, it became immediately clear that something terrible had happened. Her nose was battered and bloodied, eyes starting to swell shut, and she wasn't sure how it had happened. A kid who had been peeking through the curtains said someone had slugged her in the face as she walked to the bar.

With that, my cousin Wayne and I decided we would find the jackass who did the damage, not realizing the situation. We had to argue with the bartender to let us out, but he finally relented. Once outside, the scope and range of the fight, something we couldn't see from within, became abundantly clear. We sidled through the midst of at least twenty folks all in a frenzy, fists flying, people wrestling on the ground, bodies being shoved up against cars, with some guy having his head pounded against one of the then-remaining gas pumps out front.

This wasn't our time to solve anything, so we wandered back inside. Some things you can remember about a fight, and others don't matter, but what I remember most about that debacle was after our tour, in the light of the bar, I could see blood splatters all over the front of my brand-new ski parka. All we did was walk through the area, which tells you something about the intensity of the battle.

We loaded our lady friend up in the Jeep and headed for the hospital. The thermometer hovered around minus twenty degrees, which became an issue when we ran out of gas coming by the airport. God only knows where they came from a long time later, but a couple in their seventies, headed to Aspen on a lark, stopped and hauled us the rest of the way to the infirmary.

We made it home after daylight, a memorable New Year's Eve celebration behind us. I'd tell you the rest of the story, about how we exacted repentance from the perpetrator of the errant punch, but we're out of room.

No Dope for the Dopes

A table, big enough for twelve, on a hot, muggy August Aspen Friday night, held steak cooked rare and family, at least fourteen of us. My brother, Steve, going to summer school in Denver, had driven up for the weekend as he did occasionally, and we were making plans.

Just the two of us piled into my 1960 Plymouth Fury (which I'd given to my brother but hadn't yet changed the title) and headed to the Isis to lose ourselves in whatever was playing and then maybe get crazy uptown afterwards, drinking, chasing girls and lettin' off steam with a cup of dice and a roll of bills.

Heading in, just between the S-curves, an Aspen cop car going the other way whipped around behind us like we'd run over a baby carriage or something and kept his nose right on our butt. We figured we hadn't done anything wrong, and developed a little agitation right off at these two yahoos, but what are you gonna do? It was the early 1970s and paranoia was a state of mind for many in town, including some on the police force.

It took most of Main for them to sort out their thought processes and they finally pulled us over in front of the Monarch Building. I was trying to make reality out of watching an overweight beast of a man jerk my brother from the car about the same time a well-dressed, detective type yanked me out the passenger's side. Displaying an odious amount of arrogance that far exceeded their capabilities, these guys refused to tell us what was going on and, cuffed and provoked, we were driven down to the jail.

Sheriff Carroll Whitmire came out of his living quarters in the courthouse basement, interrupted in the middle of dinner. Despite all the bleating from Hunter S. Thompson and his band of miscreants, Whitmire was a decent guy who insisted our handcuffs be removed and explained that my brother was in serious trouble for suspicion of running drugs into Aspen and he might as well give himself up and save everyone a lot of hassle. Since the car was titled in my name, I could give permission for them to search the vehicle, rather than demand a search warrant, and they could get my brother Steve settled into a cellar lockup before the movies were out.

Receiving no objections from Steve and with a typically suave outburst of anger, I signed the waiver and told the city cops to get their "asses up there and let's see whose credibility is on the line."

If you've never had your car searched by amateurs, don't. Those clowns were so certain they'd made the big score (based on a "tip" from some jealous boyfriend or incompetent parent), they refused to let reality seep into their consciousness. They allowed us to watch, with the intent, I suppose, of letting us see how adeptly they could sniff out whatever it was they were looking for. When they couldn't find anything under the seats or dash, they kicked the backseat forward so the fat one could crawl into the car from the trunk. Then, the scrawny detective with the big ego pulled the head liner apart in the middle, allowing it to fall into the seats below. It was kinda like car rape.

"What the hell, where's the dope?" telegraphed their eyes. "Maybe you boys f--ked up," was my creative comment, and they could have apologized, but by now they were in too deep to even think about salvaging their honor. Without a word to the wise, or the contrary, they got in their official car and slunk off into the night.

Steve and I spent the rest of the weekend trying to put the car back together, and when we finally got the floor carpet tacked down and the seats close to normal, he drove it back to Denver and coaxed some charitable organization into accepting our generosity. Trust authority? Not in this lifetime.

Not Quite Lost but Found Several Times

If you've ever read John Cheever's short story, *The Swimmer*, this tale will have a certain ring to it. However, even if you haven't read that intriguing snapshot of a man's life, you may still find this recounting of survival in the Roaring Fork Valley to have some value beyond entertainment.

Not long ago, standing on the saddle near the top of the Arbaney-Kittle trail, where most everyone turns around, I decided to take a different way down and having the unerring sense of mountainous terrain that Hugh Glass, mountain man extraordinaire, undoubtedly had, I took off on this new byway without blinking an eye. About 50 yards past a crucial turn-off point and realizing my mistake, I continued on anyway, just to see what further vistas might reveal.

Soon, the Basalt (Fairview) Cemetery was in full sight, and spotting a man sitting proximate to a tombstone, figured I'd see about scoring a ride back to my Jeep, stationed at the trail head. Alas, it soon became apparent that the man, in a wheel chair near the grave, was reasonably drunk and giving a sermon to all departed souls who would listen, detailing the wrongs he personally had committed against his deceased friend, lying there at his feet.

Wrong guy to ask for a ride, so I quietly began working my way around the mountainside to my vehicle, making an effort to stay high so that I didn't end up on the private Roaring Fork Club golf course. Things went well, albeit a bit slippery, until on my way by one of the cabins lining the links, I happened to glance in a window and spy a middle-aged woman, dressed only in bra and panties, standing before a mirror. It was clear she had seen me and visions of being arrested for peeping through windows went spiraling through my head.

With that thought in mind, I headed for the golf course to take my chances with security rather than spook hell out of the neighborhood, as there were a couple of cabins yet to pass. Almost immediately, a golf cart containing an officious sort of person drove directly up to me and asked if I needed help. My negative answer triggered the offer of a ride, which I refused. (Before reaching the clubhouse, a total of three carts had asked if they could be of assistance, each more ingratiating than the last.) I felt totally out of place on the fairways, particularly going the wrong direction, but slowly began to reassess the situation.

With my salt-and-pepper hair, shorts and hiking boots, I could easily have been a guest there, and began to feel less like an intruder and more like a man who quite possibly appeared to be disoriented or lost, or both.

About dusk, I made the clubhouse and once again was stopped, this time by a young man who insisted I stop and talk to him for a while, just to let myself calm down. Knowing I had not outwardly exhibited agitated behavior, I surmised this request a little curious, but acquiesced, beginning to find this whole odyssey a bit on the wild side. The kid had grown up in Aspen and knew my family well, or so it seemed. He asked if we still had the cabin on the hill and I, thinking he was referring to our old cow camp, about 18 miles distant, replied in the affirmative. With that innocent, but misleading answer, he said he would arrange for someone to take me home without problem - it'd take just a minute to get a cart to come around.

I now knew they thought I was an uncaged guest, on the borderline of embarrassing them, and as the kid went for the phone, I bolted, up the stairs, around the swimming pool, past a couple of cabins (on the hill) and into the Arbaney-Kittle parking lot. "Let'em stop me now," I thought. "I'm off the property."

Groovy and Goat

Back in the seventies, I worked with a pair of individuals that were, if nothing else, unforgettable. Groovy and Goat went everywhere together and I imagine probably even slept in the same bed, they were that close.

To a young man, a gravel pit was a marvelous thing - big machines digging and hauling dirt, huge apparatuses crushing and screening rock into various commodities - all needed as part of Aspen's burgeoning "renaissance". A guy I sometimes drank and gambled with, Joe McCarthy, had just bought the Stillwater pit from Pat Hemann and offered me a job, skills unknown.

I could hardly wait to run the big loaders and Caterpillar dozers, but being the new kid on the block, was assigned the job of running the rock crusher. It was a good job and I loved the purr of the gigantic diesel engine, but when I think about how I used to jump over moving conveyor belts and whirring jaws and screens, bypassing every safety device, in the name of increased production, I realize I'm fortunate to have all my limbs, much less be alive.

The man responsible for clearing away the produce of the crusher and stockpiling it elsewhere was a man I knew only as Groovy. Tall, 6'5" at least, probably in his 60s, with a big, toothy grin, he incongruously wore tight jeans that were, of course, too short and altogether, he made a hulking sort of vision as he climbed in and out of his front-loader. After a time, we got to be on speaking terms, but that was about it. Every once in a while, an afternoon rain shower would roll in and Groovy would head for his 60s vintage, white Chevrolet pickup truck and I'd go sit in my red Volkswagen bug. Depending on the storm, we'd go either back to work or home.

One day as it started raining, Groovy waved me over to his truck. "Get in, you dumb bastard. It's wet out," and with that we crossed the line into friendship. Entering the cab was an unexpected experience, for there in the middle of the seat sat Goat, a small dog of unknown description, possibly some Pekingese and

Poodle mixed up with something else. A low growl filled the cab as Groovy implored Goat to be silent. "Oh, for Christ's sake, let the man sit down." And then, in the way it always seemed to be, necessity required me to be offered the role of accomplice. The vodka bottle came out, small in Groovy's large hand, and there was an urgent desire on his part for me to partake, to taste the forbidden juice, for then it would be impossible for me to implicate him for something we both participated in. It worked, and from then on, whenever it rained, Groovy and I would sit in his truck, drink vodka and pass Goat back and forth, laughing at his antics as he begged unmercifully for tidbits and attention.

What does a tiny dog do at a gravel pit all day, as his owner drives a huge loader that could smash fifty dogs at once, and large trucks of all description move back and forth? I can't say, exactly, except that he'd better stay in the pickup and wait for the boss.

It's hard to tell what happened to Groovy, but he traveled on in one way or another and soon after, we began moving the operation to the Pitkin Iron site in Woody Creek. As we pulled the office trailer away from the sandy bank against which it rested, dozens of empty vodka bottles slid down into the place where the trailer had sat, and Groovy's "secret" was there in the open for everyone to see.

Maybe Groovy drank too much, maybe he didn't, but either way, it couldn't matter to Goat, for every fiber of the dog's being existed just to please his master. There are heroes and there are heroes, and Goat could tell of one he never got over.

Of Love, Family, and Liquid Gold

When I was about thirteen, and through a diffuse network of women, my mother somehow got me hooked up with a girl in another part of the western slope, for what reason, I cannot be sure, but the relationship was a prolific one, in a sense of a different kind, as you may see.

The girl was dark-skinned and petite, with hip length black hair, seductive eyes, and a temper as fiery as the top of Mount Vesuvius. Her mother was not afraid to entrust her car and her daughter to me, a kid glowing with an infusion of adolescent hormones and an attitude that the world was somehow made for him. But this column isn't about the daughter, or me - it's about the mother.

Just as the daughter was dark, the mother was a light-skinned, tall blonde, usually clothed in long dresses and long sleeves, even in the hot days of summer, but not always. She had a way of presenting herself that could bowl over all but the strongest of personalities, and I mean that in a good light. Her energy level always appeared to be turned on high and wherever she went, things happened in fascinating ways.

She had that incredible sense that some people have, of knowing a given situation better than the players and thus, more in control of the action than most anyone else could understand. She knew that her daughter, older than I, would be able to withstand my advances, and she further understood that I, being a ranch kid, was a conscientious driver and would bring her daughter safely home.

The daughter and I never really hit it off, although we tested the limits of good behavior a time or two, but our association did create a friendship between the two families that lasted for a couple of years, or more. Summers were good for socializing and the other family would come to the ranch and either camp out down by Woody Creek, or stay up at the house in one or two of the four bedrooms while us permanent residents found somewhere else to perch for the duration. All told, there might have been 5 or 6 kids

276

lurking around and there were parties, horseback rides, moonlight hikes, hard work, swimming in the creek, and all other manner of things that might keep youngsters (and adults) involved.

Alas, the heart ache arrives when the monster, quieted for so long, sneaks quietly in the back door, unannounced and ready to rip lives asunder. During the war, the mother had been an overseas nurse and had been diagnosed with a serious infection that required extensive abdominal surgery. The recovery that followed was incredibly painful, and through ignorance or ineptness, her doctors unknowingly married her to the needle that delivered the torment-dulling morphine. "Butchers," her physician husband would later call these doctors, and although it took a very long time, she kicked the habit and appeared to slip seamlessly into an upper-middle-class life that seemed suited to her desires.

But, for whatever reasons - perhaps as Charlie Parker, the alto saxophonist, once said, "You can get heroin out of your body, but you can't get it out of your brain," - the temptation to smooth over problems with an old friend became too great, and the first of recurring needle tracks began to appear.

The telling note came on a pitch black, quiet night at our house, the daughter helping her mother surreptitiously sneak out and leave in the middle of the darkness, desperate to make a soul-calming connection way down the highway, many miles away.

I didn't understand at the time, but slowly came to realize, as I saw everything else take a back seat to the liquid gold coursing through her veins, the severity of the problem and the devastation it had on everyone who loved her, including me.

Pete Luhn and an Unknown Lady

She threw her skis down in front of me, impeding the only way forward and without lifting her eyes, loudly exclaimed, "Don't worry, I'm not blocking your way." Hmm, a prima donna with testicles, I thought, and said the first thing that came to mind, "You just flopped one of your skis down on a sharp rock." "Yeah, I did that on purpose," she replied, giving me an exaggerated look of wonderment at just how obtuse I might actually be.

She had on one of those checked, light-green snowboarder jackets that are sort of a modern plaid, and I grimaced as she clicked in, visualizing a deep dent in what otherwise may have been a finely tuned bottom. I shot my partner, who was nursing one of her better hangovers, a quick look of, "Let's get the hell out of here," and gingerly stepped my skis around in a partial 180 to avoid running over the twenty-something who maintained her ground, talking to a friend.

It can be a little crowded at the top of the Bowl sometimes, and if that girl hadn't been so obnoxious, I might have forgotten all about it, but what happened next cemented the memory in my mind. Further down, while waiting for my partner to catch up, I spied this mettlesome lass dive into G-8 with reserved abandon. Gutsy little thing, for sure, but without much form, and skiing in a manner reminiscent of the "Western Pig" style, only without the "western" or the "style" parts of the package.

Not too many people skied the Western Pig, and maybe even fewer know what I'm talking about, but it doesn't really matter, anyway. Ski bum extraordinaire Pete Luhn claimed to be the father of the Western Pig, although there were those in the late-night hallowed halls of the Red Onion who would, without compunction, nastily tell Pete to his face that he was "full of crap." But there was another side to Pete, if he liked you.

Pete never got under my skin, except when he claimed to be the better crud skier, and late one evening, at the top of our B.S. game, the two of us vowed to put the issue to rest the next time there was some almost-impossible-to-ski wind-crust on the mountain.

A few days later, I called Pete from the ski patrol shack, informing him of ugly conditions, and with the aristocratic demeanor of one who had just been challenged to dual by pistol, he soon arrived to settle our wager, a half-smile across his face.

Pete and a couple of patrolmen got in behind me as I led them off to what I had previously calculated to be the worst windswept snow on the mountain. Youth and ego have no peer and without the slightest hesitation, I bailed enthusiastically into the highly-crusted, rock-laced, steep terrain, wearing a pair of 210 cm Kneissl Red Star slaloms, the only ski more akin to a hickory two-by-four than an actual board of the same name.

Ever the gentleman, Pete enthusiastically observed until I inevitably caught a tip and then skied close while my battered, airless lungs involuntarily wheezed for oxygen. Clearly, I'd blown it, but Pete was calm. "Jesus, Tony, I thought we were here to have fun, not on a suicide mission. You're too crazy to mess with today." And off he skied, leaving our argument for another day.

Maybe the girl from the summit of Highland Bowl will eventually become a lady of the West and learn to put a little style into her neophyte presentation and maybe even improve her manners, but I'm guessing it's too late for her to grasp the intrinsic savoir-faire or class of a die-hard skier.

Oh, the Stories They Would Tell

They came from all over town, just to sit in the big rocking chair in the kitchen corner and tell their tales. The three women who lived there would hover around, making tea, getting out the assorted homemade cookies, and setting up the straight-backed oak chairs in a semicircle around the leather-covered rocker. And the honored guest was made to feel just that.

The Aspen Times came out once a week on Thursdays, so there was a need for some method of getting the news out to the folks on other days, and neighborhood visiting was the best way any of the old-timers could find, particularly for the women. At my maternal grandmother's Bleeker Street house, the great old, comfortable leather rocker was where the guest always sat.

Guests like Lilly Reed, daughter of Katie, namesake of the Katie Reed House uptown, and Iola Ilgen, who lived across Bleeker from Grandma's house. The two women were contrasts in philosophy - Lilly would send notice that she would appear at a certain date and time (and was as imperiously punctual as an executioner), whereas Iola would request permission to visit at a time and date convenient to my grandmother's household and generally arrived within striking distance of the agreed upon hour.

Such visits created great excitement with the women in Grandma's household, but generally drove my great-uncle, Tom Stapleton, to head to the Red Onion or Ski n' Spur to hobnob with his buddies. Similarly enough, when one of Uncle Tom's cronies would show up, the women all disappeared, either into the living room or the garden.

Harry Holmes, rancher and miner, would sit in the rocker, putting his booted feet up to rest on one of the oak sitting chairs, and either play with his pocket knife or complain about things he should be getting done at his house. He didn't hear all that well, and wore a huge hearing aid that never seemed to work. Uncle Tom would lay out the plan for the day, or just ask Harry how he was doing, and the usual household noise would be ruptured by the sound of Harry's booming, scratchy voice. "What? Goddammit Tom, you know I can't hear. Speak up." Harry and Tom were two guys who talked mostly in silence, occasionally throwing out words just to make sure their thought patterns were both still in the Roaring Fork Valley.

Every once-in-a-while, Harry would bring his son Russell along, which put a different shine on the conversation. Russell's nickname was Rasputin, which I always found amusing, but it didn't matter, for Rasputin, or Russell, was always after Uncle Tom about the mines on Aspen Mountain.

"You've been way deep in there, haven't you, Tom? Why the hell did they tunnel that direction, anyway? Seems like they put a bad angle on 'er, if you ask me." Russell has long been credited with having a ton of knowledge about Aspen's old mines, and he did, but that's only because those taking stock didn't have the privilege of talking to Tom or Harry before they died.

Of course, Harry would have trouble keeping up with the conversation, what with that huge hearing aid, and eventually Uncle Tom, who seemed as patient as Job, would holler out, "For Christ's sake, Harry, go wait in the Jeep while Russell and I finish this conversation. We can't yell at you all goddamned day."

As the song says, "If the rockin' chair could read the thoughts from people's minds, Oh, the stories it would tell time after time . . ." And I reckon it's true, but you'd have to know a little bit about the people to fully understand the stories.

Of Rats and Men

I'd been holed up at our cow camp, waiting out a blowing, early October snowstorm. At daylight, I awoke to at least two feet of snow, and it was still coming down.

Without too much thought, I gave my good horse, Willie, an extra ration of hay, put together a beef stew on the wood stove and burrowed in for the day. As I leaned back in my chair, a good book in my lap, there was a cold shiver of exquisite contentment tickling my spine.

As the fire crackled, there'd occasionally be a stir of life from the corner of the cabin nearest the stove, too big to be a mouse. He made a run for it once, dashing along the floor, and from the reaches of my peripheral vision, I determined my guest to be a pack rat.

If you're not experienced with pack rats (wood rats, if you prefer), you might liken them to a wolverine, only a much milder form. If given enough time, they'll completely destroy the inside of a cabin, chewing everything you cherish into bits of trash and dragging in more grass and stale humus than you could reasonably imagine. But still, he added a little diversion to the too-quiet ambiance and I determined to go easy on the critter.

There was another pack rat, in an earlier time, a vision conjured up for me by my cousin, David E. Stapleton. Imagine, if you will, a young teenaged boy, traveling the length of Owl Creek Road behind a flock of sheep, headed to the summer range on what was to become the Snowmass Ski Area.

These drives weren't the stuff of movie legend; no Border collie sheep dogs and well-trained horses for assistance. David was on foot, relying on every bit of his own will to get the job done.

His only companion was a man named Tony Garcia, a herdsman who forever spoke with broken English and who carried the proud conviction that as a Mexican, he was an infinitely better sheepherder than his Basque counterparts, men from another continent.

The sheep camp cabin, on the Divide between Brush and Snowmass Creeks, was the summer home of these men. In its last reincarnation, it was the dinner spot for the nightly Snowmass Stables sleigh rides. That was before Columbian Mammoths and Ziegler Pond.

Coyotes, the scourge of sheep ranchers, silently watched the herd by day and as darkness fell, formally announced their deadly intentions with mournful, bone-chilling wails. David slept with his .25-.30 rifle next to his bunk, a flashlight taped to the octagon barrel for emergency night work.

In the dark, he heard the footsteps, quick as a mouse but much larger, and mentally followed the sound as he pulled the rifle up to his shoulder and switched on the light attached to the barrel. There, in full luminescence, running along the ceiling rafter, was a pack rat with David's socks in its mouth. The blast awakened Tony, who wasn't too pleased with the noise, but welcomed the thought of one less rat.

Some things never change, and as the present-day pack rat in our cow camp began scurrying around after I'd snuffed the lights, it became a nuisance rather than a companion. The small claws noisily tapped about the cabin, trying my patience, and I shined the light around to see what in hell could be so interesting to a rat.

Fatally, the beam caught the creature's eye and he was immediately hooked. He came around the bunk and up onto my sleeping bag, intent on crawling in with me. That was enough.

I swatted him off, and as he stood defiantly in the corner, the last thing he saw was a flicker of mesmerizing light, shining the way for my hand-held pistol.

Our Young Racers Deserve Support
(2008 J2 Junior Nationals)

The finish line might as well have been a million miles away, so slim were her chances of crossing it. She'd just ripped through a fast flush and was two gates away from the electronic beam when, as sometimes happens when you give it your all, she got wide of the next gate, body going one way, skis the other and only a miracle could keep her from falling. Even if she didn't fall, she'd never make the next gate with the speed she was carrying. But then, through an incredible display of guts and desire, she demonstrated what it's like to reach deep inside and turn it around. Her eyes never left her goal, and in a nanosecond, she pulled her body around, slammed her knees to the right, setting her edges for a dazzling blast of compressed power, and then just as quickly, turned it all the other way, crossing the finish line with the fastest run of the day.

That wasn't the only flash of brilliance displayed during this year's running of the J2 Junior Nationals on Aspen Mountain, but it certainly was indicative of the caliber of young racers we have coming up in this country. The idea of holding Junior National events is to get the next generation of America's World Cup competitors familiar with courses they will run once they make the World Cup team. Running downhill on Ruthie's and slalom on Fifth Avenue, puts these kids on historic and legendary courses, revered over the years by some of the world's best contenders.

It's hard to say what it costs to keep a kid competitive in junior racing today, but it has to be well into five figures. That's why you see so many parents on the race course - as volunteer workers. There are a lot of local folks up there, as well, because Aspen, from its earliest renaissance roots, has been a ski racing town. As it's always been, these kids (and parents) need all the help they can get to pull these races off. And Aspen, being the town that it is, comes out of the wood work to help make it happen.

As I watched the eager spectators climb the edge of Fifth Avenue, clambering to get the "best view" from the island of trees at the bottom of Strawpile, memories of past races flashed through my mind. Strawpile wasn't always the great slice of gentle, groomed rolls that it is today, and "back when" there used to be a rather severe wall near the bottom, just above Tower Ten road. Jimmy Gerbaz and I used to thrill at near-disasters as Roch Cup downhill racers like Dick "Mad Dog" Buek flew precariously off the Wall before making the sharp turn into Fifth Avenue.

Someone mentioned that the J2's were racing on "America's Downhill" course, which is true, but long before that, it was Aspen's Roch Cup course, on which the world came to compete. I doubt today's kids care too much what it's called, as long as they have good wax and fast snow, but the deep-seated history of ski racing in Aspen shouldn't be dismissed, or forgotten.

Before the slalom, a young, local racer full of unfettered enthusiasm climbed onto the gondola with my buddy Bob Snyder and me, wondering if he'd gotten in the AARP cabin by mistake. Once he slowed down a bit, he talked seriously about ski racing and how, in his opinion, the Roch Cup meant so much to Aspen that it should be resurrected.

Maybe, but perhaps the Roch Cup has truly been run, its place in history as the forerunner to "America's Downhill" revered and cherished, talked about by the young racers with respect.

And besides, these Junior National kids are tomorrow's heroes, the one's we'll be yelling for to cross the finish line first, and that's where our focus should be. Keep your eye on 'em.

People Make Up Our Rich History

Sometime ago, a columnist at this newspaper handed me a packet containing portions of a family history going back to the 1700s. It wasn't because she was trying to impress me with the "blueness" of her heritage, but rather, there is a possibility that the ancestors involved may be common to both of us.

Her father, who put it all together, was an excellent writer and researcher, and the information contained therein is presented in a straightforward, professional manner. Once the pages are cracked open, one cannot help but become engrossed in the development of this family over the generations, and there is a curiosity to see how various family members made out, given their birth order and gender in the line of descent. I suppose what is most interesting is that it doesn't really matter if these were my relatives - it just makes good reading.

Such narratives are man's credible time machines, giving us a glimpse into lives we sometimes think were so much different from ours, but in practice, weren't. We can say, with 21st century arrogance, that such old-time existences were certainly mundane compared to ours, and in our ignorance, completely discount a certain richness and tranquility found back then, a depth of human experience that seems, with common regularity, to be marginalized by the frenetic pace of today's world.

Aspen's history is about 130 years old, but some of its pioneers are still palpable to my touch. There are warm memories of being three or four years old and visiting a nice old lady on Main Street, a woman who lived alone in a nifty, one-room log cabin, now part of the Christiania complex. Her nickname was Lollie and my enthusiastic wails of, "Let's go visit Lollie," are still fresh in memory.

Every time the Aspen Historical Society presents History 101 at the Wheeler Opera House, I think of Lollie, as she was the one and the same Ella Stallard, as played so ably by Wendy Perkins, Jeanne Walla or Nina Gabianelli. I can only think of how much more content Lollie must have been in her last years, holed up in that snug log chateau, no longer worried about how impossible it was to heat the large Stallard House on West Bleeker.

Or there was my great-uncle Tom Stapleton, brother of the first white boy born in Aspen, who was a rancher and miner throughout his life, a man who saw no need to travel any farther away from home than the top of Aspen Mountain or Snowmass Lake. Oh, he went to Denver a few times and once took a whirlwind trip to the West Coast, but his life was in these mountains and he knew the terrain as well as the next guy. He could tell you more about the underground tangle of mining tunnels around here than almost anyone, but you'd have to catch him on a stool at the Red Onion or the Ski N' Spur to glean the information from his conversations with beer drinking buddies.

There'd be a row of them, bib overalls all - Harry Holmes, Auget Ericksen, Bill Herron, Hod Nicholson - old boys with the deepest roots, who like most of Aspen's original pioneers, would rather not say much. Too many questions from people who didn't fit in, was their take on it.

We all have a lineage somewhere, and whether we think it's important, we should remember that someday it will have significance to someone. Those possible ancestors from long ago, who settled in Virginia and were leading professionals of the day, might be surprised to see that one of their descendants is a cowboy and a ski bum, but I don't think that is nearly as interesting as it is to learn how their lives developed over the years, up to and including the schooling of future-president Andrew Johnson, as a tailor.

Philosophy and Levity Do Battle

It was an odd relationship we had, almost from the beginning, and in a strange way, it never really ended, but she taught me the price of levity. I'm talking about the University of Northern Colorado and me.

I went there to play football, but through an evolution almost as quick as the blink of the eye, my surly jock persona became that of a studious English literature major. In the exaggerated euphoria that comes with flexing muscle of your own volition, sans input from parents or peers, I developed my own manner - traveling under the radar, I thought - until the dean of the English department informed me that an "interesting" character such as myself probably bore some watching.

I didn't realize at the time there was anything remarkable about my "style" and although certainly not a "hippie," I had long hair and a beard, wore a thigh-length, cowhide leather coat with wool lining and incredibly wide shoulders that made me appear far more menacing than I was. My sloppy work boots were never tied. I rode a 1957 BSA 650 motorcycle to class every day and parked it about anywhere I wanted since there were only four bikes on campus.

On a tour through northern Colorado one drunk and dreary night, I'd managed to pick up a couple jugs of raisin wine for fifty cents a gallon. Thinking it would take forever to polish off that awful swill, but unwilling to sacrifice the buck, I'd have a glass every morning for breakfast, which no doubt, gave me an aroma that, mixed with the gas and leaking oil from the motorcycle, was unforgettable in itself.

And thus it was that I arrived at a certain 9:00 A.M. philosophy class for the midterm, my second actual visit to said gathering. The well-dressed professor cast a surprised glance my way, for he thought no one could pass his class without regular attendance. I had, through knowledge aforethought, borrowed the class notes from a "genius" fellow student, and that, coupled with my meticulous reading of the textbook, made me well prepared. The academician handed me the exam with a bit of a smirk and sat down immediately to my right, making sure any performance I gave was based purely on my own knowledge of the matter at hand.

To make a lurid story short, I garnered the highest mark on the test, much to the professor's consternation and true to my style, didn't go back again until the final examination. Once more, I pulled it out of the air and proved my knowledge to be of stellar caliber, and on the board where the results were posted, saw that I had received an "A" for the semester.

Walking into my apartment with the rarefied ego of one who knows he is smarter than the average Joe, I eagerly answered the ringing phone, looking for an opportunity to brag of my latest accomplishment. Instead, it was the professor I had so eloquently fenced with on the matter of philosophy, wanting to know if I would meet him at the student union for a cup of coffee.

But, of course. Maybe he needed an assistant, or wanted to anoint my intelligence in some other suitable fashion. But what he said, very succinctly, was, "Mr. Vagneur, although you've gotten the highest possible score in this class, you did so without contribution or exhibiting any of the "pizzazz" I would expect from such an accomplishment. I respect you for your resourcefulness but think you'll agree that a "C" for the semester is more indicative of your true performance."

Somehow, I couldn't argue and quickly realized that "average" is about as far as arrogance and lack of respect will ever get you.

Football Champions from the Past

Sometimes, history comes out of the past, smacks you with a jolt and marches you back to a time you thought was forgotten. Such was triggered from a terse e-mail sent by one of my old cow-punchin' buddies, Bill Blakeslee, saying something about the 1936 state football champions, the Grand Junction Tigers. Who? The Grand Junction Daily Sentinel was looking for people connected to the team as they were writing a story about it (I missed the deadline). My dad, Clifford, was on that team and in the '36 season, they beat their opponents a total of 506 to zero. It's probably still a national record.

But, speaking of stories, how did my dad, a Woody Creek rancher's kid, end up going to school in Grand Junction? Simply, his mother and her sister, Aunt Babe, who lived in GJ, conspired to send him there with the prevailing thought that a larger school than Aspen's must surely be better. My grandmother Grace, who was a roving reporter for the Aspen Times and for a while served as Ninth Judicial court clerk under John T. Shumate, should be forgiven for her interest in furthering my father's education out of town, simply because such a notion was not that foreign back then. There was no Colorado Rocky Mountain School or other private school nearby to take up the slack, so residents were left to their own devices as to education in those days, provided they were unhappy with the Aspen schools. My dad later ended up serving thirteen years on the Aspen school board. Ironic, perhaps.

When I was in the 7th or 8th grade, my dad told me that during a routine physical for the 1936 team, he was diagnosed with a "heart murmur," a slight irregularity, the doctors thought, but not significant enough to keep him from playing. Unfortunately at the time, no one had the knowledge to ascertain that such an "insignificant" medical malady might kill him 45 years later. A leaking mitral heart valve, the bane of more than a few of his generation, was his Achilles.

Several years ago, I wrote a story about spending the day at Lincoln Park in Grand Junction, watching my daughter participate in an all-league track meet at Stocker Stadium, and throughout the narration, wove in the fact that my dad had watched me run track there, back when I was in high school. Dad, who died in 1981, was a huge presence with me that day in 2001, and I am totally perplexed that I did not remember he had played championship football in the same location.

Of course, he never seemed to talk much about that gridiron phenomenon, other than what I've mentioned, simply because to do so would have violated his conviction that self-aggrandizement was distasteful. But I have to believe that somewhere, in the unseeable dark of night, chasing elusive consciousness as he unsuccessfully fought to recover from heart surgery, he was back on the gridiron in his school colors, running the ball up the middle, past his tacklers and down the field as the cheers and yells of a frenzied crowd echoed in his ears.

Now, his ashes are gone and there are very few men left from that championship team, but there still remain the material remnants of a Woody Creek boy's high school life in Grand Junction. On my bookshelf sit the leather-bound law books of Judge Shumate, given to my grandmother as an unrealized incentive for my dad to study law in college. In the bottom of a chest of drawers, nestled next to my mother's 4-year Basalt high school basketball accolade, rests a big varsity letter "G" (for Grand Junction), in orange and black, and emblazoned across the front - "State Champs 1936." It's good, Dad.

Ranching, the Land's Good Friend

I'm not really a political nut, but I sometimes keep my ear close to the ground. Thus, I found myself watching one of the debates on Burlingame, when, after the moderator had finally declared a cease-fire and the cameraman failed to gracefully call it a day, Mick Ireland could be clearly heard to say that, "Ranching is abuse of the land."

I always like those kinds of statements, simply because they have a sense of absolute finality to them, as though God himself had actually handed the thought down to Mick - or whoever else utters such declarations, including yours truly on occasion. This meager column cannot begin to address such a strange rambling, but we'll throw what we can at it.

Whenever anyone uses the word "ranching" or some other variation of the word, it gets my attention as I am a rancher of sorts and have been all my life. Most people use the word without having any idea what it means - they sometimes just use it to fill the void in some thought-process that is lacking in definition. There is a world of difference between a large landowner and a rancher, although they can sometimes be the same. "Ranching," as it is used by ranchers, is an ability to make a living off the land by growing or otherwise nurturing a product for sale. In my experience, large landowners are more likely to pull some dumb-ass stunt with the land than are genuine ranchers. Of course, a ranch can be very small, as well, if it provides a living for someone.

To keep a ranch viable for next year, and for the next generation, requires that a rancher take care of his land, including grazing permits. Some of those less-than-educated cowboys who over-grazed the land and distorted the riparian areas went out of business (as they should have) in the last century and are no longer an accepted lot in the West with today's media and market savvy agricultural producers.

Unfortunately, many of today's "commentators" on overgrazing, cheap grazing fees and methane rich bovines (ad infinitum) have no idea of what they're talking about, other than to visit the sins of the fathers upon the producers of today in a blanket of erroneous claims and thoughts that do nothing other than to create a divide between two groups who should be working together. Ninety-nine per cent of the population wouldn't know a grazed pasture from an ungrazed one, let alone an overgrazed meadow from anything else, and that includes the group of "commentators" mentioned above. Use of such buzz words as "overgrazing" generally only serves to inflame those who are easily influenced.

For good or bad, and it doesn't matter which at this point 'cause we have it to live with, there is still a lot of undeveloped agricultural land in the valley that needs the nurture of people who love the land and the ranching life. Some people have the naive notion that we should just let the land return to its natural state, and replace active care with some kind of passive admiration of open spaces. This does not take into account the fact that much of the productive land in the valley floor has been planted with non-native grasses to make hay for farm animals and needs to be irrigated. To return to the natural state, we would have to plow up much of the valley and re-plant it with native grasses, almost an impossibility in the world of thistles, leafy spurge and other weeds that would likely doom such an enterprise to failure. To not care for the land would be a travesty, or an abuse, if you will. Besides, such care helps keep our water rights in the Roaring Fork and its tributaries rather than on some Front Range golf course.

When realtors say they're looking at the "highest and best use" of the land, they clearly mean development. So maybe ranching isn't your cup of tea, Mick, but it appears to be one of the best friends Pitkin County has.

What is a Cowboy, Exactly?

What is a cowboy, exactly? I reckon nobody really knows for certain, although the definition might be similar to that of pornography - you know a cowboy when you see one. A girlfriend of mine refers to cowboys as people with expensive trucks and trailers and no visible means of support. Another friend says she never met a cowboy who wasn't hurt, broke, or both. Still another says she gets a special thrill in finding a pair of dusty cowboy boots parked under her bed in the morning.

When I was a kid, there wasn't much difference between a cowboy, a rancher, or any of the folks who ranched for a living or worked for those who did. Guys like Roy Rogers and Gene Autry were "cowboys," made to order for the imaginations of kids, but because they sang and dressed really nice, we always considered them to be "city cowboys." Then of course, there were the real cowboys, the ranchers, like those folks out in Woody Creek who were our neighbors.

You can buy a hat uptown that'll brand you a cowboy to most folks, one with sweat and dirt painted on it's crunched-up facade, and a pair of boots to match, with artificial scuffs in the leather. But being a cowboy isn't about how you look - pretty is not the gist - it's about whether a guy or gal will pick you up from the mud after your horse has dumped your sorry ass in it. Looks take up space at the bar and provide a backdrop for wishful stories, but they can't rope a wild cow or doctor a sick calf.

The life of a cowboy takes the good with the bad. Almost every day, I saddle up a horse or two and head to the high country, either packing salt, clearing trails, or moving cattle from one grazing ground to another. Along the way, I'm graced with looking at Capitol or Daly or other majestic peaks in the Elk Mountain range, take in a lot of fresh air, and see more beauty than many people glimpse in a lifetime. I usually ride alone (which some consider folly), with the exception of my dog Topper, and could die up there as easy as not. According to James P. Owen, Wall Street financier and author, "The code of the west is based not on myth, but on the reality of life on the open range."

There used to be an Aspen City councilman who, from time to time, denigrated the wearing of cowboy hats. Those of us who considered ourselves cowboys and deserving of the right to wear whatever type of chapeau we chose, always felt the councilman dressed reminiscently of a shirt-tailed, poor cousin of Oscar Wilde and who, on his best night, was no better than envy paying tribute to genius.

We take issue with the imagination-challenged, pseudo-intellectual, journalism professionals on both coasts who, in a fit of laziness befitting skid row bums, took to calling George W. Bush "the 'cowboy' president." That's a crock, and a damned insult to every man who ever fancied himself a cowboy, as Dubya fairly well represents just the opposite of everything a cowboy stands for. In Texas, roaming cattle defecate once about every sixteen-hundred acres, so I don't know if that makes Bush a one-cow "rancher" on his 1600 acres near Crawford, or just a guy who's "all hat and no cattle." But, any way you cut it, he ain't no cowboy.

Those who bemoan the loss of our western heritage are the same people who have always used the West as a fantasy destination, a place they'd be if they could honestly live their lives as they wished. Better they not know how tough it is to scrounge an almost impossible living from land that can be so beautiful to the naive eye.

There are still cowboys around, even a few in the Roaring Fork Valley. And like good skiing, you have to get off the road to find them.

Kudos to the Red Brick School

It was mid-April, temperatures hovered in the thirties, deep snow covered the ground outside and Olympian and future Colorado Ski Hall of Famer Steve Rieschl herded us up and down the halls of the Red Brick School with a whistle and a keen eye. Ever mindful of his athletes, Rieschl preferred the hardwood floor of the hall over that of the gymnasium for running – there was more give to it. We were forced into this bizarre indoor training schedule because it was impossible to conduct track practice outside and as a consequence, the Red Brick School added one more memory to the huge bank it already held.

Today's Red Brick Center for the Arts was actually once a public school; in fact, it housed all twelve grades, 1–12. Built in 1941, it originally contained only classrooms – the gymnasium and performance stage didn't come along until 1951-52. The Washington School (5th and Bleeker), elementary school for the town's children, was closed for safety reasons (it was getting ready to fall down) and while the new building of red brick material was being constructed, grade school lessons were conducted at the Hotel Jerome. High school classes were held in D.R.C. Brown, Sr.'s old house, now burned down, which was located on the site where the Yellow Brick holds court today.

There aren't many old photos of the Red Brick, but the ones that exist are remarkably the same and express the uniqueness of Aspen, even in those long-ago days. Almost every photo shows smiling kids with skis over their shoulders, milling down the sidewalks, headed to the mountain. Early ski racing pioneers like Dave Stapleton, Max Marolt, Keith Marolt, Melvin Hoagland, Tony Deane, and others walked those hallowed halls. We were a proud, highly engaged school when brothers Max and Billy Marolt made the Olympic team ('60 & '64 respectively). Terry Morse, classmate of mine, went on to Olympic fame in 1972.

Don't start thinking I'm name-dropping or trying to impress you, but it's important to note that the Red Brick School was never a small town, podunk operation. Some kids never finished the curriculum, others went on to Ivy League schools, a couple committed suicide and even others made names for themselves in the business world. Some of us still live here. It was a hodge-podge of some of the best kids in the world, names and faces that none of us will ever forget.

There aren't that many rooms in the building, so think of the logistical nightmare of managing the place. Grades 1-6 were stationary, in the same classroom all day, but 7-12 moved from room-to-room every hour, and that's a lot of kids shambling through the locker-lined halls. Definitely cramped, but it never seemed that way. In addition, there was a state-of-the-art science laboratory and a well-stocked library that doubled as study hall. Physical education was required and taught in the gymnasium, which got a few kids out of the way each hour.

If you're a politician or tax collector, it might be important to blather on about academic achievement, but I don't think it matters much to the students themselves. School is less about academics than it is about social interaction and that is the stuff we remember most. How many love affairs were started (or ended) in the hallway during the hourly shuffle; how many camping or hunting or weekend trips planned during the day? Disagreements were hatched and resolved, tears shed, and smiles and hugs and handshakes made it all okay. We were all heroes or bums, depending on the day. So much of what my life has been about is tied directly to the Red Brick School and the people who shared it with me.

It's a big deal to have the Red Brick Center for the Arts near the middle of town, an amenity that other towns our size might never come up with, especially if you include the attached gymnasium and well-manicured lawn out front. But clearly, we need to honor the strong and lasting foundation of the predecessor Red Brick School, one that was laid long before the arts center was envisioned.

Red, White – and Bare

As far as the Fourth of July goes, it wasn't much of a plan, and the odds of incessant excitement were rather slim. It was a couple of years ago and I'd gone up to a secluded family cabin with a broken heart, delivered to me by a woman who had, in the ways of love, let me off somewhere along the path with very little explanation. We'd spent a lot of time at this hideaway, so I'd come back to purge the place of maudlin memories and get on with it.

The year before, I had started rebuilding the cabin's horse corral, so on this sunny and warm 4th, I proceeded with the project, working along the creek. The sky was cloudless and there was a perfect stillness in the air, save for an occasional songbird. Even the jets and planes at the airport were reasonably quiet, but the 5th would be the usual day of reckoning.

It was hot, even at 10,600 in elevation, and the idea of getting a little sun with my shirt off was appealing, but as I thought about it, why not just take everything off and get some full-body exposure? Emerging from the cabin in only a pair of cowboy boots, a Stetson, and with a small bandana around my neck, I felt a little foolish, but being my only admirer, felt I could appreciate it for a while.

After a few minutes of work on the corral, the realization came that it would be easy to lose track of time and get seriously burned, so a new scenario developed itself in my mind. I would walk down the trail about a quarter-mile or so, checking out a lush, green meadow and look for an owl who (who?) had made a considerable racket the night before. It would be a short trip of about thirty minutes by my reckoning, then back to the cabin, put my clothes on, and be none the worse for wear.

Deep into the open meadow and about five minutes from the log abode, a grin upon my face and the hot sun penetrating my winter-white skin, there was suddenly a sound that didn't fit. I didn't know what it was at that instant, but knew it wasn't part of the unspoiled world and that it could only mean trouble to my solace in the wilderness. As I did a 180 to ascertain the sound's source, a woman on a mountain bike came into view, giving me pause. "Oh, thank God I've found you - we're so lost," was the first thing she said, pedaling directly up to me without quite realizing the full impact of whom (or what) she was talking to at the moment.

I spied a small bush off to my left, thinking perhaps I should crouch down there and save her (me?) the embarrassment, but decided that it was more natural to remain natural in the natural world than to act civilized, and stood my ground, so to speak.

About then, her female partner arrived and observed the scene before her with a more relaxed and somewhat less-panicked eye. It was, no doubt, obvious from the color of my skin that I was not a practicing nudist and after rummaging through her pack, she handed me a plastic poncho to use as I saw fit.

Ever the gentleman, I led the way back to the cabin, wondering if the giggles behind me were of the fun-loving sort. After I regained my clothes, we sat down to a humorous pot of tea and went over some maps of the local trails. On occasion, I see one of the gals around town, who always gives me that certain look, as in, "I know what you really look like!"

The event served to lift my despondent emotions, and that night I drifted off to sleep with a smile on my face and a lightness of spirit in my bones.

Ski Cooper and the Tenth Mountain Troops

I first spotted it on a full-moon night, a beautiful, wide, glorious-looking ski run, one that was tied directly to the 10th Mountain Division. That was four or five years ago, on a winter drive to southeastern Colorado, and in that one glimpse from near the top of Tennessee Pass, a personal crusade was born that finally reached fruition last week.

My entire life has been spent in and around Aspen, a large part of it on Aspen Mountain, so it was impossible to imagine that I might be out of place at a small area such as Ski Cooper. I had on an Eider parka with complementary Eider pants and a pair of Atomic boots, all from Stapleton Sports. In Aspen, I'm just another stylin' dude, headed up the gondola. At Ski Cooper, I was a colorful curiosity, a guy to keep your eye on. "Better see what he's up to," a suspicion I didn't help by requesting a pair of rental poles. The girl behind the counter, smiling like she truly enjoyed her job, wondered aloud if I had everything else I needed, right down to sunscreen. "Are you sure," she asked?

It's hard to say where the customers come from. Some from Leadville probably, and I suspect more from Minturn and the Eagle Valley. I mean, if you had a choice between the crowded slopes of Vail or the total freedom of Ski Cooper, you'd have to think about it.

Like any good tourist, I grabbed a trail map, which almost rattled out of my hand in the strong wind, and headed up the hill on what they call the 10th Mountain Chair. There looked to be a good little run named Corkscrew next to the ski area boundary, and I figured that was a decent place to start, given an existing familiarity with a local run of the same name. In reality, it was a tree trail, more akin to Hidden Treasure on Aspen Mountain and like a gaper, I missed the entrance, requiring a traverse through the trees on set-up crud to get there.

Dodging the narrowly spaced trees put my "frozen-slush" skills to work, and eventually I skied to the bottom of the area's other chairlift, a non-high-speed triple. A smiling young lift operator, who could easily have been family, wanted to know "what the hell" I was doing over there on that trail, "in these conditions, anyway?" We had a good laugh, and when I asked where the moguls were, he cast me a sideways glance, the kind with a half-closed eye on the near side, and said he didn't think the snow would soften up that much, not unless the wind quit.

The few moguls I found had incredible rhythm and hadn't been hit hard enough to get the downhill "chop" on them, the kind that rattle your teeth, like on Summit. It didn't necessarily matter that they were rock hard. If I'd a been there the day before, I could've ripped the place apart in the spring-soft snow and left with a deep tan, but you take what you get.

We can't deny that we're spoiled here, having world-class Aspen Mountain out the back door with its great lifts and incredible terrain. Many serious local skiers have reached a level of sophistication, a way of traveling that speaks to recreational professionalism, a die-hard philosophy that comes across as arrogant to many outsiders, and probably with good reason. I may be one of 'em.

There is something refreshing about a place like Ski Cooper, where sitting in the cafeteria, one cannot tell skiers from gawkers, not without looking to see who has on ski boots, and brand is not necessarily connected to quality or "cool." The employees, just like here, are incredibly friendly and will give you the best service they possibly can. The best part, I suppose, is that Ski Cooper reminds us of our intrinsic skiing roots, particularly as they relate to the 10th Mountain Division. That's why I went.

Really, I'm Looking Forward to Summer

The winter season is similar to a fast run down the mountain - mostly a blur of great skiing with a few icy bumps and maybe a fall or hand-dragger thrown in. Upon closer inspection, some things stand out, such as suffocating face shots and the occasional big air. Winter, the time of year when I close my mind down to everything but skiing (well, mostly), had more distractions this time around than usual, but for the most part, they were welcome.

My daughter, Lauren, graduated from college at the end of the fall semester, and after several attempts, most of them requiring skilled salesmanship on my part, convinced her to move home and settle into the life of a ski bum. It may have been a successful move, as her last comment on the matter, at least the one I remember, is that perhaps another winter like this one would be to her liking. She and I managed to ski together at least three or four days a week, something we had been looking forward to for years but had put on the back burner. Be careful, kid, or you'll end up like your old man.

My ol' ski buddy, Valerie, and I mixed it up together way more days than last year and finally got our groove back. She's a really good skier, long legs and major energy, unerringly taking the fall line, no matter the pitch, and always coming up with a smile. We did the Bowl, for the first time together, after four years of talking about it, and might make it again with the extra week added onto the season. She'll shudder to realize I'm talking about her like this in public, but you should also know she's got her feet moving really fast now, in unison.

It wouldn't do not to mention my regular ski buddy, Bob, the guy who wears that friggin' Yeti coat all over the mountain. He didn't ski much this year, although he can still put a zipper on the bumps better than almost anybody, young or old, who thinks they're really good. His fashion sense remained true - without fault - as he pulled on a spanking new, pink parka, trimmed in black diamonds, the first day of gay ski week. I really felt it was unfair of him, a good-looking hetero, to align himself in that manner and besides, I think the color looks better on me. He got new boots, too, but who cares?

Last week, Tim Cooney (and friends) staged a reunion of the ski patrol/trail crew at the Red Onion. Much as I love the place, it had been a long time since I'd rattled her swinging doors, and walking into a bar full of guys and gals I've worked with since even before the early seventies was, if it hadn't been so festive, almost a somber occasion. A couple of sharp-memoried dudes I hadn't seen in years recalled conversations we'd had long-ago, late at night over beers, and could also recount the density and consistency of the powder we'd skied the next morning. Tonight, there'll be a big blowout at the Onion, but a lot of us have already said our good-byes.

And so it goes. Whatever we do, however we do it, it all comes back to the snow and the winters and the skiing. And that's how it should be. If you're in the know, you know Aspen isn't about the town, it's about the mountain. As my friend Randi Bolton said, quoting someone: "If you have to have a sport instead of a career, skiing ain't bad." See you on the slopes.

Rhythm on the Eastern Shore of Maryland

The key is rhythm, steady rhythm, like the beating of your heart or the advance of tectonic plates across the earth's surface; the tide along the banks of the Chester River on Maryland's Eastern Shore ebbs and flows with a rhythm millions of years old and the horses feel it, somewhere deep inside.

We stepped into a late October, early morning dense fog, lightheaded at the scarcity of landmarks. Carefully walking across the damp earth and trying to look around, it was as though floating through a dream, a Colorado horseman lost in the murkiness, unsure of his role.

Horses, unseen but snorting through the mist gave one a sense of home and from within my breast, an eagerness sprang to meet these new friends, to touch the familiarity of equine reality with my thoughts and feelings. Horse barns are built by men, but horses own them through the sheer force of their personalities. A barn without horses is one without romance, without purpose. The clomping of a horse's hooves as it walks the alleyway is, well, unforgettable.

A mountain boy from Woody Creek, plunked down in the middle of a Thoroughbred race horse farm back East without his western saddle, helping to break yearlings and handle stud horses, makes for an interesting scenario in survival. Nerve and naiveté help, but a sense of deep curiosity serves to keep one in the game. That and a good boss who always tried to make things interesting for that scrawny kid and his young wife.

Charlie Moloney, the manager, already had our horses saddled, and they were snuffling and pawing, eager to begin their exercise routine. As we mounted up, the fog began to lift, giving one the perception that something magical was in the works. We left the barn area, four abreast, with me wondering where the adventure would lead – the others wondering if I'd measure up.

The stout gelding underneath me, one of the fox hunting stable, was steady enough and immediately gained my trust. After a bit, we kicked up into a slow canter (lope) and the immense energy of the beast began to tire my arms as I attempted to keep him in the pack. "Put an iron cross on him," hollered Eddie Houghton, the farm owner, from the outside. Hell, I didn't know an iron cross from a wooden peg at that point, but by watching Eddie, I learned how to cross the reins over the big horse's neck, letting him pull against himself.

Harold Hall and I broke a lot of horses in the Woody Creek Canyon, and we rode some rank ones into damned good ranch mounts, but those mornings spent exercising the fox hunters back East are still powerful in my mind. Charging down wide, well-kept, sandy trails through forests of red oak, beech, maple and dogwood, standing up in the stirrups of an English saddle at a gallop, my face within inches of the light sorrel mane and experiencing every nuance of the powerful horse under me was a rush I cannot forget.

And I became aware of something I knew, but hadn't before acknowledged. To be a good rider, you need a lot of practice, but even more important, you have to develop the ability to merge with the rhythm of the animal you're riding. Horses react naturally from the heart without giving their actions a lot of cerebral consideration, a gift we humans have denigrated in ourselves, believing brain power to be superlative.

It's been almost 40 years since I traveled those Maryland trails and in the incessant rhythm of life we can't control, some of the riders have left our midst, but my memories of them will never die. Eddie, the high-energy owner, is gone, along with his farm manager, Charlie. Long ago, the horses we rode stopped clunking through the barn and galloping after fox hounds. Somewhere there's a photo, taken by my friend Buck Deane, documenting my life as an English exercise rider in the secluded woods of Maryland. I'd like to find that photo for just one more glimpse.

Road Trip and Memory Lane

First spring road trip and I'm driving down a strange street, with only an inkling of my destination, when the house instantaneously materializes before me. Through the wooden fence I see her, totally engrossed in a gardening project at the back of the yard. As my truck door slams shut, she looks up suddenly and jumps to her feet, running to unlatch the yard gate with a gentle touch and a genuine smile. An Aspen native, recently moved and my friend from the first-grade on, she looks as she always has - full of energetic beauty. Her hip length hair has grayed a bit, but the youthful appearance of her face is mostly unchanged, and I particularly notice her long, tanned and graceful fingers. Our visit is good.

As I round the bend outside another small town, a little white church nestled in a clump of large cottonwoods unexpectedly reveals itself and I pull over and just look at it for a while. Screwing up my courage, I walk across the lawn and enter through an unlocked door into a large, empty sanctuary. Before I know it, I'm at the old, almost immaculate grand piano, adjusting the bench and thinking I'm smaller than the cherub-faced woman I last heard playing it.

There's an air of friendly solemnity in the large, sunlit room, and my heartbeat increases with an unfounded nervousness as I begin to play. It's a fast-moving blues tune, a song I've wanted to play on this piano since last I heard its resonance so many years ago. Music fills the hall as the memories flood back, my mind in many places except the present, and fresh tears cloud my eyes as I reminisce the years for Jessie, my sweet Jessie, a long-ago, out-of-town girlfriend who was buried not far from this church long before her time.

It's another town, another piano, a beat-up old wreck of a thing, but the mood is upbeat and the saloon patrons are whooping it up and whistling and stomping their feet. It's early evening, just after sunset and an older gent with a bit of a list in his step from a long afternoon of bourbon wanders my way with a harmonica in his hand. He's good and I laugh with the serendipitous energy of the moment, watching this man coming to life who earlier had the look of a worn-out rag doll as he sat at the bar.

A woman in a red satin dress, standing next to me, swings her butt to the beat and keeps an eye on the already half-full tip jar, occasionally giving me a suggestive rub with her hip. I wonder if the soft fabric of her dress is the same stuff that covers the lamps casually placed on shelves and dining tables around the room. She was once a fireball, that's apparent, but there's now a sadness to her and after a while, I make for the dimly-lit backroom to take a break from it all. Four young guys playing pool look as though they've been in the place for all eternity, and spying the back door, I casually walk out, glad to be gone and glad that alcohol is no longer the draw for me. I'd bet that the lady in red scored the tip jar before I hit the alley.

Last day out and I've been invited somewhere for Sunday brunch. The guest list includes a lady that the matchmaking hostess thinks - you know how that goes. Untypically, the lady and I know each other from winters past and before the caterer can unpack his crate, she and I are roaring out of town in her car, up a dirt road on the side of a mountain, looking for a place that only she knows. We land the car and snuggle down in the grass, the first buds of spring on the overlying branches. Her lips are full, warm and wet. Hard-angled sunlight, freshly enlivened by the passions of warm weather, insistently presses itself against the reflective diamonds of civilization down below, and our smiles become the essence of springtime.

Rubbing Elbows with Celebrities

If you have a lot of time to kill, you've no doubt been exercising your Facebook account, and if you've gone that far, you've certainly come across the site, "Friends of Aspen from the 1960s - 70s." It's a loosely held-together group of baby-boomers who lived here in the described time period and who now readily admit, in the words of many of them, that "I can't remember 90% of the people on this site, but I know what they're talking about."

By my count, and that counts for very little, it appears that the subject garnering the most comments to date has been the one about "celebrities." Most of the posts detail certain Aspen encounters with well-known people, the general take being that "celebrities" back then were a bit different than many of the publicity-seeking prunes that clog our sidewalks today, say at Christmas, etc.

Many of us seem to have a certain fascination with "celebrity," although I have to say that even a good "paparazzo," trying to sell photos around here before 1990 would have starved to death rather quickly. We didn't seek celebrities out, but seemed to stumble over them with regularity.

Jeanne Lauck, long deceased but a great friend in the 70s, had put the word out to her closest friends that she was throwing a party. "Come by after the bars close," she'd said, and we huddled in a Red Onion booth, sipping and planning when some gal strolled up and wanted to know if she could bring Clint Eastwood along. "Who the fuck is Clint Eastwood?" replied Jeanne in her famously loud voice, and I looked up in time to see Clint, standing at the bar in the haze of the smoke and the buzz, trying to look nonchalant. Jeanne put him on the list.

The Red Butte neighborhood, a quiet enclave of family-style Aspenites, took on the glow of the big-time for a while, strange as that may seem today. Buddy Hackett had a house across from my uncle Victor and was known to drop in unannounced, feeling no pain, with his latest joke of the day.

Approaching that same uncle's house one snowy, winter evening, I came upon a car stuck in the ditch and stopped to help the lady get back on the road. A tall girl with dark hair giggled, cussed and invited me by later for Christmas cheer. None other than Cher, it turned out, who had bought the log house next door. The possibilities were there, I always imagined.

Not everyone gets the respect he or she might desire, and this was apparent at Jimmy Buffet's wedding at the Redstone Castle back in the 70s sometime. There was, of course, security and a gate you needed to be checked through to gain admission. Apparently, one of the guards inquired of his partner as to who had just wandered through and the reply, obviously extra-loud and well-elucidated for those of us within earshot, was, "That was Hunter "Asshole" Thompson." Ouch.

With adulation comes derision, even in good ol' Aspen town, no matter how smart, cool or famous you might happen to be. Some 70s wise-guy, married to a woman of physical fame, once bragged to a friend and me that he was worth twenty million dollars. My buddy, gentleman that he is, replied that such a sum wouldn't get you much more than a cup of coffee in this town.

If you look into it, one theory is that we admire celebrities because they live decadent lives filled with spontaneity, lives which make our own look rather drab and uninteresting.

Whoever thought that up seems to have it backwards, if you ask me. That's why the celebs come to Aspen - to prop up their own lives, dull by comparison to the local shuffle.

Ski Lessons and Schools Days

The other day, waiting for a meeting at the Red Brick Arts Center, I happened to walk around behind the building. The memory of a scared first-grader, wandering the grounds, wondering where his skis and poles had disappeared to, crossed my mind and a bit of that boy's young soul tugged at my emotions. The boy had somehow missed the instructions, coming back to school from a Wednesday afternoon on Aspen Mountain, on where the skis would be left and was asking himself how he'd ever explain to his dad what had happened. The worst fear was knowing that once lost, the skis would never be replaced and my skiing days would be over.

The Aspen School District used to have a Wednesday Afternoon Activities Program, designed to get kids out into the world of winter delights and to partake in the benefits of living in this, even then, legendary town. The choices were sparse, but opened up a huge world to most of us: skiing, ice skating, or study hall. Skiing was by far the most popular event, but believe it or not, there were a fair number of kids who preferred ice skating or study hall.

It was kept very simple and plebeian. Imagine a town-full of students, first grade through twelfth, coming to school dressed for their chosen afternoon sports, somehow keeping gloves, hats, goggles, boots, skates, etc., within the confines of the very small spaces allotted kids in those days. We lined the skis and poles up in the snowbank along Hallam Street out front - there was no going home and coming back - you lived it from the first bell.

Right after lunch, skiers loaded onto buses, bound for Aspen Mountain, the skaters walked kitty- corner to the ice rink on Bleeker, and the rest went to study hall, which was held in various rooms, including the science laboratory. Volunteers from town were our instructors/chaperones and we generally had a blast, learning to ski and getting the savvy of the mountain. Saturday, Sunday, and Wednesday afternoons - we were living pretty well.

When I was nine, tucking Spar Gulch from the dam (bottom of the FIS lift), for the umpteenth time in bear-trap bindings, I finally fell, and as my buddy Terry Morse said would happen, broke my left leg in a deforming fashion. Needless to say, I found out what went on in study hall the rest of the winter, along with Tommy Moore, who broke his leg twice, once at the Junior Nationals in Whitefish, Montana; Gerry Morse, who broke his training on Aspen Mountain; and a couple of other broken legged guys whose names are the stuff of lost memory.

Tommy and Gerry, who were several years older, gave me lessons in balsa wood model building, how to "fake" people out by throwing steel-tipped darts into each other's casts, how to walk on hip-length plaster casts (forbidden by the doctors - we all had to get replacement casts much earlier than technically indicated), and how to otherwise occupy ourselves through the warmth of an inside room at the bottom of a world-class ski hill.

The next year, Terry and I joined a powder skiing class, and had fresh powder every Wednesday, every week. It didn't snow all that much - the mountain just didn't get the traffic and we really didn't think about it.

On that day long ago, and through the window of an empty classroom, the young boy spied some skis stuck in a snowbank out behind the school and wondered who the kid was lucky enough to leave his skis anywhere he wished. It turned out, with exhilarating relief, that I was the kid.

Strongest Memories of the Strongest Woman

Like most kids, the outdoors was my playground and as I wrestled toy cars and trucks along winding dirt roads made by my own hand, the sound of music would slowly catch my ear, enticing me up the front steps. Three-quarter time on an old upright piano pounded down the bass while a beautiful, unmistakable and strong soprano voice carried the melody out the open window, through the porch rafters and into the yard, finally disappearing behind the lilacs and cottonwoods along a small irrigation ditch.

She could hold me endlessly with her music, but like a young and energetic filly, was reluctant to let me too close. If my interest was too keen, the singing would stop and she'd disappear into another part of the house, to "do the housework."

"Oh, of course I remember her, a unique woman," people will say, if her name comes up in conversation. She had her causes and her ambitions and she worked tirelessly to accomplish those things she thought important to the community.

We went to the music tent at least once a week in the summer and every Sunday listened to the music students sing in the Aspen Community Church choir. Maybe music was our elixir, for in the summer, we had great times together. Her aspirations for me to become a polished musician were dashed by my paternal grandfather who, in a larger than life image of the old west than even John Wayne could project, purposefully instilled in me a ranching heritage that I cannot break, not even today.

Her health began to fail while she was still in her thirties, compounded myopically by the western slope's main medical facility, run by a pack of nuns who refused to allow hysterectomies, no matter how serious the need. Maybe it was naiveté that kept her from going to Denver, or maybe just a young woman's faith, not yet corrupted, that people always had your best interests at heart. For weeks, maybe months, she would be gone, not once but several times, bedridden in a faraway hospital, trying to recover from the butchery that posed as modern medical science.

Such absences, perhaps, were the catalyst that began our slow drift away from each other, but on deeper reflection, the seeds of estrangement were already there. She still kept me in piano lessons, with an attempt at strictness, but never again would I hear her playing on those lazy summer afternoons, and the brilliant timbre of her voice had descended to a delicate hum, when it appeared at all. The music tent and church disappeared from our rounds.

In her early fifties, maybe it was the loss of her youngest child, coupled with the death of her husband soon after, that brought her down, but it was ugly any way you wish to fathom it. Sometimes, unkind words are said in an attempt to gain sympathy for one's own predicament, and such accidents of human nature, no matter how well understood, rend wounds that never seem to repair themselves and leave once-staid accomplices as strangers in a continuing, life-long relationship.

Somewhere in my mind, I had visions of us repairing the rift, although I knew it would be impossible. Death waits not, and while I procrastinated, she faced the shrouded reaper in a lonely Denver hospital room. I missed seeing her by mere hours, but would it have made a difference? Upon my sister's beckoning call, I cried myself to Denver, nonstop. Were the tears because of someone dear I had lost, or more likely, did I weep for the woman who, even in her own setting sun, didn't want to go, for there glimmered still a hope for fleeting contentment, no matter how brief.

A lifetime of challenging circumstances couldn't break her heart completely, but in the end, she must have realized the fragility of what was left.

Transitions

It's a simple thing to drop off a uniform at the Ski Company offices and be on my way. The end of winter is here, another season almost over, but that can't explain the melancholy.

There's a burning in my eyes, maybe because Iris DeMent's CD is providing one of her inimitable tear-jerkers as background to my mood, but I suspect it runs much deeper than that. Did a susceptibility to such moods start early in my life, at a time my memory cannot access, or did it develop over the years from seeing too much . . . something?

This event, or that event, taken by themselves, walk through our lives with some sort of expectation that things will happen, can't be helped, but when they start cropping up, we are left open to the realization that some situations will never come our way again in this life.

It wasn't that long ago, deep into the cold of January that a matriarch of the Vagneur clan died. Ruth Vagneur gave it up after a long life, leaving behind a vital, and still local family. At Red Butte Cemetery, as we prepared to lower the coffin, the undertaker opined that bitter winter was preventing his electronic machine from doing its job. My cousin, Kent, pulled four lariats from the back of his truck, and in a manner befitting a ranching family of five generations out in Woody Creek, we gently lowered Ruth down in a style consistent with the old times around here.

A week or so ago, lifelong native, Sam Stapleton, died at his house after putting up the good fight for the past few years. Or for a lifetime, I guess, if you want to look at it that way. "A kaleidoscope of stories," was how Gregg Anderson of the Prince of Peace Chapel put it last Friday as we listened to friends and family pay their last respects. Sammy Pete was a cousin of mine and we shared some stories that might, in the proper company, bear repeating. We once worked in tandem to save a little girl from potentially life-threatening injury on a spooked horse, but talking about heroic things he'd done wasn't the stuff of Sam, so I'm not going to mention it, either. But, you know, a guy like that leaves a hole when he ducks out on you.

Yesterday, we took the time, for the second Friday in a row, to visit the Prince of Peace Chapel, this time to say our last goodbyes to Norbert Anthes, a good friend who put sunshine into our lives since almost before we knew him. The usual drive on a Friday night, just to get home, and when it turns into a nightmare, the lives of many are unalterably changed. Wouldn't you like to grasp that powerful handshake and see the twinkle in those eyes, just one more time?

If nothing else, we learn equality from death, for we each leave for the next world with about the same accoutrements. Forget monuments and things named after you - it's the repetition of your name on the lips of friends and family that provides lasting memory in this world of ours.

The tears can't be held back, but the grass is greening up, the horses slicking down. The cutting pain of these deaths, and others, will slowly dull, and no matter how far inward our thoughts may have been turned, life moves on and we continue our participation. My daughter will be coming home from college this summer, a special friend is arriving soon for a rendezvous, and spring, however incongruously, signals a rebirth of life.

Maybe the uniform won't fit next year, or I may not be here to wear it, but the life that has been partially intertwined with it is good and appreciated, and already, I'm worried about being in shape for next ski season.

Summit, the Run

The other day, on my way out of Bonnie's on Aspen Mountain, a fellow skier, whom I'd never met before, grabbed my arm and asked, "You're the guy who likes Summit, aren't you?" Summit is a non-descript name for a ski trail, totally lacking in any description of what it's all about or why it was cut, other than it's near the top of the mountain. Trail names are like that - not even Corkscrew equates with its original vision and layout. Mention Summit to those in the know and the almost immediate feedback is, "You mean 'Vomit'?"

Jimmy Gerbaz introduced me to Summit the winter I graduated from college. Red Rowland had cut the trail sometime during my university years and one day after a good snowstorm, Jimmy and I got first tracks down the mother in about a foot of wet, heavy stuff. I swore I'd never go back.

I'm not much of a tally man and it would be impossible to say how many times I've skied Summit since, but if you take my youthful years on the ski patrol when I religiously skied it at least once a day, just for discipline, and then take the 14 years lately when I've gotten back into skiing (and hit Summit 3 or 4 times a day when it feels right, but at least once), a good ball park number is 3000, more or less. Sometimes my back tells me it's nothing to brag about.

My buddy, Bob Snyder, who matches me run for run, once lapped it thirteen times in a day, which may be a record. The man mentioned in the first paragraph (anonymity is sometimes good), has meticulously kept written records of his runs down Summit since the winter of 1987-88 and claims over 3500 successful conquests of the brute. I readily concede to such dedication and fastidious attention to detail. He wrote it down, dammit!

There's a reason some people have nicknamed it "Vomit." Most like to say it has a double fall line, unaware that it's actually the triple fall line that gives them all the trouble. And by fall line, I don't mean the latest fashions out of New York – I'm talking the

316

direction a rock would roll if tossed down the hill. Also, it's narrow and due to its ever-changing topography, the bumps have absolutely no rhythm.

There are three basic entrances to Summit, the first being a simple traverse off of Dipsy Bowl. The more adventurous can drop in off the Buckhorn Cutoff road, but my favorite is just past the trail sign, down to the left of a lone pine standing there. Other people sneak in from either Ankle Grabber or the side of Midnight, but that's like skiing Little Nell and saying you ripped Aspen Mountain. At any given time, you might have one great run down the SOB and go back for seconds only to exit totally frustrated by its capricious bruising of your ego.

A lot of guys look good and feel confident about themselves blasting down the Face, the Ridge or Perry's, but the great equalizer is Summit. No matter how you might try, you cannot bullshit your way down its twisting, off-kilter terrain. You have to be on your game the whole way down, alert to each turn. Many a skier, smooth and controlled everywhere else on Aspen Mountain, has been exposed as the true intermediate he is once he dips his tips in Vomit, er, Summit.

My favorite day on the mountain, which hardly ever comes around, is dropping into Summit when it's about twenty below on top of 8-12 inches of fresh snow. Launch off the road high, hard and fast and your smile will be a mile wide. Miss a beat and you'll be picking up after a yard sale of your own making.

Talking about Summit with a friend who skis it all the time is like listening to two men talk about the woman they are both sleeping with. Every nuance, every caress, every iniquitous move is appreciated by the other in a way that only one who has been there can truly understand.

And in the end, fidelity to the cause and respect for Summit itself makes it about smiles, laughter, love, cuss words and oaths to never return, depending on the day.

Tale of a Wolf Hunt

It's a gray, foggy morning in mid-April as the wolf silently pads her way over the pine-covered Montana mountainside. She weighs about a hundred pounds, a little heavier this time of year, but glides effortlessly on feet that appear too big for her body, her back undulating almost indiscernibly as she moves with a single purpose toward a place she will know immediately on sight. With all probability, she is the alpha female of a small pack, a group who, for whatever reasons, is seeking out new territory beyond the relative safety of Yellowstone National Park.

In a chance encounter that belies fate, a Montana hunting guide (or an anachronistic rancher, or simply a ruddy-faced, squint-eyed defender of an aberrant, modern-day West) sees the lone female crossing a portion of his land and takes aim with a high-powered and well-scoped rifle, allowing himself to become judge and jury over the worth of the animal's life, not realizing that his knowledge of this, or any wolf, is highly subjective and may be inferior to that of a city-slicker who has actually read up on *canis lupus*.

If he is a hunting guide, he shoots the wolf out of fear that predation will deplete the elk herds he depends on for a livelihood, somehow unaware that overpopulation and drought are far more deadly to an elk herd than a wolf pack.

Montana outfitter James Hubbard, worried about wolves "killing the industry" and as quoted recently by the Associated Press, says: "They (hunters) used to see so many (elk) it was unreal." If Hubbard and others like him listen to knowledge about wolves as well as they listen to themselves, it's no wonder wolves are in danger. "Unreal" numbers of elk may be in direct correlation to a lack of "real" predators such as wolves, not to mention the natural rise and fall in herd numbers.

In November 2004, the Alaska Board of Game, in its infinite wisdom (and in capitulation to outfitters), opened more land in eastern Alaska, near the Canadian border, to aerial and ground wolf hunting. Today in Alaska, 60,000 square miles are now open to the hunting of wolves and it is estimated that 2000-2500 wolves may be killed in 2005, roughly a third of the Alaskan wolf population.

Catching the wolf in mid-stride, a poorly placed bullet tears into her haunch, knocking her to the ground. Killing wolves is a new thing, just recently legalized in parts of the lower '48 (due to de-listing of wolves as an "endangered" species and being put under state, rather than federal control), and it will take some time to sharpen up the marksmanship skills needed to be an effective "wolfer."

With her backside paralyzed, the frantic wolf tries valiantly to raise herself on still-agile front legs to escape the terrible nightmare enveloping her, but it's useless. Struggling to fulfill an ancient desire, she wants only to find the den site and deliver her pups, giving life to a new pack in a new territory. She doesn't understand why she can't.

The man with the rifle warily approaches his "trophy," afraid something still alive like that, even though half–paralyzed, may offer a danger to himself. Originating with the mother who bore him years before, a glimmer of compassion momentarily overcomes the man and he timidly puts the last bullet home, causing instantaneous death. The five pups in her belly die soundlessly, with hardly a squirm, as their lifeline, the umbilical cord, shuts down. Just as quietly, the future of this wolf pack becomes almost as bleak as the now-lifeless body lying on the cold ground.

That night, the remaining wolves may howl toward Sirius, the "Wolf Star," not only for the loss of the pregnant female, but because they feel a sadness for the insecure and misdirected humans who, lacking a desire to understand, cause so much pain and destruction to North American wolves.

It has been suggested that wolves are second in intelligence only to man, but when one realizes that wolves are not compelled by fear and ignorance to destroy their brothers upon the earth, that ranking may be suspect.

The Dark Trail

The span of a lifetime isn't much in the grand scheme of things, and the trail I'd been looking at has existed for at least five generations, a well-worn cut, down a precipice consisting of more rock than dirt.

Its intrigue has mesmerized me for a very long time, a path whose existence is undeniable whenever I glance that way while driving by. The last time I walked down that track has remained clear in my mind for fifty-five years and its continued existence has enticed me, stronger and stronger over time, to revisit its very dimensions and to reclaim the memory for eternity.

Last week, my big horse Drifter took me to the edge with long, clomping steps and then he hesitated, as if questioning the wisdom of traveling so far back in time. I answered with my spurs and down the corridor we headed, a rush of adrenaline flooding my being. At last, I was there.

Clawing its way up from the depths of my mind, I could almost hear and see the busy scene behind us; a huge threshing machine, powered by a John Deere tractor, chopping and blowing oat straw into a tall, delicious golden pile while the separated seeds were augured into a truck parked alongside. Teams of mighty draft horses pulled neatly laden wagon-loads of bundled oat stalks up to the giant contraption and strong-armed men from neighboring ranches tossed the bundles into the ravenous maw of the incessant machine.

It was a hot, mid-afternoon September day, and my dad had sent me down the trail to fill a couple of gallon containers with Woody Creek water for the thirsty men. It was a difficult job for a boy of ten and a steep walk of about half-mile, but there was no arguing with the old man.

Trudging back up the trail, it seemed impossible to make the top with such heavy cargo, but at last the threshing machine and my father came into view. I soon rued the sight, for my dad wanted to know what "the hell" had taken so long. With that, I impetuously tossed one of the full glass jugs at his feet, which immediately exploded into a million pieces. Then came the thrashing I probably deserved, which in the end, embarrassed both my father and me. He always underestimated the depth of my obduracy.

The path was now laid before us, narrow from disuse, and Drifter went cautiously, stiff-legged, testing my resolve. Long ahead and steeply straight, the trail got gloomy as it entered a willow patch and its murkiness seemed uncaring.

Other thoughts rolled across my mind, injustices that had been perpetrated upon me in those days, either real or perceived, the most glaring of which was, years later, the sale of our original Vagneur ranch. I argued passionately with my dad to prevent it, but he had siblings to assuage and the tables were stacked hard against me.

I prodded Drifter down further, spurs jingling and chaps slapping my legs, wondering if it was that ten-year old boy I sought, to soothe his bruised ego, or if I thought somehow I could right all the distant wrongs by facing the past from the future.

The darkness ahead seemed increasingly precipitous and more ominous, as though it might swallow Drifter and me up, and my curiosity stalled. Blessed by recent events, I'd traveled most of that iconic Vagneur ranch this past summer, investigating nooks and crannies important only to me. This spot, on the very edge of the ranch, was the one remaining place I had not explored.

Half-way down, we stopped and pondered a bit, my horse and I, before turning around and heading back the way we had come. Perhaps in everyone's life, there is a dark place best left alone, a stash of demons better left buried than resurrected, the notorious Pandora's box that shouldn't be opened.

I still see that trail when I drive by, but the burning quest to explore it has been sated by the power of intrinsic considerations too ethereal to question.

Tom Munn

It's an easy-going tempo these jazz musicians work through, a gathering of old friends putting together their best stuff during a live recording session along the bayous of the Mohawk in upstate New York. They'd never guess, if any of them are still living, that their soulful lyricism wafts itself daily through my Jeep stereo speakers as I wind up "Killer 82," headed to Aspen Mountain.

They don't monkey up their repertoire with crafty lyrics, the piano player being clearly the most talented at creating poetry out of wordless sound, although the man on the clarinet gives him some competition on a couple of tunes.

As they play, one can almost hear the rustling of autumn leaves against the stark vitality of relentless time, detect an occasional riff of brutal reality from a white-walled car tire cruising the damp country road, and the piano man's youngest son boards a Greyhound bus bound for Colorado, the enigmatic land of cowboys, itinerant do-gooders, and freedom.

"That guitar ain't gonna do you much good, resting in a hand-carried case while the rest of your belongings are slung in a pack across your shoulders. Son, you've got talent and it won't do to travel out west. Stay near the cities."

There's a home waiting over the Continental Divide, high on a mesa above Woody Creek, at the end of a narrow, winding road, and the folks ranching there are glad to see a big, stout kid who wants to work. The bunkhouse "boys," they stack up neat; L.C., the old man who's been through it all and is now relegated to cabin cook; Jay, the American Indian, a man you could trust to cover you in the worst of times, but if you made an enemy out of him, you'd better sleep with one eye open; and the new hand, the one with the guitar. "Hell, every kid comes west has a damned guitar, seems like."

The boss is a tough case himself, one who often drinks too much, sometimes knows too much, and who frequently rides his men harder than they deserve. But, he'd back them up to the death against an outsider, including the law, right or wrong.

With time comes change. Ol' L.C. gets dragged out boots first and Jay ducks to get out of the way before trouble starts. Mostly it all happens because the ranch is being sold. The bunkhouse, once their home and gathering place, becomes unfriendly and cold. The handshakes are firm, promises to keep in touch polite but meaningless, and the kid, who's learned to ride a bronc with the best of 'em, knows he doesn't want to work for any more outfits with a "V" in the brand.

The years pass, and the kid finds himself in a middle-aged way. Somewhere along the path, just as he envisioned it would be, he gets billed as a nationally renowned cowboy-poet, famous not only for the poems he writes, but also for the music he puts to the words, making the old west come alive for his listeners. The years in the bunkhouse and riding with the big boss and his family have given him enough material to last forever. Also, due to a resolve developed in his early youth, the U.S. Marines make him an honorary member, perhaps the only one, ever.

And he says to me the other day, "I'm proud to give you this CD of my dad playing the piano. He's good, matter of fact, some claim he was a genius. Wonder what the hell happened to me?"

Yes, I hear your dad, and his talent has inspired me. And I hear your poems about the cowboy life, set to music, and it's clear nothing "happened" to you. Just like your father, the expressive poetry flows from your heart and you too, could be called a genius.

Tom Munn died in 2009, before this column was written.

The Great Gatsby

We grew up, at least around here, with the notion that the American dream was about individualism, discovery, and the pursuit of happiness. Somewhere along the way, a concept known as the "Aspen Idea," the nurturing of mind, body and spirit, got thrown in and we began to juggle and teeter, but the two abstractions weren't that mutually exclusive and for a while, Aspen and her citizens managed a melding of the two.

But times were changing, and the anti-growth policies adopted in the 1970s, perhaps unwittingly, cemented the demise of the above ideals and ushered in an era of rampant materialism, still hauntingly upon us even in this recession. The change took until the 1980s to truly gain flight, and by then property values had exponentially soared and new wealth had put a strangling finish on the dying carcass of a once-diverse, vital community. Suddenly, Aspen was a town ostensibly off-limits to all but the best-heeled and became one of the premier gathering places of those prone to an obnoxious display of affluence and moral decadence.

At the time, there wasn't enough "old" money left in town to hold the lid on the "newly-minted" rich folks, who came with ideas destructive to the tried and true methodology that had held Aspen together through thick and thin. Town lots once big enough to hold a "miner's cottage" surrounded by ample yard and garden plot suddenly looked like pants stretched too tight around the ample fat of McMansions, built lot line to lot line. The surrounding mountains sprouted houses the size of military barracks in war-prone countries.

Increasingly rare were the days when you could philosophize with your new neighbors in front of the post office, or trade barbs with them at the next table over dinner at your favorite restaurant. They weren't that kind of people anymore. It wasn't that they had an ability to look through the locals, they just couldn't discern the difference between substance and appearance. Many of the new breed were vulgar, ostentatious bullies lacking in social manners and taste, who cared for little other than what Aspen could give them, unconcerned with giving back to the community.

"C'mon, I'm not like that," you cry, but you know someone who is. If you were like that, you'd be soaking up these words as though they were the sweet, warm oil of manna, slathered upon your skin. As you and I know, it's not about money, but rather grace, and if blessed by grace, the amount of worldly goods you have doesn't much matter.

It's interesting to note a colorful and dichotomous change occurring within the Aspen community over the last few years, out of necessity. It used to be thought that any person from any social background could make a fortune, but not necessarily be accepted by the ruling (wealthy) aristocracy.

The long-time "locals," those who actually live here, have become the ruling arbiters, those who scrupulously grease the seating assignments at restaurants, cater the "A" list parties, decide who gets what perquisites when, determine when the garbage gets picked up, and in the end decide who gets accepted locally. And consequently, not all of those desiring status in our little mountain town get it, not in this lifetime.

Just as the protagonist of F. Scott Fitzgerald's *The Great Gatsby* behaved at his parties for the fabulously wealthy, those who are the true heart and soul of the Aspen community stand apart, witnessing the gaudy, misdirected display of the overly pretentious, being entertained while at the same time plotting their own dreams and schemes, hoping the objects of their desire are worthy of fulfillment.

A Packing Fool

"If you ever need any help, give me a holler," he'd said from under a big, black hat and for some reason, it stuck in my mind. Like so many things Aspen, the aura of somewhere else seems to carry weight with those who are from somewhere else, and they think those of us who grew up here should be impressed. "Yep, I learned to pack in Wyoming, spent a summer in Montana, too."

As the old saying goes," push came to shove" on a job I couldn't handle alone, trailing six heavily-laden pack horses through the mountains near Lyle Lake, around Hagerman Pass, and I took him up on the offer. We were meeting a large group of hikers who had been in the wilderness a week or so, re-supplying them for the remainder of their journey.

The guy seemed good, ten years older than me; he had all the lingo, the right scuff on his boots, a great pair of batwing chaps (just shy of rodeo fancy), and a wiry grin under a full mustache that might have made even Calamity Jane drool a bit.

He scoffed at my insistence we use a scale to balance the weight in the sawbuck panniers and it unsettled me a bit, but everybody has an idea about how to do things, especially "experts." He tied his canvas-covered loads down with double-diamond hitches and truly, they were a thing of beauty.

Loaded and ready to move out, my helper insisted I tie all six pack horses together so he could get going. "You get the stock truck turned around and parked and catch me on the trail." And he took off toward Hagerman Pass instead of Lyle Lake. "You're going the wrong way," I shouted, to which I could only hear, "Bullshit."

It's amazing how fast things can come unraveled and this trip was no exception. By the time I caught up and showed him the map, a half-hour had passed and instead of going back down to the trailhead, my "assistant" insisted we could cut across the face of the mountain and still make the lake. "I'll show you how to get things done," he said. I was starting to see him as a deficient dunce, crippled by an oversupply of hubris and lack of brain power.

We'd divvied up the pack horses, but I wasn't having much of it. We were traversing through large boulders, up a steep mountainside, and the switchbacks, as always, were creating a dangerous situation for the horses on the end of the string. It doesn't matter how you do it, the rope between horses gets shorter on the corners, the further down the line you go. A good hand goes slow enough to allow his ponies to all get safely around the switchback.

That's what a good hand will do. However, this guy seemed oblivious to the problem and on one particularly bad corner, the last horse just couldn't deal with the lack of lead rope and available trail to maneuver around the hairpin. Without choice, she pulled back, broke the rope and tumbled backwards off the ledge, landing about ten feet below, stuck between two humongous rocks, feet in the air.

I could feel his itchy breath on my back, and while he fingered his .357 with an unfaltering throwback attitude to dime western novels, he spit it out. "We'll have to shoot the bitch. Goddamn clumsy mare."

"You stupid bastard, put that gun away and get back on your horse." With a lot of cajoling, cussing, and downright physicality, I finally got Sourdough out of the mess she was in.

In spite of the broken pack saddle, and with no further "help" from my partner, we managed to make our rendezvous with perfect timing. I couldn't get out of there fast enough.

He said something about wanting to go back to Wyoming, and I replied that I'd do everything I could to make that happen. And we never spoke to each other again.

The Bell You Can't Unring

My brother killed himself in 1977. The other day, an acquaintance asked how long it took to get over his death. I said I didn't know; I was still working on it.

We ask a lot of questions about suicide, expecting answers that don't exist. "Why! Why did you do it? What drove you to that point? What could I have done differently?" Is there a straw that breaks the proverbial camel's back or does the seductive thought of infinite release bludgeon a susceptible person into seemingly rapid submission, with little warning? Ah, if only we knew.

Coming from a ski town, we've often heard it said that the only true experts in the field of avalanche prediction are those who've been killed by an avalanche. It sounds brutal, but all the experts on successful suicide are dead, as well.

Generally speaking, people don't go out and kill themselves on the spur of the moment. To the general populace that may appear to be true, but there is usually a series of events, of clues preceding the death that can make some sense of it. Such events or clues don't necessarily mean that suicide is inevitable, but they do signal a possible problem and suggest we should at least have the conversation with whoever is involved. I've visited with family members of friends after a loved one has committed the dreaded act and invariably someone says, "It wasn't a complete surprise."

There are two things about suicide that make it particularly painful for survivors, other than the obvious loss of someone they loved. First, in almost all cases, the survivor(s) have to deal with the fact that they were totally helpless to prevent the completion of the act. We tear ourselves up inside, having thoughts of "if only I had done this or that" or something similar. We should be comforted by the fact that the "if" conversation leads nowhere. If a person is intent on killing him- or herself, he (she) will eventually accomplish the act.

The other difficulty to deal with is the knowledge that not only is the loved one dead, but was killed by the very hand of the one we grieve. We're dealing with a perpetrator and a victim, both the same person, which sometimes leads to the sentiment, "If I could, I'd kill him for doing that."

We often hear the assertion, "If they knew how much hurt they left behind, they would never have done that." I'm not so sure about that statement. If they lived in our rational world at the time of the suicide, they truly wouldn't want to cause the hurt, but they don't seem to look at the world from our viewpoint. Maybe their own pain is so great, so unbearable, that their inward focus won't allow them to see past the immediate problem, themselves. In the scheme of things, suicide is one of life's options.

My brother grew up in a house full of guns. He knew how to use them; he liked to hunt grouse and was familiar with firing ranges. At the time of his death, he had ready access to firearms, but yet chose a different method to end his life. To me, this puts the lie to those who say that if there were fewer guns there would be fewer suicides. It just means that another manner of self-destruction would be the preferred method of choice for those intent on the final act of their lives.

As I searched my brother's house for clues, I was struck by that fact that in the fridge sat an unopened six-pack of Coors, something neither one of us seldom went without. Was it defiance or did he leave it for me? Later, the toxicology tests came back negative. With chilling intent, my brother went to the dark side fully sober and explicitly clear on the path he was taking. He wanted out and he went. It would dishonor him to not respect that decision.

The Magnificence of Highlands

Aspen Highlands has an allure that just can't be quenched, no matter the span of years or change in base area ambiance. My cousin, Don Stapleton, and I started skiing there the first year it opened (1958) and all things considered, we charted a good course for the years to come.

That first year set the tone for Highlands, at least in our minds, as many of the trails hadn't been fully cleared of dead fall or stumps, and skiing the edges for a few powder turns could truly be hazardous to one's health. Even then, there were little chutes through the trees that no one knew about. From day one, Highlands had that aura of danger, of incompleteness, of being just a little off the wall that it still has today with the Highland Bowl and Deep Temerity.

It was about personalities then, almost as much as it was about skiing. Later on, Stein Eriksen became the ski school guru for a time, and we occasionally followed him around the hill, taking pointers when offered and always striving to impress him when he was watching. Sometimes, he'd take us for a run off the Cloud Nine lift, just to tune us up, I guess, although he never said much. "Follow me," was about the most of it. Somehow, ski pro Tony Woerndl became one of our mentors and always seemed to be there, never criticizing, just always encouraging us to hang it out a little further.

In high school, we were into apres-ski as much as the adults, although our interest was solidly in the music being played in the Rathskeller Lounge, upstairs from the main cafeteria. One winter, an accommodating trio let me have some serious time on the piano every week and I began to think I might want to be a musician. The drummer was a smallish guy whose mouth was always open, with big eyes behind coke-bottle glasses and who had an unfocused nervousness that only beating the drums could tame. An hour or so before the show one afternoon, he leaned on me hard to help him score some "horse" (heroin), as his regular supplier had skipped town. I wasn't quite in tune with his plight and couldn't have helped anyway, but in the nick of time, there he was, back behind his tympanic inspirations, hammering the hell out of 'em, pupils constricted as snake eyes, even behind his thick glasses.

The next year, management hired me to play the piano for the kid's ski school at Highlands. I played for an hour at lunch and got a lift ticket and sandwich for my troubles. And got to spend all the time I wanted with sexy Mitzi, the day school director, who seemed to like talking to me more than listening to my playing. Of course, I had a crush on her that wouldn't quit, but as tangled as her love life got (she kept me up to date with a running commentary), she never quite got down to taking on a high school kid.

This past Tuesday, my buddy Bob Snyder (the big mogul champ) and I hiked the bowl for Erik Peltonen's retirement party from the City of Aspen. Think about it - over-zealous youngsters hyping the bowl as a young man's game, and there we were, a group of well-seasoned, lifetime skiers who could kick butt on all but the best of the young turks. Well, maybe on all of them, at that. And, I have to say, the Bowl never skied any better for me than it did that day. Of course, and as Erik will tell you, Bob and I got there late due to circumstances beyond human comprehension and missed the potluck lunch and the patrol-sanctioned avalanche depth charges.

But, what the hell, we all skied the same mountain, just like we've been doing every year since it opened. We'll be skiing it for a long time to come, too.

Murder in 1966

Murder seems to be in the air this fall, and whether real or imagined, it brings up thoughts of past tragedies visited on our small community. Murder, a simple word, easy to commit, but there is no going back, not once it's done.

Shortly after midnight on a warm August night in 1966, good-natured ladies' man Jim Griffin and his girlfriend either slept or were making love in a two-story house on Waters Avenue, when suddenly, Griffin's estranged wife could be heard outside. At about the same time, what sounded like two rocks crashed through windows in the house.

Reacting as any person might, adrenalin pumping, Griffin hurried downstairs in an attempt to console his irate wife, from whom he had been estranged for approximately two weeks. None of us can say we knew the wife, a big woman with long, dark flowing hair and a good-looking smile, like he did, so it's unknown if he approached the door with trepidation in his heart, or rather with anger at being so rudely disturbed in the middle of the night.

As Griffin opened the kitchen door and started outside to assess the situation, he met his wife in the darkened doorway, coming at him with a long, bone-handled hunting knife. And she did a number on him, too, stabbing him at least twice, once in the chest and again in the abdomen.

Apparently the girlfriend, Gay Prior, had followed her lover down to the kitchen, undoubtedly wondering just exactly what was happening. In the dark of night and at the lateness of the hour, she may have had nothing in her mind but curiosity, but it was a deadly posture to take. Mrs. Sonja Griffin looked up from the job she was doing on her husband, and spying the blonde, slender figure of his paramour, changed the direction of her rampage.

Quickly stepping over her downed husband, Sonja violently thrust once to Prior's chest, directly into the heart, and Ms. Gay Barbara Prior, the lover, was instantaneously killed by the long, sharp cutlass of death. In the time that took, Griffin had regained his feet long enough to seize the knife from his estranged wife and pitch it out the door. He then collapsed, semiconscious, onto the kitchen floor, critically but not mortally wounded.

Mrs. Griffin then fled the scene, driving away in her husband's Jeep, which had been parked outside. At 12:28 A.M., Aspen Valley Hospital received an anonymous call from a woman, saying an ambulance may be needed on Waters Avenue. "There's blood all over. Someone might be dead." According to then-assistant DA, Albie Kern, the scene was indeed messy. "I never want to see anything like that again."

Sheriff Carroll Whitmire transported Griffin to the hospital, where he was placed in the intensive care unit, struggling to overcome the wound in his abdomen, which if you think about it, may originally have been more directed at his maleness than anywhere. The police began their investigation, having little to go on other than what Jim Griffin could tell them. Mrs. Griffin was nowhere to be found. Had the police been a little quicker, they might have caught her at home, but she wasn't there long.

The next morning, as Jim Snobble left his house near the City of Aspen shop under the Castle Creek Bridge, he found Mrs. Sonja Griffin lying on the ground in front of her husband's Jeep, dead from a self-inflicted 30.06 rifle wound to the heart. She'd returned to her apartment for the gun after she had left her husband for dead and murdered his lover.

You have to wonder if she realized the incompleteness of her campaign, or if she pulled the trigger on herself thinking she had completed the trilogy of murder-suicide she had envisioned.

Saturday Night at the Old Eagles Club

There is a shell of a building in Aspen that has about as much history to it as anywhere in town, a watering hole now gone forever. When you're walking around some night, stop in front of 312 South Galena (now Prada) and give a moment of silence to a grand old place, the past home of the Aspen Eagles Club.

Back then, there were no fancy windows out front, just narrow concrete steps going up about three feet from either direction on Galena, leading to a narrow, locked door off a very small landing. There were a buzzer and intercom to the right of the door, a token "members only" set-up, but no one except naive novices used the intercom as everyone knew everyone else, and it would have been virtually impossible for a nonmember to sneak his way past the gazes from the bar that witnessed his arrival into the foyer of the club. If the interloper looked reasonable, he was in for at least a drink on the house and an informal quizzing by those at the old-time bar.

It wasn't fancy by any means, but was originally what a quiet, burned out mining town with a few leftover miners, some merchants and a sprinkling of ranchers needed; a place to blow off steam and have some fun. Like every bar in town before noon, it had the smell of stale beer, spilled whiskey, spent cigarettes and the lingering body odor of last night's crowd. But get a few people in there, have a couple of rounds, and soon the well-oiled social interaction overcame any shortcomings and it became a home away from home, a place to catch up on the day's news with people you knew very well. A working man's club.

Early on, I used to sneak in there on Sunday afternoons with my girlfriend, Norma Just, hoping my grand-dad would be there for the Sunday dance and buy us a coke. He'd let us sit in the booth with him and his lady friend, Jennie, and Norma and I'd secretly hold hands under the table and maybe dance a time or two.

When I came back after college, I found the Eagles to be a little different from how I remembered it with Norma. I discovered

334

what a 10:00 A.M. to 2:00 A.M. shift in front of the bar could be like, more than once, and was always grateful that the kind people in there never reminded me about what a moron I might have been the day or night before. But I also discovered the stronger parts of the Eagles, like the charity that is so freely given, the fundraising efforts that seemed to be going on almost continually. Not only did we give money to national causes like the cancer and heart funds, we took on local organizations like the Aspen Valley Visiting Nurses and the Aspen Camp School for The Deaf.

There was almost nothing like walking into the old Eagles Club on a Saturday night, seeing everyone dressed up in their dancing best, smiles on their faces and mischief in their eyes. The sounds from the ballroom would slowly entice you past the long line of friends at the bar, past the lounge area and to the edge of the dance floor, where the voices and nimble guitars of the Rainbow Playboys would hold your attention.

For many years, it was one of the few live bands in Aspen and had a Sunday afternoon radio show on KSNO, broadcast live from the Eagles Club. Brothers Dub and Eb Tacker, along with Carroll Whitmire (the sheriff), Glenn Smith, Little Joe Phillips, Jim Hamlin and Twirp Anderson made up the band over the years (Dusty Seaton and Smokey, too). They could play just about any country song from the fifties on, including whatever was hot at the time. Saturday nights were special.

And now, if you listen quietly on a lonely Saturday night, you may feel the warmth and hear the memories of the past rumbling around in the building one more time, just for the hell of it.

The Storyteller

Some say it's a curse, others a blessing, but we all have it in one form or another. Clinging to us as a snake to the earth, slithering through the grass with steady, silent, random and beautiful purpose, open to the slightest suggestion, it has us in its grasp.

I refer, naturally, to our creativeness. Sometimes we call it imagination, originality, or for lack of a better word, creativity. Curiously, efforts to define it are to throw a wet blanket on that of which we speak, for creativity is the ability to mold, develop or envision outside the predictable bounds of definition.

Whether it's an architect devising better ways of building to match the landscape, a painter bringing out a glimpse of one's soul on canvas, a poet transcending language with deft, evocative flourishes, or us columnists who appear before you week after week, we are all in it together.

At nine years old, I crafted a ten-page dissertation on the crack in the Liberty Bell, something about an errant Daniel Boone rifle shot creating said deformity. It was an early attempt at humor, soundly rejected by the several magazines who received it. To this day, I console myself with the thought that such denials had more to do with my graphite scribbles on Big Chief writing paper than the content.

Motivated by the writing spirit, I kept a daily journal (including short stories) through most of my high school years, detailing my views on everything from sex to love, older women, tragic events, weather, my emotions, horses I was breaking, days on the range and myriad other subjects. Dreadfully, and I say that with every ounce of conviction implied by the word, someone very close to me years later, threw those journals out in a fit of jealous pique. You can buy new shoes or skis, but that was different.

As a college freshman, I had notions of becoming the next Hemingway, writing earthy, gritty novels that would pull on people's inner emotions as I fleshed out the underbelly of life, taking them places they otherwise might not go. I shunned established convention, in a misguided attempt to keep my thoughts true and uncontaminated.

Eventually, and prosaically, I left Hemingway and the hallowed halls of literature behind for a degree in marketing and business administration. To be blunt, as the man responsible for my own education, I was tired of being broke and figured I'd starve to death before I ever completed my sought after Ph.D. I continued to write well into the midnight oil, composing complicated dissertations on how to revitalize various problematic American enterprises, or coming up with advertising slogans for products being newly released to market.

Although we don't always think so, especially when we're young, the world moves at a frightening clip, and one afternoon, well into my forties, I found myself hanging out in the West End while waiting for my daughter to finish gymnastics classes. The familiarity of the neighborhood coupled with views of Aspen Mountain stimulated many childhood memories and it wasn't long before I'd spend time in the West End on other days as well, sitting in my truck, drawing forth seemingly infinite recollections.

Like a long-lost native son, beat up but better for it, I emerged from the immense, history-filled, old-growth forests of my mind with an armload of stories and revelations begging for light. The gods smiled, took a roll of the dice, and this space became that light.

Each week is a journey of discovery, a peeling back of the layered synapses, looking and waiting for that spark, the tiny grain of creativity that might grow and turn itself into a weekly column. There is nothing I would rather do.

Broken Neck

Come take a nightmare run with me on Aspen Mountain's Silver Queen and I don't mean the gondola but rather the run commonly referred to by some locals as "The Bitch." Personally, I'm a Summit man, at least 2 or 3 laps a day down that chute, but there's nothing like the end-of-the-day freedom and lightness of ripping down International, culminating in either the Queen or Corkscrew Gully.

Famous last words always bite or they wouldn't be famous, I guess, something along the lines of, "Yeah, let's just take it easy," as I turned 'em down the Queen, loving the texture of the snow, the size of the bumps and the angle of the sun.

It was too good, I'm telling you, and I felt tremendous, sucking up some humongous bumps in the middle before deciding to take a chance on the right. I always stop on the flat above Elevator Shaft to wait for my compadres and as I came across from the right, flying like a midnight bat out of hell, one of those sideways moguls the devil surely creates jumped into view. There was no choice, I knew it was going to hurt, but you know, I've absorbed worse, but then!

The crack of my helmet was deafening as it hit the snow, and I remember thinking it probably saved my ass as I gave myself up to the fall and tried to relax. Quietly and quickly, I flipped into the air and landed on my chest like a wet towel dropped from a second-story window.

Face buried in the snow, I couldn't breathe, and as my buddy Bob Snyder said, all it would have taken to denote a dead body was a chalk line around my lifeless form. It was impossible to help myself - I couldn't get any air, couldn't move my head, and most noticeably, couldn't move my arms or legs.

Paralyzed. That's a scary proposition, but I took it with a certain amount of equanimity, along the line of "You really fucked up this time." Hurry up Bob, and dig my airway out of this damned snow and then I'll think about this predicament I'm in. A buddy like that is worth a million bucks, for damned sure.

Bob was great - he removed my skis, and then at my request, unfolded my arms from the awkward positions they were in. I was thinking it was going to be a little rough getting down the steeps in my condition, but then ever so gradually, feeling and movement began returning to my arms and legs. Hallelujah! With that I was back in the groove, but still functionally unable to help myself.

I'm an Aspen Mountain ski patrol alumnus from the 70s and can only hope we performed with the same level of professionalism that greeted me on the mountain last Saturday. I love those guys and girls in a way that those of us in dire need quickly come to appreciate.

Aspen Valley Hospital staff hovered over me like the injured pup I was and got me through an MRI, a CT scan and fed me a delicious IV. No doubt tired of my sense of humor, they let me go home a few hours later. Those folks, too, are the epitome of professional.

This column is almost over, but my travails are not. I have two prolapsed cervical discs choking my spinal cord and a beat up vertebrae between the two, all requiring surgical removal, but first I have to allow the swelling to subside for six weeks. In the meantime, there's not much to do what with the constant pain, a cervical collar that seems elephant-sized and strict orders to stay home.

Six weeks of recovery after surgery, and I'm back in the game. Just so you know.

Footnote: I had surgery much earlier due to a change in doctors. I sincerely thank my daughter, Lauren Vagneur Burtard, for nursing me through a long recovery. The wreck happened on 3/13/2010.

Death Penalty Cause Celebre

When is the orgasm so good that murder is incidental to its release? Is the life of a 12-year-old child worth it, or the life of anyone, for that matter? We'll never know the answers, of course, because we're not the ones motivated by such hideous insanity.

Aspen did indeed, however, play a pivotal role in this chilling saga, and I suppose we'd all like to forget it, but as columnist Paul Andersen once wrote, "We have a celebrity climate here that even includes mass murderers." It doesn't seem right to talk about it, now that we know how it all turned out, but that's why we'd like to forget, I reckon.

For me, it started out innocently enough. Headed to Carbondale to replenish feed for the T Lazy 7 horse herd, I suddenly found myself pulled up short in a long line of vehicles at the Old Snowmass Conoco. Soon enough, the solemn-looking law officers manning the site left no doubt they were serious about something, as they looked in trunks, pried open hoods and peered behind seats with an efficiency seldom seen in local enforcement. Such aberrations always put me in a bad mood 'cause I figure if someone hadn't screwed up somewhere along the line, we wouldn't need the hassle of a road block.

Up until then, rapist and serial murderer Ted Bundy's presence in our local jail hadn't made much of an impression on me, but his escape that morning and the sudden realization that my wife, Caroline, was home alone on the ranch (which was along a possible flight route), parched my mouth and cranked up my pulse rate. Over the phone, I instructed her to keep my lever-action .30-.30 close at hand and to be extremely suspicious of anyone coming by. "Finish your errands," she'd said, and had I been "Terrible Ted," I'd have made a wide swath around her, she was so confidant.

Which is exactly what he did, shortly after my telephone call. He went up the far side of Maroon Creek, directly across from our house, not a hundred yards away. We didn't know this until days later, when a sheriff's deputy thought such information might be welcome. It made me cuss, I remember that.

Later that afternoon, we drove up the road to see what kind of big deal the manhunt had created. At the lower end of Henry Stein's meadow, near the mouth of East Maroon, we spotted a roaring fire, stoked up for a pep rally it seemed, surrounded by beefy, squint-eyed men in wool shirts, jeans and leather boots who amateurishly spit tobacco, stroked their high-powered rifles as they might rub morning erections, and slurped on cans of beer.

The fact that I'd walked the couple-hundred feet down to the gathering, rather than bouncing a big four-wheel-drive vehicle into their midst, marked me as one of the unwashed, but when I told 'em they were on private property (looking out for Henry's better interests, I was, thinking they were a bunch of nut cases from over the Divide), they looked at me like I'd lost my mind. They had been "deputized," the story went, and were gonna catch Ted Bundy that night, or soon thereafter, and I'd best not interfere. Turning on my tall-heeled boots, I offered that if they built a bigger fire, Ol' Ted might be drawn to the flames, like a killer moth.

Bundy, who once said, "So what's one less? What's one less person on the face of the planet," and who couldn't drive around the block without screwing up, was arrested six days later when he drew attention to himself near the Aspen Grove subdivision in a stolen Cadillac.

Only in this civilized world is it possible, but he went on to kill at least two more women and another 12-year-old girl. Those clowns with the big bonfire should have caught him first.

Jubilation and Despair Meet Here

Sometimes it's hard to reconcile the great joy and tremendous sorrow that can exist, side-by-side and day-to-day in a town full of people who live, work and play in the mountains. The contrasts and contradictions are not always opaque, but more often cast shadows of translucence that move us alternately through myriad feelings of strong emotions as we each follow our own path.

Thursday last week, I had the extremely good fortune to ski with Penny Pitou, the double silver-medalist at the 1960 Squaw Valley Olympic Games, a member of the visiting International Historical Skiing Association, and one of the heroes of my youth. She is the embodiment of the tenacity and talent that has shaped the history of skiing in the United States and around the world. One thing the IHSA members don't like to do is sit around and shoot the breeze, not while the lifts are running, and if you stop to find a tree, you'll have to catch up later.

Friday, my friend Valerie and I had just slung our skis for the Highland Bowl hike when a serious-faced youth on a snowmobile began ferrying fellow ski patrolmen up to the closure gate. Such a focused concentration of energy alerted us that an event of potentially catastrophic proportions was unfolding. We later learned that 22-year-old Aspen native Wallace Westfeldt, pioneer snowboarder of a younger generation, had died.

By Monday, some folks had developed theories about how such an accident could have happened and how it might have been prevented. Such conversations ran the gamut from "kids will always be kids" to "it's about time those types of activities were banned or strenuously regulated." Too, the powder was perfect, the mountain almost deserted, and the pure joy of lap after lap through untouched stashes brought forth the juxtaposition between pleasure and sorrow. My friend, photographer Burnie Arndt, always the philosopher, tried gently to engage my interest in writing a column examining the relationship between independence and safety, but I felt ill-prepared to engage intelligently with anyone about such a sensitive subject.

I do know, however, that the split second between jubilant high-fives and dejected feelings of deep despair is immeasurable if it goes the wrong way, but doesn't count unless misfortune appears. The beauty of a well-executed run, the thrill of watching a daring drop off a cliff, draws our attention, and always we must remember that such grace originates from within, from the spirit of the person catching our eye. It's a gift, from them to us. Sadness emanates from the heart, but so does the raw elegance of putting the moves out there for the world to see.

"Who are you to say I can't do things like that?" There is no consolation in the knowledge of freedom of choice when it ends in tragedy, except that the integrity of all our lives is held sacred by such freedom. The days will go on - skiing, riding, laughing, taking it to the edge. It doesn't eliminate the pain or fill the void, but as time goes by, it gives you increasing strength to keep going on.

I know what it's like to lose a brother in his early 20s, but not a child, and I can only imagine the profound thoughts and feelings that Wallace's family must be enduring.

Inherent danger is what makes riding and skiing exciting sports to watch and participate in. As it's always been and forever shall be, some will be called to pay the ultimate price in realizing their dreams. For those of us who remain, the laughter and sorrow all come together in a powerful vortex of swirling hopes and desires, all pinned to the snow and the blue skies.

Trudi Peet

Sometime in the 1950s, Trudi Peet (April 23, 1935 – April 7, 2013) and her then-husband, Hank Pedersen, bought the neighboring ranch, just up the Woody Creek road from us. The canyon was big cattle country in those days and it was rather difficult to get our minds around the reality that our new neighbors, newly-weds at that, were comprised of a good-looking, sexy woman who rode horses in the English manner and a muscular, blond fellow who spoke with a thick Danish accent and raised flowers. They renamed the place St. Finnbar. We didn't get that either, not for a while.

Sometimes it takes just one person to change a neighborhood, and Trudi Peet did it, without intention. We put up the hay for Hank and her, as they had no machinery or interest in that, and my developing adolescent hormones appreciated the sight of Trudi riding around the ranch, always with a smile and a friendly hello.

It was difficult to find a suitable arena location on their property so Trudi appealed to the neighbors in Little Woody Creek for a spot to build a combination polo/performance arena, allowing some public demonstrations of horsemanship to take place. It sat right next to the road, a guaranteed conversation piece in those pre-glitz-and-glamor days.

By the time Trudi decided to give a dressage performance during the dusty haze of the annual W/J Rodeo, she'd moved on from Woody Creek, but those of us who knew her were able to talk up her horsemanship skills in the face of opposition from those tough performers and organizers who didn't think dressage and rodeo were compatible. She brought the bleachers down with applause after her first performance and thereafter rodeo and town people alike talked about Trudi Peet and dressage as though the two were one.

Appreciation and understanding of animals is inherent in those who are successful in working and living with them. One day Trudi came out to the ranch to visit Buck Deane and me, where we'd offered to take her on a sleigh ride. I thought she might be bored with it all, but as we harnessed the team, she picked up on how responsive the horses were to voice commands and was hooked. As we ripped through cold, fresh snowfall in the upper meadow, enjoying the creak of the sled in harmony with the sound of leather against leather, tug-against-double-tree and the deep breathing of the horses, I handed the lines to Trudi, telling her to take a turn at being a teamster. After a bit, she handed the lines back with tears in her eyes, "Oh my God, these horses are magnificent."

The last time I saw Trudi was at the annual Woody Creek Hounds hunt at the Chaparral Ranch in 2011. Neither one of us rode and as we visited, waiting for the riders to come in, she told me the story of looking for a certain horse in California. As she put it, "They showed me a couple of good horses, but refused to bring out the one I was really interested in. They said he was unruly, unbreakable and wouldn't be fit for sale. I finally demanded they bring him out, and bought him on the spot." More or less, that's what Trudi said.

She and the horse headed for Colorado with Trudi spending time each day, gentling the horse down and slowly getting him into the idea of what he needed to do. She'd work him each morning, then load him in the trailer and move a little further toward Colorado. On about the fourth day, they awoke to the first snow of winter, white against brown, and there was something different in the dynamics of their relationship. Trudi saddled her mount and they headed across the Utah desert, the horse at last ready to take his place in Trudi's stable of excellent steeds.

Trudi loved that story and as I thought about it later, decided it would make a good column. I tried to get in touch with her once to refresh the details, without result, but figured I'd see her again at last fall's (2012) Woody Creek Hounds event. She wasn't there and now both the story and Trudi are gone. So long, dear lady. Rest in peace.

Disturbing Dichotomy in Woody Creek

It was a blustery Thanksgiving weekend near Livingston, Montana, even with a brilliant cobalt sky overhead. Three of us rode with purpose, ostensibly trying out a highly recommended horse; but as we rode over rolling hill after rolling hill, I was awestruck by the number of abandoned homestead houses that still stood, silent sentries to the days when a man could yet make it with grit in his gut and a good woman by his side.

Without the forsaken buildings still standing proud, it would have been difficult to imagine what kind of lives these people lived 50 or 100 years ago, but the weather-beaten houses held precious clues to those days past, evidence as to levels of relative success, how many children they might have had and whether they had running water. Somewhat like reading a book, we knew much more about life in that area after we returned to the main barn. The buildings and corrals told, in unforgettable scenes, the history in a way that books and bare land never could.

As people travel up Woody Creek Road, enjoying a leisurely bike ride or admiring the scenery from a motorized vehicle, do they wonder about the history before them in a way similar to my Montana discoveries?

If you've traveled that Woody Creek path much, you undoubtedly noticed the two log houses that were summarily demolished this past summer, one a small two-story with totems and wind chimes out front, the other a much larger one-story with a full basement, protected from the afternoon sun by two large cottonwoods. Like stately cedars standing sentry on either side of a ranch entry gate, the two log structures stood almost side-by-side, looking over the ranchland below, separated only by a small, jack-oak covered rise along Woody Creek Road.

It's hard to imagine now — and impossible for those searching out the history of Woody Creek to know — how robust and lively those two log houses were at one time. The smaller was used by the Elkhorn Ranch to house hired hands, and over the years, it was witness to several single men falling in love with women from town, marrying them and bringing them out to Woody Creek to share in the ranching life. Young, fresh-faced brides rode the winter feed sleds with their husbands and my dad, rejoicing in the cold air and the beauty of the quiet life they had chosen. Deep into those frosty midwinter nights, families were started, and the women's cheeks, once flushed crimson from the cold, took on a rosy inner glow from the life growing within. So many years ago, that was. But they couldn't stay. There wasn't enough money in the job for some, the solitude threatened others and for the last couple, the new owners had other plans.

In 1949, yours truly was three when we moved into the larger of the two houses. My father, a thoughtful young man of 29, wanted to get out of the homestead cabin we lived in, without water and dimly lit by kerosene lamps, and had a new house built for his family. The excitement, the joy that must have pervaded their lives when finally they moved into a house with inside running water, even though they had to rely on a generator for electricity. Two more children followed soon after, an indication that things were going well, and I learned to cuss, listening to my dad start the temperamental generator each evening.

At some point, my dad planted the cottonwood trees out front and gave me the sacred job of watering them each day, an assignment I never missed for fear of a spanking. As I got older, my dad and I would walk outside on winter nights after dinner and look up at the brightest stars in the world. He'd put one arm around my shoulders and point with the other as he explained the mysteries of the constellations to me. Maybe we were never closer than we were on those nights.

My mother kept a well-maintained yard, with rose bushes, sweet peas, petunias, tulips and other varieties unknown to a rambunctious kid, who was forced to mow the lawn with a hand mower. Her vegetable garden was the pride of Woody Creek, and it kept more than one hungry family smiling at meal time. That remained our home until we moved into the main ranch house in 1958.

Now the two houses are gone, smashed and crumbled into extinction, because to someone, they seemed out of place. It's not my position to tell another how to manage his property, but I can disagree with the destruction of historic ranch buildings.

And on a mesa high above, overlooking the Woody Creek Canyon, a man is building a $20 million house he will never live in, not for more than a couple of months a year. The contradiction is chilling.

A Timeless Gift from the Aspen Times

It came in the mail the other day, an issue of The Aspen Times, and with well-focused rhythm, I took it straight home and laid it out with wide-eyed excitement. As you might expect, there were stories in there about people whose names are very familiar, but it's not what you think. This was the first issue of The Aspen Times ever printed, Volume 1, No. 1, Saturday, April 23, 1881. Not a copy, nor a picture or any other facsimile, but the full and honest first edition.

Despite years of being maligned by well-intentioned curators and docents, hell-bent on keeping the curious from touching our antiquities, history remains a living, breathing chronicle of where we've been and maybe also about where we're headed. And holding that four-page issue in my hands was almost as though I'd just picked it up as I walked down an Aspen street, headed to my favorite coffee emporium. It brought history to my breast (and mind) in a way that a hundred books and photographs could not.

You might think it coincidental, but judging by the advertisements back then, there seemed to be a plethora of attorneys at law, at least nine of them, closely followed by real estate brokers, against a population of very small size. And, of course, there was a front-page article about Aspen's wealth. Apparently, some things are steeped in consistency.

In the flowery vernacular of the times, and well before the surrounding mountains were almost totally denuded of their aspens and evergreens, we can feel the cool breeze shimmering through the aspen trees, hear the grandiose chirping of wild birds and relax our thoughts with grazing livestock, even as we read of the first death in Aspen.

Sara James Rilleau, daughter of the well-known William James family that lived in Aspen during the '50s and '60s (Spook, Sara and Jemima), sent me a simple message, asking if I'd like to have that rare and priceless first edition of The Aspen Times, as it had been among her mother's treasured items. Sara's mother, Julie James, a well-known artist and community leader, was one of the founders of the Aspen Historical Society in 1963, along with some other notable characters such as Joan Lane, Herbert Bayer, Luke Short and Dorothy Koch Shaw.

The trail of history can sometimes be confusing, as it seems we always have a penchant for taking a straight line to what seems to be the easy solution to complicated stories, conveniently glossing over the sweat and anguish that goes into every account or merely repeating only those stories that tend to bolster our own sense of history.

To that end, may I say that, according to the first edition of The Aspen Times (and later bolstered by other writers), there isn't much that gets glossed over, except that so early in the game (1881) great things were already being dreamed about for Aspen, its isolation and political unrest receiving only passing reference.

There's a rather detailed account of how B. Clark Wheeler, a promoter of shady disposition (or, as some have said, strong enthusiasm), pungently upset the original settlers of Aspen (then called Ute City) by going behind their backs to create his Roaring Fork Townsite Co., which renamed the town Aspen in a most unilateral fashion and took over the collective property of the fledgling settlement. This left many of the "old-timers" fuming, and there was serious talk of physically taking out B. Clark as payback for his aggressive style. This was, clearly, the first corporate takeover in the valley, and many established residents left in frustration, slowing Aspen's early development.

In addition to local politics, there is mention of Czar Nicholas II having two wives and how he got around that with the church, of mine disasters in other states and the capture of outlaws and the lynching of murderers. Reading a published list of area mining-claim names is to sit in on the dreams and hopes of tough, willing-to-gamble prospectors.

Not to pick on B. Clark Wheeler, for in the end he did the town a lot of good, but he got eternal comeuppance when his surveyor for the Aspen townsite, a man apparently in an elliptical hurry, used magnetic north instead of true north to align the streets (an engineering no-no), and forever more the streets of Aspen will be catty-wumpus and off-kilter to proper street layout, the worst kind of conversation starter.

There's tons more in that paper, and I suspect that you'll be hearing more about it from time to time. Thank you, Sara James Rilleau, for such a grand gift!

A Very Special Event

He's out there somewhere, a young boy I'm dying to meet. For now I'll have to be patient, but he'll hit town soon — my unborn grandson.

In cowboy vernacular, I'm building a big loop, like a pair of strong arms to caringly place around him to comfort and encourage him when necessary, creating an island of safety to keep him from wandering too far and to keep danger away. As he grows, so will the loop, until this granddad rides off into the sunset, leaving behind what he hopes is a good legacy.

These special moments are saved for old bastards like me, I reckon. Our faces are lined with all that we've been through, virtual lifetime works of art that are etched with worry and smiles, tears and laughter, and our eyes, which have seen so much and are stained with jade and cynicism, crave the return gaze of a young one who can look our way with a touch of wonder and a bit of awe and innocently call to us, wanting answers to questions about all things in the universe.

Today's youngsters are pushing, wanting me to move over, and I'm resisting, still riding horses that snort and buck and still snaking turns down kinky, snow-covered steeps and deeps. Maybe this is the day that's due, when I can ease up on the throttle a bit and take the time to watch and grow with the youngest in my family. Reliving life through the eyes of a child is an excellent form of rejuvenation — my daughter taught me that.

My family has decided that this grandson will likely call me "Grumpa," this originally from a daughter who has publicly thrown the term "curmudgeon" my way with a smoothness that is unsettling. I've had a couple of women friends who, when approaching the threshold of grandparentage, informed me that they had picked out names they expected to be called by their grandchildren, none of them denoting a "grandmotherly" role. As they learned, expectations are easily undermined by reality.

Never was there a bigger hero in my life than my own paternal grandfather. He taught me how to enjoy life however it came at me, and with patience (mostly), he taught me many of the things I needed to know as a man: how to saddle my own horse, how to doctor a cow in the middle of the forest, how to find good worms for fishing and always to have a date on Saturday night. He died when I was 11 years old, and there hasn't been a day since that I haven't thought of him. Grandfathers are important.

"Aren't you excited?" people ask. To be honest, I think "excited" is the wrong word. Honored, yes. Curious, of course. Excitement is for my daughter and son-in-law. This is their project — I'm but a bystander at this point. And no, I haven't been trying to influence the naming of my grandson. That's not in my bailiwick, either.

I've learned that it's difficult, if not impossible, to explain the joys of children to those who don't have any. I also know that if you're a parent, it is ultimately futile to date or have an affair with someone who doesn't have children. They never seem to understand the necessity of sharing the last cookie with your kid or that weekend athletic contests at school take precedence over romantic interludes in the woods. It's probably true that I won't appreciate being a grandfather until the day arrives — and I promise not to become too obnoxious about it all.

For the moment, we don't know what his personality is going to be like or what he'll even care about, but we do know he is going to be one of us. That is the magic.

It's a new trail I'll be traveling with my grandson, the path ahead unknown, but my foot's in the stirrup and my hands are on the reins, ready to mount up for what I anticipate to be the ride of a lifetime.

Made in the USA
San Bernardino, CA
14 September 2016